GONE TO POTT

GONE TO POTT

Derrick Brooke

The Book Guild Ltd
Sussex, England

First published in Great Britain in 2001 by
The Book Guild Ltd
25 High Street
Lewes, East Sussex
BN7 2LU

Typesetting in Times by
Acorn Bookwork, Salisbury, Wiltshire

Printed in Great Britain by
Bookcraft (Bath) Ltd, Avon

A catalogue record for this book is available from
The British Library.

ISBN 1 85776 561 3

CONTENTS

FOREWORD

Pott Shrigley is situated on the edge of the Peak District overlooking the Cheshire Plain. The National Trust Property, Lyme Park, on the northern boundary completes its most impressive position.

In addition to a most picturesque cricket ground and church it also boasts a 500-year-old school which is probably unique in having a bar in the cellar, which overcomes the problem of not having a village pub – the cricketers are very grateful!

Derrick Brooke, who has been associated with the club for 50 years, as player, secretary, groundsman and chairman, has also been connected with the High Peak & Cheshire Junior Cricket League as secretary, chairman and president.

With an ageing population of about 250 currently living in 80 dwellings, Derrick's and the club's aforethought 30 years ago in recognising the need for a strong junior section has paid tremendous dividends. The system has provided players for not only Pott and other clubs in the area but also the county junior teams.

Pott Shrigley typifies the current enthusiasm for the game in Cheshire where we are seeing increased participation at all junior levels. The continued growth and development of the game is assured when we have people like Derrick, his club Pott Shrigley and the Macclesfield Cricket Development Forum of which Derrick Brooke is a key member.

Peter Hancock
Cricket Development Officer – Cheshire

INTRODUCTION

A lot of books have been printed about cricket by players, some interesting, others not so, but not many are about 'grass roots cricket' which, after all, is the mainstay of this great traditional game.

In deciding to write this book, which basically tells of my involvement with the village club of Pott Shrigley for almost 50 years, this is my own personal view of events, some funny, some serious and some which could easily have caused the club to fold up.

While my story is about my club, I think this book should be dedicated to the many hundreds of people who have given part of their lives to keeping clubs, leagues, and competitions alive for cricketers and cricket lovers to enjoy. Hopefully, as more young people take up the game, the sport will prosper.

WHEN DID IT START?

Cricket has always been a part of my life. In the back yard of our house, five houses shared toilets and ash pits before the days of plastic bags and wheelie bins. This toilet block was set down the side of the houses with a high wall on the other side with a garden to the farm next door. With wickets painted on the wall this made a good practice area. It took a bit of doing hitting the ball into the farm garden, but it did happen. The 'Please could we have our ball back' usually worked with the farmer's wife, but the farmer liked a pint or two and tended to get a bit violent when he had had one too many, so this could be a risky operation.

Across the street was a larger yard with about 20 houses round it so this allowed us scope to play games, but with all the windows round, this was not popular with the residents with no children, and the rule of 'Pay For Your Own China' was adopted. We always used a pile of coats for wickets, and on one occasion one elderly lady who lived on her own came and chucked a bucket of water over the jackets. Family holidays in those days were always taken at Blackpool so apart from buckets and spades, a set of wickets and bat and ball were essential.

Most of the children in the area went to the same school, Bollington Cross Church of England School. The headmaster as a Mr Pendlebury

1

Annual Wakes holiday at Blackpool, 1937.

(Pengo his nickname), an imposing man whose discipline came from a big black ruler he carried with him and if you stepped out of line a whack or two with the ruler ensured you didn't do wrong again for a while. He always encouraged games and sport and loved to join in, particularly with a game of cricket. The playground was only cinders, but he had installed a concrete wicket and teams would be picked to play each playtime until the match was won or lost. Pengo liked to be on the winning side and hated getting out, so everybody knew if he was batting, the whistle would not be blown for the end of playtime, so many was the time we had to remind him it was time to go home. Anyone who bowled or caught Pengo out was in deep trouble.

One incident he was always remembered for was in the winter time. The school yard was on a slope and you could always make a good slide and Pengo used to come out to join in and have a go on the slide, and on one frosty evening felt it was not very good, so he told us to put water on it. The following day at playtime, after a hard frost, he was the first to try it out, but it was so good he could not stop and he hit the wall at the bottom and broke his nose.

Nowadays we hear a lot about genes and sports, so a lot of my ability and keenness for the game was handed down from my dad who was obviously a useful batsman and a pillar of Bollington Cricket Club where he was the chairman for many years. There should have been no time for an anonymous letter telling him to resign. This spoiled for him a lifetime work for the club. I was the only person that saw this letter but he was convinced he knew who had sent it. He may have been wrong, but it did not help Bollington cricket in any way.

Before the 1939 war, local sport was always well supported. Bollington being a cotton town which employed hundreds in the mills, cricket in the summer was very popular attracting large crowds, the hero being the 'pro' Joe Rogers, who ran off about 30 paces and was to us the quickest bowler in cricket (no helmets then!).

The committee held their meetings at the Conservative Club across the road and on special days I used to help to move the chairs from off the dance hall to make a special enclosure where the 'better off' paid a bit extra. The Bollington vs. Macclesfield matches always played before a full house. Another highlight was the Cricket Club's New Year's Eve dance at the Conservative Club. People used to be coming to our house for tickets as early as September. Music was supplied by the local blacksmith Ambrose Wood and 'The Melody Makers'. Ambrose played the piano accordion usually with his eyes closed and the last waltz was always 'Whose Taking You Home Tonight?' unfortunately locals no longer support these institutions as in those days. The Conservative Club is being sold and the Cricket Club does not get the support from old players like it used to.

CRICKET BEFORE POTT SHRIGLEY

With war coming in 1939 a lot of clubs could not carry on, but Bollington made the effort with the help of older members like my dad who had been in the 1914–18 war. Fixtures were played against some works teams, the Home Guard, the ARP and the RAF at Wilmslow. Naturally there was a shortage of players, so I was always being sought after to play at the last minute. One snag being I delivered orders for the local co-op and the manager would never let me leave until I had taken the carrier bike up to the storeroom, cleaned it and he had inspected it!

I remember my first game was against the Home Guard.

In 1944 when I was just 14 years old, I was offered a job at Slater Harrisons Ltd, Paper Coaters, and like most families in Bollington had worked in the cotton mills, but most people felt that there was no future in this and after the war this proved to be correct, and I was encouraged to take the job, so I did.

3

At the same time another 14-year-old girl, Kitty Snape, started work in the office. We went out together at 16 years old and recently celebrated 48 years of marriage. Not only did she put up with my cricket but has helped with teas and secretarial work and still sees to it that we get 11 players in the proper place at the right time, which is not always easy. I am not sure if I got her interested in cricket or if it was the Test players of that era, like Denis Compton and Keith Miller etc.

With the war over, 1946 saw the resumption of league cricket and during 1946–48 I was a regular player mainly with the 2nd XI and had a lot of success with the ball. Large crowds again turned up, even to watch the seconds. In one game against Macclesfield (this team included Fred Millet who went on to captain Cheshire and the minor counties and was considered one of the best players outside the county game) the collection box was taken round and I was handed 15 shillings. Then the president, local builder Harold Cumberbirch gave me a ten-shilling note, this amounting to more than a week's

Before going on patrol round streets of Luneburg, 1949.

4

wage for a match-winning performance taking 5 wickets for 16 runs.

In 1948 I was called up to do National Service and eventually found myself in the Royal Military Police in Germany. Although the HQ was in Hamburg I was in the section at Luneberg, a large house which had belonged to Himmler and had plenty of grounds where we could play cricket and football as most duties were at night. A visiting officer must have been watching and sent for me and asked me who I had played for and I told him Bollington. He came from Staffordshire and played against Bollington so I was later informed I had been selected for the Hamburg and District police team. Whilst I enjoyed this experience it was a bit stuffy as cricket in the army tended to be more a game for warrant officers and above. One advantage was that if I went by train, I travelled Friday and arrived back Monday. On a couple of occasions I was taken by the RSM in his VW Beetle. He used to drive as if he was on parade, sitting bolt upright, peak cap facing forward and never speaking one word, and as the autobahns at that time carried hardly any traffic, they were boring journeys.

About this time I received a letter from my sister Jean, telling me her husband Fred Wrigley, who like myself was keen on cricket and football and had accompanied me to matches, had started playing cricket at Pott Shrigley (who were in those days considered to be a 'joke club' by most Bollington supporters).

At the time of writing, Fred is on his fiftieth year at Pott Shrigley; treasurer for many years, chairman, and 1st and 2nd XI captain. Treasurers are not always the most popular officials but, like Fred, are essential to the good running of a Club.

AND SO TO POTT

After leaving the army in the summer of 1950, I was obviously keen to play at Bollington who were then under a new regime. A school teacher, Bill Goodwin, who had been made captain of the 1st XI was determined Bollington should win the league and had recruited new players from other areas, one being Brian Jackson who later opened the bowling for Derbyshire, so with the abundance of players I only got an odd game with the 3rd XI.

I had gone back to my old job at the paper mill. Also returned after service in the navy in the war was an old friend of the family Geoffrey Harding who had married Eileen Bennett and gone to live with her parents in a cottage facing the cricket ground at Pott Shrigley, and was secretary of the Club.

5

Geoff was a popular, well-liked chap and in those days there always seemed to be a lot of fun and togetherness in factories, playing in workshop knockouts etc. Geoff had recruited several to Pott Shrigley so I said I would play for Pott until the end of the 1950 season, never thinking I would stay there until now.

These workshop knockouts also attracted large crowds at both cricket and football matches, with nearly all the workers and bosses going to watch. In one game against Pott Hammonds, who had no players but always entered a team, they turned up with bats one foot wide. Barracking was part of the game with some of the barrackers bringing megaphones.

On the day of a football knockout game for which I had borrowed some strips, some of the lads dressed up 'Little Bobby' who was about 40 years old but unfortunately had not grown very much, got the cart horse out of the field across the road from the mill, and led him through the factory. One wonders what would happen if this occurred today.

EARLY DAYS AT POTT

Any illusion I had about being too good for Pott Shrigley did not materialise, as the top bowlers were Geoff and Brian Hayman and the batters were R. Whittaker, K. Burgess and H. Furness, who was the only player with a car – a 'baby Austin Seven'. He would only carry one passenger and there was 'No Smoking'. Harry was a real old time stonewaller and as 'overs cricket' was not thought of, he played some marathon innings. He would infuriate the opposition by going down the wicket, blocking the ball and laughing at the bowler. Ross Whittaker was the captain of the 1st XI and owned The Holly Bush in Bollington. At the end of the season, Kit and I were married on the Wednesday after the last match. The hospitality must have been good because my uncle, Harry Shatwell, and the parson, Reverend Jones (a former naval chaplain), both had a drop too much to drink.

The annual dinner was always held at The Holly Bush and Ross was presented with a cheque and a table lamp and his wife was given a salad bowl. Even though I did not feel committed to staying at Pott Shrigley and I was probably one of the youngest players in the team, I was appointed 1st team captain for 1952.

BEFORE 1300

The oldest thing about Shrigley is its name, which was coined centuries before the house and its estate existed. 'Shrigley' comes from two words in Old English, the form of the language spoken before about 1100: *scric* (the missel-thrush) and *leah* (a woodland glade). Translated with a little poetic licence, the name must originally have meant something like a 'woodland glade where missel-thrushes sing', and is evocative of the very earliest history of the area. Eventually the glade would have had a small farm within it, from which over the centuries farmers gradually cleared more land for growing crops and grazing their animals on the hillside where Shrigley Hall and the golf course are now located.

In the Middle Ages all this part of the Cheshire Pennines lay within the forest of Macclesfield. Medieval 'forests' were not simply woodland, but rather areas governed by special laws which protected the hunting rights of their owners. Much of Macclesfield was rough moorland bare of trees, and among the woods on the lower slopes there were many small clearings like Shrigley, called 'assarts'. Macclesfield forest belonged first to the Norman earls of Chester, and after 1237 to the Crown. The farmers made a small payment for their assarts to the Crown as lord of the forest, and came to hold their land by a form of tenure called 'copyhold'. The first family that we know were landowners in the Shrigley area took their name, as did many similar families, from the place where they lived: the Shrigleys. Almost nothing was known about them.

About 1300 the main copyhold estate at Shrigley passed, probably by marriage, from the Shrigleys to the Downes family, already important landowners in the area at Taxal, east of Shrigley, and Downes, to the south, and one of the eight families which acted as hereditary foresters of Macclesfield under the Crown, guarding the Crown's rights in return for certain privileges of their own. Their copyhold estate at Shrigley was at first small, covering only about 150 acres, which is rather less than the size of the present golf course and grounds. The rest of Shrigley, extending to some 1,720 acres, consisted of other copyhold estates in the hands of other families. Several of them are documented from around the same time, including Pott Hall near the church (now a nursing home), and Berristall Hall, a farm on the hillside south of the village. All the copyhold farms of the area were said in 1348 to have originated as assarts in the forest of Macclesfield.

The Downes family eventually bought up most of the rest of the copyhold land in Shrigley and became undisputedly the most important family in the area. They also either founded or acquired control of the church just along the road from Shrigley Hall (now St Christopher's but originally called St Mary's). The place where the church was built was called 'Pott', referring to the hollow formed by the

7

steep-sided valleys of streams tumbling off the moors. The first written reference to the church calls it 'Our Lady of Downes chapel in Pott'. The name Pott stuck for the church and then for the hamlet which grew up round it, so that Shrigley soon became known as Pott Shrigley. Today the parish and the village are called Pott Shrigley, though what was once the Downes family's home is always plain Shrigley.

1

Pott Shrigley From the Beginning

Pott Shrigley Cricket Club was formed during 1919 when there was an upsurge countrywide in forming and reforming clubs and societies, many of which had been disbanded due to the First World War.

There had been cricket played earlier in the vicinity. Shrigley Vale had played matches on a field, also used for football, close to the Cheshire Hunt public house, but eventually they amalgamated with Bollington Cross Cricket Club to form the present Bollington Cricket Club.

Speaking at the Pott Shrigley Cricket Club annual dinner in 1963, Mr Isaac Cooper, former member of the Club and then chairman of the village parish council, recalled the days of the Club's formation when, 'Colonel Lowther was approached with a view to using part of his estate [which covered most of the village at the time]. One shilling a year was paid for the use of the area now occupied by the Club. Previously it had formed part of the old Pott Shrigley golf course. The playing area was not as big as it is today [1963] and often the outfield was in long grass, but they were happy days, in fact Pott Shrigley had always been a happy Club'.

He also recalled some of the early team members, men like Jack Kirk, Frank and George Tinsley, Ted Lidbetter, George Cooper, Charlie Cooper, Hugh Mayers, Hedley Snape, Harry Burt (first captain), Lew Roberts, William Leigh, Walter Kirkham, Alf Gardiner and Archie Brown, who continued playing until he was turned 80 years of age.

These are the men and more besides who we have to thank for all their initial industry and foresight in providing us with the perfect picturesque setting for playing the game which has come to captivate us all.

The first recorded press release was printed by the Macclesfield *Courier & Herald* on Saturday 24 July 1920 stating the following:

Pott Shrigley Cricket Club met the Manchester Ramblers last Saturday. The score was Pott Shrigley 53 and Manchester

Ramblers 42. The weather was favourable and there was a good gathering of spectators.

There will be no cricket today (Saturday) being the Wakes.

The next item discovered was the report of the first annual general meeting, appearing in the Macclesfield *Courier & Herald* on 8 January 1921, under the headline:

CRICKET AT POTT SHRIGLEY
The Annual Meeting of the Pott Shrigley Cricket Club was held in the school last week, when Mr. A. Harding presided. The Secretary read the accounts of the past season, which showed that out of a turnover of over £114, there will be a small balance in hand after the cricket pavilion has been erected. This, on a first full working year, reflects great credit on the Club. The officials were elected for the coming season as follows:

PRESIDENT	COL. W.G. LOWTHER
HON. SECRETARY	MR J. KIRK
TREASURER	MR A. HARDING
CAPTAIN	MR H. BURT
VICE CAPTAIN	MR F. TINSLEY

COMMITTEE: Messrs A. GARDINER, W. LEIGH, D. WOOD, A. BROWN, G. TINSLEY, L. ROBERTS, W.H. BENNETT, W. HEAPS, W. BARTON, W. KIRKHAM, F. FULTON, T.C. LIDBETTER, A. HOWE.

TEAM COMMITTEE: MR H. BURT, MR F. TINSLEY, MR W.H. BENNETT, MR W.H. HEAPS

Although Colonel Lowther accepted the presidency he could not have been a fit man, as the following month, when asked to carry on as president of Bollington Conservative Club, he wrote, 'I am now such a hopeless cripple that I could not attend Meetings and would be a figurehead only and it would be in your interests to choose another', so resigning.

Even so, he did continue to be our Club president for another seven years, until his death on 25 January 1928.

The first recorded scorecards also appeared in the local press on 27 May 1922, the 1st XI playing at home against J.E. Ogden & Sons Ltd, whilst the 2nd XI travelled to Adlington.

Ted Lidbetter, who opened the batting for Ogden's, eventually became 1st XI captain at Pott, just a few years later.

P.S.C.C. FIRST XI

H. MAYERS	c GRIMSHAW	b BUTTERWORTH	0
B. CASEY	LBW	LIDBETTER	0
F. TINSLEY	c WATSON	b LIDBETTER	0
S. HOWE	c & b	BUTTERWORTH	1
A. BROWN		b BUTTERWORTH	11
E. CROMPTON		b EASTWOOD	9
H. BURT		b EASTWOOD	2
G. TINSLEY		b BUTTERWORTH	2
J. KIRK	Run Out		4
G. COOPER	c WATSON	b BUTTERWORTH	0
W. LEIGH	Not Out		0
		Extras	2
		Total	31

J.E. OGDEN & SONS

E. LIDBETTER	Run Out		0
C. OGDEN	c TINSLEY	b CROMPTON	3
W. GRIMSHAW	c KIRK	b CROMPTON	14
E. WATSON	LBW	KIRK	0
H. BUTTERWORTH		b TINSLEY	1
F. EASTWOOD	c CASEY	b CROMPTON	7
J.E. OGDEN		b CASEY	0
A. HURSTFIELD	Run Out		0
I. TIMPERLEY		b CASEY	0
B. HANDS	c & b	HOWE	12
A. HOWELL	Not Out		2
		Extras	1
		Total	40

P.S.C.C. 2nd XI

F. FULTON	c ASTBURY	b WAINWRIGHT	10
BARTON	c JACKSON	b WARD	5
MAYERS		b WARD	0
EVERALL		b WAINWRIGHT	8
J. COOPER		b WAINWRIGHT	3

11

N. FULTON		b WAINWRIGHT	7
C. COOPER		b BAILEY	0
BARLOW	c ASTBURY	b BAILEY	0
GARDINER	Not Out		7
R. FULTON		b WAINWRIGHT	0
HARDING		b WAINWRIGHT	0
		Extras	13
		Total	53

ADLINGTON

BROGDEN		b L. FULTON	3
JACKSON	Run Out		11
WESTMACOAT	c COOPER	b N. FULTON	6
BOOTH	c COOPER	b N. FULTON	9
GRIFFITHS	c N. FULTON	b L. FULTON	0
WAINWRIGHT		b N. FULTON	39
DARBYSHIRE	c N. FULTON	b BARLOW	4
WARD	Not Out		5
BAILEY	c MAYERS	b BARLOW	0
ASTBURY	c COOPER	b BARLOW	0
DAVIES	c L. FULTON	b BARLOW	2
		Extras	1
		Total	80

ADLINGTON BOWLING

	O	M	R	W
WAINWRIGHT	8	1	17	6
WARD	4	1	14	2
BAILEY	3	0	9	2

P.S.C.C. BOWLING

	O	M	R	W
L. FULTON	7	–	38	3
N. FULTON	10	1	30	3
C. COOPER	5	–	11	–
BARLOW	1.3	–	1	4

The following week saw Pott Shrigley 1st XI at home to Langley 2nd XI. Batting first Pott Shrigley struggled to score 36 runs with W.

Holland, for Langley finishing with the remarkable figures of 9 wickets for 21 runs, but not to be outdone Pott hit back with E. Crompton taking 6 for 5 and E. Tinsley 4 for 3 thereby tumbling out Langley for only 14 runs.

As in common with other village cricket of the time, the matches and playing staff were dominated by the quick bowler. On the early uneven wickets, cut if you were lucky, on the morning of the match, or just before play began, the bowlers held most of the aces. Any team reaching three figures recognised this as a major achievement and nearly always a sure sign of success.

Declarations were very rare indeed and in most instances sides batting second completed their innings, even though they had passed the opposition's score.

The 1922 fixture list was a full one, with matches being played on most Saturdays throughout the season. The opposition was mainly local, but varied between 2nd or 3rd XIs from larger Clubs, Clubs on an equal footing, works sides and church or Sunday school sides. The Sunday schools had a long tradition and involvement in organising all kinds of sports and pastimes with much of our sport today evolving from these early links with the churches.

With enthusiasm bursting at the seams, the results of the 1922 season were regularly printed, with the match on 24 June meriting a full report.

The season went off as follows:

1922

JUNE 3rd	POTT SHRIGLEY	36	LANGLEY 2nds	14
JUNE 17th	CHRISTY'S			
	STOCKPORT	97	POTT SHRIGLEY	32
JUNE 24	PRESTBURY versus POTT SHRIGLEY			

The fixture between local teams was played on Saturday last on Prestbury's ground. When a low scoring match left the home team the winners by 14. The batting on both sides was weak. Without the splendid addition of 25 by their genial skipper, Prestbury would have looked pretty poor and similarly Snape's 16 for Pott Shrigley saved the side from leaving a hopeless score on the board. The bowling was difficult and went far towards securing the quick despatch of the teams, towards which smart fielding played an important part.

13

PRESTBURY

H. JANSEN	c FULTON	b LIDBETTER	4
FINDLOW	b TINSLEY		0
COLLIER		b TINSLEY	0
NEILL	Run Out		4
SILLAVAN		b LIDBETTER	25
J. JANSEN	c COOPER	b LIDBETTER	6
BUNYAN	Not Out		5
HOLT	c FULTON	b LIDBETTER	3
STEARN		b LIDBETTER	0
MILLNER		b TINSLEY	3
DARLINGTON	c LIDBETTER	b TINSLEY	4
		Extras	1
		Total	55

POTT SHRIGLEY

E. LIDBETTER	c HOLT	b JANSEN	0
K. SNAPE		b DARLINGTON	16
F. TINSLEY	LBW	DARLINGTON	3
J. KIRK	c HOLT	b DARLINGTON	3
L. FULTON	c & b	JANSEN	2
H. MAYERS	Not Out		12
HOWE		b DARLINGTON	0
G. COOPER	Run Out		0
W. BARTON	c COLLIER	b JANSEN	2
F. GARDINER		b DARLINGTON	0
		Extras	6
		Total	44

JULY 1st	POTT SHRIGLEY	41	WHALEY BRIDGE 2nds	65
JULY 15th	J.E. OGDEN & SONS	22	POTT SHRIGLEY	39
	Crompton 7 Wkts and Tinsley 3 Wkts			
JULY 22nd	POTT SHRIGLEY	32	ADLINGTON	30
	Ward 9 Wkts for 18 Runs and Tinsley 6 Wkts for 17 Runs			
JULY 29th	POTT SHRIGLEY	27	ST GEORGES	89
AUG 26th	POTT SHRIGLEY	69	LANGLEY	45

SEPT 2nd   POTT SHRIGLEY   57   PRESTBURY   15
          Lidbetter 7 Wkts

AVERAGES FOR 1922
Played 16   Won 8   Lost 8   Runs for 749   Highest Score 98
Lowest Score 20   Runs against 847   Highest Score 117   Lowest
Score 14

BOWLING

	OVERS	MAIDENS	RUNS	WICKETS	AVERAGE
E. LIDBETTER	106	24	188	41	4.58
F. TINSLEY	122	36	178	38	4.68
E. CROMPTON	41	9	77	18	4.2
G. COOPER	46	13	91	15	6.06
J. KIRK	29	3	80	8	10.00
B. CASEY	24	2	59	5	11.8

BATTING

	INNS	RUNS	H.S.	RUNS	AVERAGE
R. SNAPE	11	–	32	107	9.7
E. LIDBETTER	13	–	22	96	7.38
B. CASEY	10	1	14	64	7.1
F. TINSLEY	14	1	18	68	5.23
E. CROMPTON	8	1	12	41	5.8
J. KIRK	11	1	16	47	4.7
A. MAY	9	1	11	33	4.1
A. BROWN	12	1	13	40	3.63
H. BURT	15	2	21	47	3.61
H. WRIGHT	7	–	10	23	3.28
L. FULTON	9	2	6	23	3.28
G. COOPER	10	2	5	11	1.37
W. BARTON	6	–	2	4	0.66

By 1924 the Club had joined the Adlington and District Cricket
Association. An early attempt at league cricket by a few local clubs,
these games were interspersed with normal friendly fixtures so as to
ensure a full fixture list.

The final tables for 1924 showed us next to bottom, to which we
eventually sank the following season.

1924 LEAGUE TABLE

	P	W	D	L	PTS
WOODFORD	5	4	1	–	9
NORBURY S.S.	5	4	1	–	9
ADLINGTON	6	3	–	3	6
LANGLEY 2nds	6	2	–	4	4
POTT SHRIGLEY	5	1	–	4	2
OAK GROVE	5	1	–	4	2
WHITLEY GREEN	WITHDREW				

1925

	P	W	D	L	PTS
POTT SHRIGLEY	12	3	1	8	7

Cricket being the complex game it is, has always thrown up controversy. Here is one from the early days of our Club and just as today, the press, albeit local, played their part by giving it prominent coverage on the sports pages of the day.

13 September 1924

Warrington who are running Macclesfield close for the championship of the Manchester & District Cricket Association, turned out with only ten men at Bollington on Saturday last. They required twelve runs to win and nine wickets had fallen, so a Bollington man was asked to go in and bat, and he knocked up a score that won the match for Warrington.

Will Macclesfield Cricket Club protest? I hope so.

signed (BOLLINGTON CORRESPONDENT)

20 September 1924

Your correspondent of last week should have made sure of his facts. We do not dispute that Warrington had to find a substitute, but he went in when seven wickets were down and not nine as stated. Moreover he plays for Pott Shrigley and was merely at Bollington as a spectator.

We never did find out who our player was, or if Macclesfield CC protested or not, but they did win the league that year, though Bollington got their own back by pipping Macclesfield to the title the following year.

Funds were always required during this period and the popular

16

efforts of the time were whist drives. These seem to have been held on a regular basis at the school and were well attended by the local men and womenfolk, with prizes donated by the members. The whist drive and dance in January 1927 was attended by the Member of Parliament for Macclesfield, Mr J.R. Remer, who addressed the gathering. Mr Remer was also well-known for his connections with the local crown-green bowling societies of the day, who played annually for the Remer Cup.

Only four results are known for 1927:

21 May   Saw Pott scoring 62 then tumbling Adlington out for only 11 runs. W. Hough taking 5 for 4 and J. Vare 5 for 5.

11 June   Pott had their second win scoring 55 to Oak Grove's 47. This game saw J. Vare taking 7 wickets for 18 runs and in doing so beat the league leaders.

25 June   A close game saw Pott beating Offerton by only 3. 38 to 35 with no player on either side reaching double figures.

16 August This was an even lower scoring game, in which Shrigley just beating Oak Grove for the second time. Pott could only score 27, but it proved to be enough, as the opposition collapsed to 22 all out. W. Hough was top scorer on both sides with 6 runs.

The annual dinner on 21 January 1928 was held at the Merridian Hotel Bollington, and it is recorded that:

There was a good gathering, the dinner and singing was greatly enjoyed by all. The minutes read by Mr Ford drew attention to Mr Archibald Brown, the veteran of the club, who would attain his 75th birthday on Thursday and wished him good health, hoping he would reach his century. F. Tinsley gave an inspired speech in which he appealed for juniors to come for a trial and to be *coached*.

Only four days later on 25 January it was announced that Colonel W.G. Lowther JP (our first Club president) had died at his residence Shrigley Hall in his 79th year. Colonel Lowther was replaced as Club president by Mrs Higson who, living at Pott Hall helped to start the local Rose Queen tradition and served as president for two years before moving to Windermere.

1928 also saw a new Adlington and District Cricket Association being announced with new management and conditions, though what they were remains a mystery.

Two landmarks were reached during the season, on 5 May away to Trinity Wesleyans and Shrigley bowlers dismissed the home side for 47, then Pott themselves were bowled out for 47 also, resulting in the Club's first tied game.

Then on 30 June Pott hit their highest score to date, with Walter Hough hitting the Club's first individual score over 50. His innings of 54 away at Adlington, took Pott to 129 then after sufficient tea he proceeded to take 5 wickets for 26, along with A. Wainwright's 5 for 32 sending Adlington back for 62.

Shrigley's 1st XI finished mid-table with 12 points from 12 games, but the 2nd XI finished top of division 2. Their record of played 10, won 7, drawn 1, lost 2, pts 15 ensured the Club's first success.

Unfortunately for the players concerned no trophy existed at the time for the Division 2 winners, but this was to be rectified by the Pott Shrigley president Mrs Higson the following season.

It was interesting to note that some Clubs played two games on the same day. Now there's keenness for you.

All the effort and input of the early years by the many enthusiastic members began to come to fruition in 1929. The Adlington and District Cricket Association Division 1 was increased to nine teams with eight in Division 2.

The sun shone brightly on the first half of the season and Pott Shrigley must have had their share of luck. Several keen and tightly contested games were played with the 'Hillmen' coming out on top. Bundled out for 29 by Trinity Wesleyans, Pott bowlers hit back dismissing the opposition for only 25 and in another low scoring game against Christys Stockport, Pott could only make a total of 45 but this proved enough as the visitors could only muster 38. An even closer game was played later in the season when playing at home to Grove Lane and batting first Pott could only raise 35 runs, but again the bowlers triumphed securing victory by the closest margin of 1.

To their credit the 2nd XI matched the results gained by the 1st and at the halfway point in the season neither team had lost a match, reflecting a strength in depth not achieved before.

Though each team did lose one game apiece, the final tables show Pott Shrigley teams sitting proudly on top of their respective divisions, winning a trophy for the first time in the Club's history.

On the first Saturday following the season the champions met a league XI at Adlington and the event was reported as follows:

18

21 September 1929

On Saturday the Pott Shrigley Club met the Association XI at Adlington, when a very entertaining match was held. The champions certainly played as such, being comparatively easy winners.

During the interval, Mrs Higson presented the medals and the Mather Cup and mentioned that as President of the Pott Shrigley Club she was particularly pleased they had secured the championship of both the First and Second Divisions, an achievement which had never been equalled by any Club in the Association.

The Adlington and District Cricket Association is very greatly indebted to Mrs Higson for her splendid offer of an additional Challenge Cup, which will undoubtedly create a greater interest in the competitions and will prove especially attractive for the first winners next season.

As the following scoreboard shows, Joe Fisher was a fine strike bowler and must have commanded respect wherever he played. He regularly took wickets, both at home and away. Joe eventually was to become 2nd XI captain and was still playing in the 1951 side.

Walter Hough was more of an all-rounder than Joe, but had many 5- and 6-wicket hauls himself as well as scoring the Club's first 50. Together they must have made a formidable pair of bowlers on which much of Pott Shrigley's early success was founded.

CHAMPIONS POTT SHRIGLEY

R. JACKSON	c HEATHCOTE	b BARTON	5
W. BROGEN		b TETLER	5
A. GARDINER		b TETLER	1
F. KIRK		b BARTON	6
A. LEWIS	c BUXTON	b TETLER	1
E. LIDBETTER (Capt)	LBW	b BUXTON	7
C. CHADWICK	Run Out		5
C. RILEY		b BUXTON	12
C. COOPER	c BARTON	b HEATHCOTE	3
J. FISHER		b BARTON	4
H. MEYERS	Not Out		9
		Extras	6
		Total	64

19

BOWLING

A. HEATHCOTE	1–19	W. TETLER	3–15
F. BARTON	3–12	A. BUXTON	2–12

SELECT XI

W. TETLER	c RILEY	b FISHER	18
BARKWORTH		b FISHER	0
SUTTON		b FISHER	0
A. HEATHCOTE		b FISHER	5
F. BARTON		b FISHER	0
MELLOR	c RILEY	b FISHER	0
A. BUXTON		b KIRK	11
W. HOUGH		b FISHER	11
I. SMITH	c COOPER	b LEWIS	2
G. TOMLINSON		b KIRK	1
C. HOUGH	Not Out		0
		Extras	3
			—
		Total	51
			—

BOWLING

J. FISHER	7–17	A. GARDINER	0–10
A. LEWIS	2–20	F. KIRK	1–2

UMPIRES:	MR BAKER	CHRISTY'S C.C.
	MR PLATT	HIGHER POYNTON C.C.

FINAL LEAGUE TABLES 1929

1ST DIVISION

	P	W	L	D	PTS
POTT SHRIGLEY	16	14	1	1	29
CHRISTYS	16	9	6	1	19
GROVE LANE	16	9	7	–	18
TRINITY WESLEYANS	16	9	7	–	18
KERRIDGE	16	8	7	1	17
HIGHER POYNTON	16	7	9	–	14
ADLINGTON	16	6	9	1	13
NORBURY	16	–	14	2	2

2ND DIVISION

POTT SHRIGLEY	14	12	1	–	26
TRINITY WESLEYANS	14	10	4	–	20
KERRIDGE	14	10	4	–	20
OAK GROVE	14	8	4	2	18
HIGHER POYNTON	14	4	8	2	10
CHRISTYS	14	4	8	2	10
GROVE LANE	14	2	12	–	4
ADLINGTON	14	1	12	1	3

During recent years our the Club has been fortunate in the help given by our ladies. Village cricket more than most relies on wives and girlfriends in many areas of Club life. This also seemed to be the case back in 1930. As the champions began their defence of the trophy, the ladies of the day were determined to play their part to the full as the following newspaper report shows all too well:

10 May 1930
POTT SHRIGLEY 134, ADLINGTON 33 (Ainsworth 7 for 9)
Adlington visited Pott Shrigley on Saturday last, the weather being very dull. They were unfortunate to lose the choice and Pott Shrigley decided to bat first.

Adlington's luck seemed to have deserted them, or was it the home teams lady supporters' vociferous encouragement to the homesters that upset them, anyhow they were badly knocked about and it will not be the Pott Shrigley ladies fault if the Cup leaves the village.

As the end of the season approached the ladies must have been quite hoarse for Pott went into the last game to Trinity needing a win to clinch a second championship. This they duly did and Captain Lidbetter received the Division 1 trophy from the league president G.E. Gardiner, celebrating afterwards the Legh Arms, Adlington. Well done Ladies.

1931 proved to be another successful year for the Club, skippered by Ted Lidbetter with vice-captain Walter Hough. Once again on these early wickets the bowlers had the upper hand. Two remarkable performances were reported in the local press of the day:

29 May
The outstanding feature of Saturday's matches was that of Walter Hough of Pott Shrigley, who was mainly responsible for

21

the first defeat of Higher Poynton this season, by taking six wickets in six consecutive balls, all bowled, so taking Pott Shrigley to the top of the League. All told he took nine wickets for only four runs.

The second superb return was by G. Tomlinson for the Second XI, against Adlington, he won the game by taking eight wickets for only ten runs.

It must have been a close run thing for the 1st XI, as it was reported that the Club had objected to taking part in a match with Higher Poynton, to decide the championship, claiming that by the rules of the league they had already won the championship.

This was confirmed at a meeting of the league committee and the Club captain was congratulated and presented with the Mather Cup for a third consecutive season. The 2nd XI also finished as Division 2 champions, again taking the Higson Trophy, celebrations being held at the village school.

The following season saw Club's entering both 'A' and 'B' teams in the same league and on 5 August Joe Fisher for Pott 'B' took 8 for 24 versus Kerridge 'A'; then, two weeks later came the 'crunch' game as Shrigley 'B' Team beat Shrigley 'A' 50 runs to 21 runs in another game dominated by bowlers.

The 'B' team eventually ran out winners of the league with the 'A' team finishing as runners-up. The 'B' side went on to beat a rest of the league side 45 runs to 20. Celebrations this time were held at the Turners Arms, Mr Isaac Smith presenting the trophies and medals.

From 1933, Clubs started to form their own fixture lists and continued to play friendly games and, as far as we can ascertain, the Adlington and District League trophies were used for the last time for a knockout competition, the finalists being Woodford and Pott Shrigley. But this time Woodford carried the day scoring 54 to Pott Shrigley's 30. Top scorer on the day was Green hitting 10 for Woodford who were awarded the Mather Cup with Pott being presented with the Higson Trophy. The Shrigley team on the day were W. Brogden (captain), F. Thorley, W. Hough, F. Kirk, J. Gumm, F. Brogden, L. Hough, C. Riley, J. Whitehurst, R. Jolliff and F. Lonsdale.

During the mid-1930s, most of the local minor Clubs were finding it hard to survive. Prestbury were struggling, appealing for players as well as funds and Langley had to merge with Brocklehurst-Whiston Amalgamated in an effort to continue playing. Similar pressures must have existed at Pott Shrigley as people found it hard enough to live, let alone fund cricket teams and the club committee felt it necessary to put this press release in the local sports pages at the start of the 1936 season:

Rumours that Pott Shrigley C.C. had approached Bollington C.C. to be absorbed into their Club and become a Bollington 3rd XI are officially denied. More efforts will be made to raise money to put the Club on a more secure basis. Meanwhile, work to improve the ground will continue and friendly fixtures only will be played, in the hope that the Adlington and District League will be re-formed.

The same season saw the first mens vs. ladies match in which the ladies were represented by: L. Hewitt, Miss Tilson, Mrs Brogden, G. Lomas, J. Jackson, Mrs Hough, V. Tinsley, I. Bennett, N. Henstock, M. Sheldon, I. Bradley, A. Lomas, M. Brown, E. Ainsworth and W. Hough, but despite their numbers the ladies still lost 76 runs to 89 by the men.

The Club did continue, playing local friendly cricket and the scores recorded show that the bowlers in general kept the upper hand. The highest pre-war individual score we could find was an innings of 58 by Hough in 1939, at Lyme Park, but it didn't say which Hough: Walter or Les. The Houghs were cousins living in Bollington.

A match later the same year received a mention on the sports pages under the headline FIREWORKS AT POTT SHRIGLEY. It reported that a team called Macclesfield Educationalists had been shot out for 7 runs – of which 5 were Extras. Les Hough took 6 wickets for 1 run and A. Hurrell took 3 wickets for the other run.

Arthur Shepley at 79 must be our oldest ex-player, though you would find this hard to believe, as Arthur can still be spotted, regularly walking through Bollington as sprightly as ever. His memory is clearer than many half his age and his eyes light up as he recounts games past.

He tells of a visit to Adlington, which resulted in his third 'duck' in a row. Vowing never to play again, he threw his boots under Adlington's pavilion. By the following Monday, Arthur had relented so he trudged all the way back, crawled under the pavilion to retrieve his boots, cleaned them off and carried on playing.

Unfortunately Arthur passed away recently, whilst this book was in production.

2

The Friendly Years

Like most village clubs, the war had taken its toll with the ground and pavilion neglected. However, one significant thing did happen: someone parked a caravan on the ground and, very unusual for a small village, no one seems to remember a name only that they came from Manchester to avoid the bombing.

The Shrigley ground after the war, showing the caravan, photo supplied by Kirks, a name associated with Pott for many years.

The move to get things going again at Pott appears to have been started by two old members, Jack Barton and Hubert Dalzell, later joined by Geoff Harding who became secretary and instrumental in getting the clubs fixtures, obviously a difficult job. For a small village,

Pott had a remarkably good bus service, with buses from Macclesfield to Stockport every hour and buses through Bollington regularly going to Pott, so a lot of games could be arranged with works teams, Hovis and Scraggs of Macclesfield, Mirlees and Albert Mills of Stockport being regular opposition.

There is also evidence of a second team playing in this period, one member being an apprentice plumber – Bryan Holmes, who later started his own business and has given hours of his time helping the Club, mending burst pipes, repairing windows etc. He almost lost his life helping the club (more about this later).

In 1949 the Club joined the North Cheshire cricket division but with Clubs forming and disbanding at an alarming rate, this organisation folded.

As tends to happen with older members, when one retires, several of that era seem to follow suit, taking up bowls and golf. One I remember was Joe Fisher, a nagging bowler, who had taken nine wickets. We had given a few runs away before the last man was run out and Chelford were 26 all out. However this backfired with Pott skittled out for 13 runs. In retrospect this was a time when village clubs like Pott Shrigley could soon go under or survive and try and improve.

The few youngsters who were taking the game up were generally from grammar schools and were directed to the bigger league clubs in the area. We had two good young players in Reg Payne and Ted Cooper who performed well before joining Bollington. Ted was a big strong Pott lad who bowled quite quickly and in his National Service days won several boxing medals. He later went on to build up a successful transport business but always took interest in the Club, buying a house quite close to the cricket ground. The last time I spoke to Ted, he said he could get a set of gang mowers cheap and was the club interested? At that time the club was having huge problems regarding the 'right of way' to the ground with all our funds being swallowed up on solicitors' fees. (A lot more of this later.) Ted said if the committee were interested, he would put the money down and we could pay him back as soon as possible. The committee agreed, so I called at his house to inform him, but as there seemed a few people about, I left it to go back after lunch. When I got home, Kit told me that Ted had died. Obviously it was a big shock for Jean and the family, but shortly afterwards Jean telephoned to say it was one of the last things they had discussed, and she hoped the club would carry on with the arrangements we had made. Shortly after, I met her walking the dog round Pott Shrigley and Jean stated she would like to donate the mowers in memory of Ted, a gesture which we all appreciated.

25

The ground, particularly the outfield, was in a poor state, not being cut until about June and then only by an old chap who had a small-holding about half a mile away, using a scythe. However, we did get an older member who worked for a local builder to lay a concrete practice wicket. Arthur Shepley was the chap always remembered by visiting teams, as along with his cricket tackle, he nearly always turned up with his shotgun so he could shoot a few rabbits; with rationing still on, rabbit pie or stew were popular. Arthur was a survivor of the Burma campaign and his other claim to fame, if you could call it that, was that he and Gerv Coe got one run each and two byes when Pott were bowled out for four at Stockport parish.

As you could imagine most games had low scores so there were plenty of early finishes. Hence we usually ended up at Bollington watching their game with the local bigmouths saying 'Here come Pott, they have lost the ball down a rabbit hole'. With their ground always beautifully kept (they had a professional to look after the wicket plus two other council workers) I did begin to think I had 'missed the boat'.

One thing that I had insisted on was players should wear whites which did not happen at times with village clubs, but in my mind it made the opposition think you could all play a bit. The season finished as usual with a Sunday game at Didsbury. Ross Whittaker came back from Devon to play, only to play cards all afternoon.

I was again appointed captain for 1953. I accepted not thinking I would do the job for the next 12 years.

With the ground showing no improvement, the back of the old wooden pavilion was now rotting away. As a club we have been lucky with getting members to help in situations like this and an engineer – Norman Hodson – devised a plan to make an angle iron frame with asbestos sheets. On the Saturday we did the job. Norman and an apprentice, Donald Hackney, carried the angle iron down to Maccles-field bus station, put them in the luggage boot and transported them to Pott.

Norman was a huge man about 6'4", weighing approximately 16 stone. He stood and held the roof up while we knocked the old back out and inserted the framework. Funnily enough for such a big fellow he was another great stonewaller at cricket and table tennis.

If I could name a year when the seeds were sown to start improving the club, I would say 1954. With two or three years behind us, and Geoff still the secretary, it was apparent that all the village organisa-tions were virtually controlled by a couple of families who, in most members eyes, preferred to keep the village in a time-warp with no development or improvement anywhere.

As quite a lot of members did not live in Pott Shrigley it was difficult but you could not carry on a cricket club still using ideas from the 1930s. What members wanted was firstly a proper balance sheet as the name of Jack Barton was always given as treasurer, but he was never seen and some 20 years later Jack told me he had never held office. One is not suggesting any fiddle was going on, obviously the money involved was negligible but we wanted to get the club on a better footing.

Although I did say 1954 was the year the club really started to improve, I did not think so a few hours after the meeting. I woke up with terrible stomach pain and sent for the family doctor in the early hours. He poked around and said 'Derrick, you will have to get that appendix out' and a few hours later I was operated on. Strangely enough it did start an improvement on the ground as we had now purchased a second-hand Acto 16 motor mower and as I was still off work I went to the ground, got the mower out and started cutting the outfield. As the weather was good for all the time I was off work, progress was made and even though it was not a big area it was certainly an improvement.

I missed playing in the early part of the season, but a local businessman Eric Burgess had joined the Club and had encouraged two new members to the Club: Joe and Graham Higginbotham. Joe was a good swing bowler and Graham was one of the best all-rounders that have played for Pott Shrigley.

Apart from their playing ability both were enthusiastic about the club. Joe was a bit of a wanderer changing houses and jobs at frequent intervals. However, on one of his jobs he had worked on a golf course and set about improving the wickets. There were only three at the time and at the graveyard end there was only a run-up of about four-yards before a sharp fall of about a foot and a half. Joe turned the square round a bit and squared it up so we now had five wickets of a sort.

After good weather when I was not playing, the summer turned into a wet one. Two more members came about this time: Shipley Broster, a big hitter from the next village of Rainow, and Philip Hammond who had not played before but was a fighter (I gather in more ways than one). He turned out to be an exceptional worker for the club. He always said he looked like Alan Ladd but nobody agreed with him although he was about the same size.

The club now appeared to be on the up and Joe, Graham and myself started to do work on the square. At the end of the season Joe managed to borrow a hand-operated aerating machine. Joe held the handles while Graham and I had a rope over our shoulders pulling it along. Each time the tines dug into the ground, it felt as though it was

27

pulling your neck off your shoulders. We then decided we had to get rid of the worms.

By this time Kit and I had managed to buy our first car – a 1939 Austin Cambridge – so off we went to Hadfields in Macclesfield and bought 1.5 cwt of lead arsenic. Joe and I chucked the stuff on and needless to say we have never had a lot of trouble with worm casts in that area. I would think that we would be breaking EU regulations today.

At the AGM of 1955 a lot of discussion took place regarding the state of the pavilion, with many ideas about getting hold of second-hand sheds etc. Every idea met with rebuff from the locals who were stating the Peak Park planning would only allow anything the same size and it would have to be put in the same place which seemed unbelievable as the only toilet facilities were two sheets of corrugated iron by the side of the wall which was only about 2' high, so anyone behind the sheets could be seen from the road and cottages across the road. The nearest ladies toilet was in Bollington. The secretary was asked to find out from the Peak Park the proper situation regarding planning permission. Not before time, Fred was appointed treasurer and was not pleased when the club was £9 in the red. He never let this occur again.

Also it was passed at the meeting and agreed that we should hire a coach for all Sunday games although this was not popular in all quarters. Most people look back to those days which seemed to bring a terrific atmosphere to the Club, always a sing-song on the way home, and there were a few memorable incidents. One player's father-in-law (a heavy drinker who always wore his hard hat) had a drinking session with the coachdriver who, when it was time to go, just stood up and fell over, so we had to stay a couple more hours to sober him up. When some of the clubs booked fixtures they would ask if the man in the pot hat would be coming, no doubt thinking about their bar takings! Although we now had only one team it was quite successful with most players knowing what cricket was about.

We had also purchased another 16" motor mower so with two people mowing, the outfield improved a bit more.

The closed season saw the start of more effort to raise funds with a Christmas draw and a football competition.

The state of the pavilion was again discussed at meetings, but in general it appeared we were banging our heads against a brick wall.

1956 again saw good progress. Looking at the AGM for that year subscriptions were fixed at 2/6d, match fee 1/-. Cash in hand was £122/17/6d at the year end and the first indication of our intentions to do something about the pavilion. Materials for the new pavilion

(£36/14/0d) having been purchased there was still a feeling among the players outside the village that the locals on the committee were not keen on this progress and with G. Harding, B. Stewart both son-in-laws of Mr Bennett and Mr Stewart, chairman, we knew we would have a fight on our hands to get things moving. Fred heard that Mr Bennet's name had been put on the committee without being proposed. Fred told them in no uncertain words this was wrong and Mr Bennett said it didn't look as if Mr Wrigley wanted him but even though his name was not on the committee as being elected at the meetings, it did turn up on the fixture card.

It always seemed sad that divisions between some of the villagers and people who were prepared to improve the club and ground existed, but we had good playing staff who were also willing to work to improve things. Most had been in the forces and now wanted to enjoy their life and sport under the best possible conditions. It was generally decided that if we were not allowed to improve, particularly with the pavilion, we would look at the old ground at Adlington, whose Club had never started again after the war.

After the meeting we were still discussing things and somebody remarked they were glad that Fred shot the sheriff down. From then on Mr Bennett was always known as The Sheriff of Pott Shrigley to Club members and as he appeared to do most of his business in the phone box by the church, this became the sheriff's office.

The 1957 season was probably one of the busiest in the clubs history. At the AGM most of the officials stayed the same. Subscriptions went to 5/-. We were determined to make headway with a new pavilion and the idea of building one with concrete blocks was agreed. The season went well and we managed to get some plans drawn up, so on the Saturday after the last game seven or eight of us went up to the ground, tied a rope around the old wooden pavilion and pulled it down. Naturally, this caused a bit of a stir with the locals, but it gave the message that we intended to build a new pavilion, or there would not be a cricket club, the idea being that we could build it by ourselves with these blocks.

The new pavilion was allowed to be built on another site and was about double the size of the old wooden one, so all we had been told about only being able to build it on the same site and the same size was a load of rubbish. Although we had no one in the club in the building trade, Philip Hammond had done a bit of labouring for a builder and we paid him £25 to come along and start us off, so by Christmas it was halfway up. When it came to the windows etc. Philip said he had a cousin – Percy Barker – who had a building firm who could make the windows and doors. Percy had a reputation as a top-class builder and also we managed to get a joiner – Arthur Pickford – to help.

One problem we had was getting materials across to the ground as the farmyard and croft could be a bit of a nightmare in the summer and in the winter it was like the Klondyke. However, with horse and cart and tractor we struggled on. With a bit of bad weather and Christmas, it was soon February and you start talking about eight or nine weeks to the first match.

Not only were we building a pavilion we were also having to raise money running a series of dances on Saturday nights. The ladies, organised by Ethel Burgess, held jumble sales, coffee mornings etc. On the Saturday of the annual dinner we had a day off, but I had a walk round. When I got to the ground there was a photographer from the local paper taking a photo of Geoff with a trowel in his hand pretending to be pointing up, and the caption read 'Pott members working in the day, then attending the dinner at night'. The reality was he was doing neither but it made good publicity. Still Geoff was well liked and easy to get on with. Unfortunately he was a chain smoker who always seemed to have a conversation with a cigarette butt in the corner of his mouth. Whether this did his health any good I am not sure, but it was him that got most of us to Pott in the first place.

With time going by and the walls more or less finished, the big problem was the lintels over the windows and glass front, so we asked a joiner to board these in. Obviously he did not work in the building trade but spent all one Saturday and most of Sunday making a box. When he finished it, it did look a bit like 'The Bridge Over the River Kwai'. We were getting ready to put the concrete in when Arthur and Percy came up, had one look, and said 'That's no use like that'. Percy picked a piece of wood up, knocked one stay out and the lot collapsed. These two gentlemen, both of whom had spent a lifetime in the building trade, then more or less took charge of the project giving hours of their time and expertise. However, the Sheriff nearly ruined this for us. Percy's firm had started building some new houses in Bollington on Shrigley Road. He had a good reputation and had them all designed differently. However, even though they were not in the Sheriff's territory he put an article in the local paper calling them 'Monstrosities'. Naturally, Percy was upset at the idea of giving and doing so much for the club and then having as he thought an official of the club denting his pride.

However, both Percy and Arthur became superb members of the club, Percy taking up umpiring and Marion, his wife, putting on coffee evenings etc. in the top 'Monstrosity' where they were now living.

30

Arthur had one or two claims to fame in the club. He always came armed with a bag of Nuttall Mintoes and as it was the time of the Colonel Pinto affair, Arthur became 'Colonel Minto'. He had also served in the Royal Navy so he only drank rum stating it never made him ill, until one night we had to stop the bus for him about four times. He never lived that down. Probably the most important thing he did for the club was bring his 13-year-old son John along, who not only became the only member I remember to get all ten wickets (a feat emulated by Rick Mattock) but as you will read later he was one of the most influential officials we have had. Unfortunately for Pott Shrigley John chose a career with Customs and Excise and I know everywhere he has lived it has been their cricket Club's gain and our loss.

Even though John had no boys his eldest daughter, Sarah, followed in his footsteps by playing, while John still runs juniors in Horsforth and Sarah also played for Yorkshire Ladies. When her mum, Pam, died a few years back she lost interest for a while. John has recently remarried and brought Alison, his wife, to watch Pott playing in an important promotion match in September only to see them all out for 65 runs and lose by 10 wickets.

Back to the pavilion. With all the help we had received this was virtually completed a fortnight before the first game, but not painted. However, the next time we went up 'noughts and crosses' had been painted on the walls so we had to set to and paint it. Everyone blamed me for this but I suspected Joe Higginbotham who was working nearby, a fact which Joe admitted to a few years later. Joe was a great Club man but had a bit of wanderlust and at the end of the season we presented him with a barometer. He made an emotional speech, some of the ladies even had tears in their eyes, but then he was back for the start of the next season. The balance sheet for the end of the year reflected how much effort went into the club, with £527/13/0d being spent on the new pavilion and increased expenditure on the ground. We still had £43 in hand. Also on this balance sheet was an item in the income 'Ted Blair Billiards'. Ted was a top class billiards player which was popular in those days, and he gave an exhibition with several top-class players. He also had been a good wicket-keeper having played minor counties cricket – not in the Jack Russell mode but a thick-set man who wore big wide pads, and with his nose on top of the bails you never hardly got a ball past him. He was about 60 years old when he joined us and obviously past his best with his eyesight going a bit and on one occasion Graham Hackney (Pott's Derek Randle) went for a run out with a fast throw from close in which Ted never saw which luckily slid off his bald patch leaving a scratch from front to back. Ted gave us about three years good service, hardly ever missing a game and eventually when we left him off the team one weekend, he went and joined another Club.

One thing he did do was to bring his next door neighbour, Bob Fairhall, to the Club. Bob was later to become a pillar of the Club and also the chairman of the Cheshire league. Sometimes he could be a bit controversial, but I am sure he was well-respected for it.

At the AGM in 1958 we had decided to close the pavilion and the 'Buy a Block' fund at 2/6d a block brought in about £130. A plaque with the names on still hangs in the pavilion today.

The pavilion was opened on 10 May 1958 and of course in a small village several of the 'knockers' were on the photograph of the opening ceremony.

Another feature was the floral displays in both the marquee and pavilion arranged by a Mrs Metcalfe of the Old Vicarage who seemed to appear from nowhere for this event. Even though we had a new pavilion we had no water or electricity so we had to buy chemical toilets and still carry water from the churchyard.

Looking at some of the minutes for that time discussions did take place regarding these services but a letter from the Water Board stated no new connections could be made until the supply was improved to the village, so it was some years and a lot more in-fighting with the natives before this was achieved.

I have named this chapter 'The Friendly Years' because we virtually played only 'friendlies' playing five-hours cricket. Practise was on a Tuesday night when nearly all the members turned up. Sunday games were always played away. For Sunday games on the bigger grounds we always tried to get a couple of outsiders from Macclesfield to play and Philip Hough, who had games at the Lancashire, turned out. However this did not always go down well with the opposition so we began to rely on our own ability, made a lot of friends and usually giving a good account of ourselves. Also during this season one or two more members, including juniors, came along so we had to start discussing restarting a second team.

Another aspect of these so called 'friendlies' were the local Derby games, particularly against Langley, Prestbury and Chelford as most of the Clubs at that time seemed to possess an umpire who had been with the club for years. It is difficult to say they cheated, but they liked to see their own club win. Langley had a chap called Harold Goodwin who had given me out so many times, one day it hit me on the pad, there was a big shout so I thought I may as well walk, and in the pub afterwards he bought me a drink for being such a good sport.

Another incident I remember was at Prestbury. One day they had an

32

umpire, Dennis Scott, whose family had been associated with Prestbury for years. Dennis had moved from Prestbury but still umpired for them. He always came on the train and was usually about ten minutes late arriving. He always seemed a bit eccentric and when officiating sat on a shooting stick and when giving the opposition out, stood to attention. On one particular day Philip Hammond was batting, Dennis came out, sat on the shooting stick – a big appeal for LBW off the first ball, up he stands with his finger up and Philip said to him 'I thought you had put that bloody stick down with the wrong end up'.

Ernest Hackney umpired for us for years and both his sons were regular first team players. Don kept wicket and if he got caught behind off Graham's bowling, many is the time he had said to the opposing batsman 'You didn't have a lot of chance with our kid bowling and our dad umpiring'.

Another funny incident concerning Ernest and Phillip was when Ernest had given Phillip out. Coming home on the coach we called at an old-fashioned pub for a pint. Phillip as usual, was the first in the bar where there was a sword hanging on the wall. Phillip took it off the wall and said 'Now where is that bloody umpire'. The landlord didn't see the funny side of this and we all got thrown out of the pub.

After all the activity of 1958 the 1959 season seemed a bit of an anticlimax. The chairman, Albert Stewart, who had seemingly got divided loyalties with both Pott Shrigley and Bollington, resigned.

The previous season I had recruited a workmate – John Vernon – to the club. John was born in Pott Shrigley and although he didn't have much idea about sport, he stayed with the club for over 40 years and was sadly missed when he passed away at the age of 60. We always called him the catering manager even though his language could be a bit colourful in the kitchen. He was very popular with the tea ladies and usually made the scones at home and over the years must have made thousands of them. They were always excellent. In later years when I was not playing, if I was brushing the wicket, he always left a couple of scones on a plate for me. One Sunday we were playing Mere and they brought some spectators with them. One of them saw the scones and went to pick one up. John saw him and shouted 'Keep your bloody hands off'. The bloke turned round and burst into the song 'We'll Keep a Welcome in the Hillside'.

We had hoped that John would take on the job of secretary in 1959, making Geoff the chairman, but he stated he would only be assistant secretary, so Geoff landed up chairman and secretary.

In the early spring we had another showdown with the Sheriff. Graham Higginbotham and myself were digging a drain across the 'square' so he came to us and asked what we were doing. We refused to tell him so he stood watching us nearly all afternoon. It was a bitterly cold day. He was always smartly dressed and when he was laying the law down always had his coat open with his thumbs in his waistcoat. He seemed to have got some idea we were going to allow sewage in the river which was about a quarter of a mile away. As we only had chemical toilets I don't know where that idea came from.

On one Sunday about this time, Graham and myself decided to ride round Pott to contact people from the larger properties to come along to the annual dinner. First we called at the president's house, Mr Ruddin, who we had not seen before. He invited us in, got two tumblers and half filled them with whisky. Next we called on Mr and Mrs Hulme and out came their whisky. From there we called on Geoff and Barbara Taylor who we did not know at the time but Geoff was a real character, somewhat in the David Niven mould. He got the whisky bottle out and by the time we left we were nearly legless and I had to drive home. It was a good job that there was not much traffic on the road in those days. Some people think this approach should be carried on more but we have tried it recently with catastrophic results (more about this later).

It worked in those days with Mr Ruddin, Mr Hulme, Mrs Hulme and C. Taylor all being presidents and along with the Rev. Siviter and his wife, gave the club great support. There was hardly a Saturday when the Siviters missed coming across to the ground, admittedly nearly always when the water was boiling for a cuppa but I feel things like this are part of our heritage. Mobberley CC, another beautiful ground, when you visited them that well liked personality of cricket, Canon Randle would always make an appearance.

Another member who joined the club was Pakistan Eagles player, Asghar Hussain who waited on at The Highwayman up the road. A prodigious spin bowler and a brilliant fielder, when not bowling he did not appear to be interested and usually had to be woken up when it was time to pad up. One thing I remember, he always insisted on a short extra cover and certainly seemed to pick up a lot of wickets there and he did his part in another successful season.

Another offer to buy the ground was made to the Lowther Estate but this was refused.

The 1961 season saw Geoff Taylor made chairman and to try and improve fixtures, I myself took on the job of fixture secretary and I am still in that position today. Occasionally someone will ring and ask if I am still the same chap his dad used to deal with.

Graham Higginbotham was vice-captain in place of Eric Burgess who was getting the golf bug. One incident I remember was we had decided to improve the roller by adding two small rollers front and back, so one Sunday afternoon we arranged to take it to Ambrose Woods. As it was all downhill to Bollington the biggest problem was holding it back but the noise it made was frightening, particularly down the last hill in Queen Street which was cobbled. Front doors were opened all along the route to see what was happening.

For the first time for some years we now had a second team (P. Hammond, captain) and a Sunday XI with a full list of fixtures.

One bitter pill we had to swallow was being bowled out by Langley for 34 but on the same day the aforementioned Bob Fairhall took 8 for 5 for the second team.

I had encountered problems with our groundsman Joe early in the season. He did a superb job but did not like to see his 'square' messed up and early in the season both captains felt the ground was playable but Joe didn't and cleared off home, so I wrote to him and informed him he would not be selected again until he apologised, which he did.

Unfortunately, with the club improving, some of the members who had worked so hard in building the pavilion were finding it difficult to keep their places in the team and a couple left, seemingly not too happy, which was sad but I suppose we had to progress on the field to survive. Prior to the season we all attended a sportsmans' service on the first Sunday in April. As I stated, the vicar was a good supporter of the club and was very keen on this service. He asked us to mention it in our 75th year brochure but it was unfortunately in print.

The 1962 meeting brought about quite a few changes. Mr Ruddin, who had been president since 1949, resigned through ill health. Also Geoff resigned as secretary and at the meeting it was requested that the following be recorded of the outgoing secretary: 'We cannot let Geoff go without saying something. Pott Shrigley Cricket Club would not be where it is today if it had not been for Geoff Harding. He has worked hard and has done this job well for many years'. A vote of thanks was passed.

Mr F. Hulme, who lived in the house near the ground which was the clubhouse when it was a golf club, became president.

As usual, a lot of time was spent discussing the hiring of coaches. Fred was an exceptional treasurer but travel and touring were never considered one of his favourite pastimes and he did not like to see money spent in this manner, but the general feeling was that hiring coaches so that all the wives and families could support us was part of the success of the Club. At one meeting the chairman of the parish council, Isaac Cooper, a founder member of the Club, joined in the discussion and stated they had never had these problems before the war. Shep Broster called him a bloody fool because they only travelled as far as Adlington. Calling the parish council chairman this did not endear us to the council, but again it showed the out of date attitude they had towards us.

However, we were not allowed to use our own ground on Sundays and with all the games played away (looking at the fixtures for the season these included games at Llandudno, Port Sunlight, Blackpool, Winwick and Bob Fairhalls' old club, Balderton in Lincolnshire, plus a tour of Kent based in Margate with fixtures at Sandwich, Nonnington and Sibton Park) we decided to try and get a contract for the season. This we did with Hopley of Wincle. They had two coaches. Dad drove the old one which had a separate cab at the front. It was a bit noisy and he was slightly deaf so it was difficult drawing his attention when you felt he was taking the wrong turning – Heaton Mersey always seemed to pose problems. I think we went past the road the ground was on four times before we could get him to turn round.

Another ground we never seemed to find was Prestwich but this caused amusement. One Sunday when Ernest Hackney saw some droppings on the road he shouted to him to follow that horse but Shep Broster said it was not horse muck but elephant muck. This brought howls of laughter, but as we turned the next corner in front of us were eight elephants all joined together.

The son, Brian Hopley became part of the club, turning out for us on many occasions. He also played a musical instrument which was similar to a mouth organ, but with a mouthpiece, at which he was quite professional, as he was driving. When playing up at Sherrif Hutton we always stopped in York and Brian drove through the archway in the walls. Bob Fairhall guided him through with about an inch to spare either side. Neither of them had seen a huge policeman watching them. When we eventually got through the arch the policeman came up and said 'Well, I've been here twenty-five years and never seen that done before – now turn it round and get it out again'.

The season began well, the 1st XI not losing until we met our old adversaries Prestbury on 9 June. Prestbury were always a bit unpredictable but had some good players. Their opening attack of John Rowson and Keith Henshaw I considered as good as any, and both were excellent batsmen.

On 23 June we set off in good spirits on the tour. Shep Broster was late as usual so things didn't go quite as planned. We were hoping to attend the Lords Test Match, but by the time we arrived, the ground was full and the gates were locked so as the ladies went into the City and we had our own Test Match in Hyde Park.

On the Sunday we beat Sandwich Town, then on the Tuesday drew

36

with Margate Police who invited us back to their Club where the hospitality was first class. I don't know what time the bar was closed but it didn't please the landlady the time we came in, particularly when the driver started to play music between 2.00 a.m. and 3.00 a.m. in the morning.

On Wednesday we played Nonnington who we had been informed were a good side, but we had taken with us Pott Shrigley's own Frank Spencer, a lad called Barry Clarke, who could bowl the occasional good ball but generally did not know where the ball was going. On one occasion at Port Sunlight he bowled one that went so wide the wicket-keeper split his trousers trying to avoid byes. Harry, the wicket-keeper always expanded on this by saying he ran as far as the square leg umpire, dived and still missed the ball.

However, on this day at Nonnington the home team had collapsed to about 40 for 5 so I thought being as though Barry had come all this way I would give him a bowl. Of course, what does happen, he takes 4 wickets for 10 runs and spoiled the game. Another thing Barry was well known for was his singing of 'Ramona' on the bus. After walking round Margate one night we went into a club where some of the lads had gone for a drink. The orchestra was playing 'Ramona' with Barry singing into the mike, but after a hectic night Barry had great trouble keeping his eyes open at breakfast the following morning. Everybody had a great time except the landlady who was not very pleased regarding some of the 'goings on' and the noise, and always seemed to blame Bob Fairhall who probably did make a lot of the racket. After we paid up on the Friday, we did not see her again, not even to wave us goodbye.

Another character on the tour was Gordon Lomas, just the opposite to Barry. Up at the crack of dawn cleaning his shoes, washing, shaving and annoying others who fancied a lie in. Gordon was also remembered for purchasing some oriental soup spoons he saw in a Chinese restaurant, thinking his wife would like them, probably to act as a peace offering for him coming on the tour. He ordered half a dozen off the waiter to take home and arranged to collect them the following evening, but there was no happy ending – a couple of days later we found the same spoons on sale in Woolworths at half the price and the story goes his wife didn't like them either and threw them at him.

The other amazing thing was that most people had enjoyed the tour and wanted to return the following year, and at a meeting shortly after it was agreed we would return in 1963, but I stated we would have to find somewhere else to stay. Bob Fairhall proposed I write to the same place and much to my surprise received a reply stating that the landlady would be pleased to see us all again.

37

On the playing side, the way the club was progressing was shown by the fact that the 2nd XI played 18 games. One outstanding Sunday performance was by John Barrow who took 5 wickets for no runs. Keith Arnold scored most runs with 848.

Very little change took place at the 1963 AGM, most officials being re-elected but a young John Pickford was appointed 1st XI vice-captain.

For the first time in the Club's history, the meetings and after-match drinking were moved from the Cheshire Hunt to the Turners Arms in Bollington. I think Hedley Snape the landlord from the Cheshire Hunt had been caught up with his excessive drinking habits. The Turners Arms had been taken over by Corris Mawer who had joined the club when he moved here from the Blackpool area. I still meet Corris on many mornings when I call for my newspaper and we discuss old times, so I do not think he will be offended by my description, but when *Fawlty Towers* came on the television, Sybil and Basil reminded me of Peggy and Corris. Peggy always looking super-efficient while Corris was always one of the lads. He and Geoff Taylor struck up a good drinking partnership.

On the field Keith Arnold again scored a lot of runs with a then record individual score for the ground of 122.

The second tour to Kent went ahead but was plagued by poor weather so was obviously not as enjoyable as the previous year.

One sad occasion during the year was the death of Mr Frank Hulme, our popular president, who was only in his second year of office.

At the 1964 AGM Mrs Hulme had informed the club she would be happy to accept the honour of being president as Frank had always been interested in the club and she felt he would have wished her to do so. I was replaced as captain by Bob Fairhall with Don Hackney as vice-captain. The minutes read: 'The Chairman extended his thanks to D. Brooke on behalf of all members for all the work he had done over the years he had held the office of captain'. I replied acknowledging the fact that the Club had made great strides over the years and the efforts that had been put in by many people.

At this meeting a deputation of six members was proposed to attend a debate on the need for a village hall in Pott Shrigley.

With no captain and selections problems, Graham Higginbotham and myself had more time to concentrate on the square as Joe again had departed. We now had an 'Atco' sit-on mower for the outfield which members cut on a rota system. Also another expensive improvement was the laying of two 'En-Tout-Cas' practice wickets. These lasted years and I still feel were as good as any artificial wicket you can get today.

Pott Shrigley C.C. dinner

Mrs E. Hulme (President) centre top table with guests at the annual dinner of Pott Shrigley Cricket Club on Friday

One of leading village cricket clubs in area

Pott Shrigley Cricket Club, which in recent years has become one of the leading village clubs in the area, possess a ground which is the envy of many, but as was stated at the annual dinner in Bollington Conservative Club on Friday, this has been made possible only by hard work.

Mr. Isaac Cooper, present Chairman of the village Parish Council, and Mr. Wilbraham Baxton, spoke of the days in 1920 when the club paid a shilling a year to Colonel Lowther for the use of the ground and of the tremendous amount of work that had to be done to put it in playable order. At one time it formed part of the old Pott Shrigley golf course.

EARLY MEMBERS

They recalled the names of some of the early members, men like Jack Kirk, Frank and George Tinsley, Ted Ledbetter, George Cooper, Charlie Cooper, Archie Brown (who continued playing until he was turned 80 years of age), Hugh Mayers, Hedley Snape, Harry Burt, Lew Roberts, William Leigh, Walter Kirkham and Alfred Gardner.

The playing area was not as big as it is today and often the outfield was in long grass, but they were happy days; in fact, Pott Shrigley has always been a happy club.

There was an attendance of about 70 and members brought along their wives. Mr. Robert

A. Fairhall was toastmaster and extended a welcome to all the guests.

At the outset the guests stood in silence to the memory of their President, Mr. Frank Hulme, who died during the year.

GOOD SEASON

Mr. Geoffrey Taylor, Chairman, submitted the toast to the President, Mrs. E. Hulme, who has taken over the duties following her husband's death. Mr. Taylor said the club had experienced a successful season and had played more games than in the previous year, due no doubt to the fact that their ground was in such excellent condition. The finances were also sound.

Their President, Mrs. Hulme, was well-known to them all for her excellent work for the club and also for her activities in other directions. Although she had now gone to live at Poynton she still retained her interest in the club. It was a great blow to the club when Mr. Hulme died because he had been so interested in the club and loved his cricket.

living in Poynton she always had her happy memories of her association with the Cricket Club with her. She had always been made welcome by the cricketers and their wives.

She then presented a cricket bat to the club.

Mr. Norman Holt, proposing the toast to the club, said he had very long and happy memories of Pott Shrigley Cricket Club. It was good to see that night some of the old founder members. They had much to thank them for.

Replying, the Captain, Mr. Derrick Brooks, dealt at length with the season's performance and said the first team played 45 matches and did exceedingly well. They lost more games than they usually did, but perhaps that was due to the fact that they had played better clubs. The second team also had a good season.

The outstanding batsman was Keith Arnold, who scored 848 runs. One of the most consistent performers was Graham Higginbotham. It had been suggested that the reason they lost some games was because

Graham did not play in them.

There were some outstanding bowling performances — John Barrow's five for 0 against Ashburton and John Franklin's eight for 28 against Kerridge. Bob Fairhall topped the bowling averages, with Graham Higginbotham second.

FIVE FOR NONE

The cup for the outstanding performance of the year was presented by Mrs. Hulme to John Barrow for his five for 0 bowling performance.

Tribute to those who worked so hard with the catering was paid by Mr. John Vernon, the Secretary and the man in charge of catering. He called upon Mrs. Hulme to make presentations to Mrs. Kathleen Higginbotham, Mrs. J Wrigley, Mrs. W. Broster, Mrs. M. Hackney and Mrs. Pickford in recognition of the work they had done.

Afterwards, t h e r e was dancing and some excellent singing by Miss Sylvia Dixon and Mr. Don Towle, of the East Cheshire Operatic Society, who

The *Macclesfield Express*'s report of our annual dinner at Bollington Conservative Club, 1963.

39

POTT SHRIGLEY DEBATE NEED FOR VILLAGE HALL

Representatives of the Parish Council, the Church, the Cricket Club and the Parish Council met in Pott Shrigley Schoolroom on Tuesday to consider whether they were prepared to support the erection of a village hall, first mooted in 1952.

After a long discussion it was agreed that the Parish Council should go ahead with investigations into the cost, site and the preparation of plans and then, when something definite has been obtained, to call a further meeting.

There had been a suggestion that the church should erect a suitable building for their youth and various speakers felt that there would not be room for a village hall and a youth hut.

County Councillor Mrs. Nattio presided and invited views of representatives.

BACK TO 1952

Mr. G. Taylor, Chairman of Pott Shrigley Cricket Club, said he was completely in the dark and would like to know what they were expected to express their views on.

Mr. W. H. Bennett, Clerk to the Parish Council, said the idea of a village hall was first brought forward in 1952 when, through the efforts of the late Mr. F. Hulme, they staged a village wedding pageant in Pott Shrigley which attracted good crowds and it was decided that the funds should go towards a village hall. A small committee was formed to see it through further. At first the idea was to have it as a commemoration hall to the present Queen. Up to the year ———— and 55 it went

extremely well. Then interest waned, but it had never been lost sight of and now the Parish Council had decided to make a further effort to bring it to fruition.

GROUND AVAILABLE

There was the ground available for the purpose. They had a beautiful piece of ground which the Cricket Club used, which was also available for the use of the children at the day school. There was always the probability that land would be left in perpetuity to the village. The Cheshire Community Council had been seen regarding the matter.

The object of that meeting was to ascertain the views on how far the Parish Council could go to provide a village hall for the benefit of the village.

Mr. Taylor said they had no idea the village hall was going to be put on the cricket ground.

NO DEFINITE SITE

Various representatives said this was not so, and when asked if there was a definite site, Mr. Bennett stated there was not. The village green had been suggested, but there the provision of parking ground would be the difficulty.

Mr. Taylor said the Cricket Club would be very interested

but at the moment they were faced with a big expense. They were to have a new wicket which would cost £200.

"RIDICULOUS"

Mr. J. A. Gibson, a member of the Parish Council, said that when they were discussing a matter at the Parish Council meeting he felt it was ridiculous that they should have a youth hut and a village hall being discussed in the village and he suggested they should get representatives present to see if they were prepared to discuss having one hall. His idea was to get the views on whether the Parish Council should go ahead and not to discuss costs, sites, etc.

Mr. K. Penney, Dramatic Society, felt there was a need for a village hall. There was so much that could be done if they had such a building. Through it things would develop. What they needed was the co-operation of all organisations. A village hall could well be the salvation of the village

VICAR AGAINST

The Vicar said there was the cost of the building to be considered and also the maintenance of it. That was always a headache. They did not want to have to organise bingo sessions to maintain it. Personally, he was not in favour of a village hall. Pott Shrigley was not a village; it was a series of hamlets.

The Chairman said she remembered a figure of £5,000 being mentioned as the cost of a hall.

Mrs. K. Penney said that not so many years ago the village was faced with having to provide a new vicarage. Many shuddered at the thought of the cost but they raised the money. If they set out to do it they would raise the money for a village hall.

Mr. Fairhall, the Cricket Club, said they would like to know where the site was going to be.

Councillor Mrs. Mosley, J.P., felt that youth had to be considered. She saw no reason why they should not have a building for the youth until a village hall was built.

In reply to a question as to how much money there was in the bank, it was stated that it would be in the region of £100.

Mrs. Sliviter said she wished she could say she was 100 per cent in favour of having a village hall but she did not think Pott Shrigley could support a village hall. The villagers did not support the Cricket Club by attending their matches. She had been very concerned about the youth. She was aware they could use the school but it was not ideal. They had table tennis and darts in the garage at the vicarage which they now used. If they used school premises they could not leave the things they needed lying about

HUT FOR YOUTH?

During the past two weeks she had felt there had been some very bad feeling in the village over the suggestion that they should have a hut for the youth. There had been little murmurs going around causing strife. They had a meeting of the Youth Fellowship last Friday and invited parents. They decided that, under the present circumstances, they would not go ahead with having a hut because they were afraid it was going to stir up unpleasantness.

Some people thrived on rows but they did not. They were more concerned with building characters than youth huts; therefore, they had decided against the hut.

Even though they were not wholeheartedly in favour of a village hall they would not be the people to put a spanner in the works.

ACTION NOW

Mr. Fairhall said his sympathy was with the youth. The young people would be turned 20 by the time a village hall was built. Youth wanted action now.

Mr. B. Stewart said they wanted everyone's help now if they were to have a village hall

Report on the meeting regarding the village hall project from the *Macclesfield Express* in March 1964.

Looking at the results for 1964 it seemed an amazing year weatherwise. We played our first game on 11 April and the presidents match against Bollington was on 3 October with only two Saturday matches and two Sunday matches cancelled.

The 2nd XI was getting stronger all the time with a full Saturday list and a few Sunday fixtures. On the field it was another excellent season with Graham Hackney now becoming a force scoring 954 runs. G. Higginbotham had 84 wickets, R. Fairhall 78 wickets and D. Brooke 75 wickets.

1965 saw G. Taylor appointed president and as with everything he did, he threw himself 100 per cent in to the job and still remained 'one

Langley's opening batsman faces the bowling of Graham Higginbotham.

Lovely setting

Pott Shrigley has one of the most ambitious village cricket clubs in the area. Possessing a ground in a delightful setting, its members, most of whom come from Bollington and Macclesfield, have worked exceedingly hard to provide a wicket and amenities which today are second to none in their class of cricket.

They raised more than £1,000 for the handsome pavilion, have laid down practice wickets at a cost of £200 and this season have a new motor mower which cost £195.

Mrs. Frank Hulme formerly of Pott Shrigley now residing in Poynton has succeeded her late husband as President and takes a keen interest in the club's activities. They are also fortunate in having an excellent Chairman in Mr. Geoffrey Taylor and a hard working committee. Much credit for the work that has been carried out on the ground must go to Mr. D. Brooke the former Captain, who has striven painstakingly over the past few years to put the club in the position it at present occupies.

The club has a ladies committee which looks after the refreshments and they are ably led by Mr. John Vernon. The club runs two teams who both have a full fixture list, while there are also games for a Sunday eleven. The Captain of the first eleven is Bob Fairhall, with Donald Hackney as Vice-Captain. So far this season they have drawn three, won three and lost one. The captain and vice-captain of the second eleven are H. Lawson and J. Franklin respectively.

Skipper and fast bowler Bob Fairhall in action.

A rest from preparing the tea to watch cricket in comfort.

A feature on local clubs in the area from the *Macclesfield Express* in 1964.

41

of the boys'. His son, Peter, played but never really committed himself to the game. Mrs Hulme had now moved from the village and was made a life member.

On the playing side the results were reasonable, the weather being not quite as good and we were without Graham Hackney who unfortunately had to spend a year in hospital which was obviously a worrying time for his family who were pillars of the club. As fixture secretary I had arranged more games with clubs like ourselves who were fielding first and second teams and we were tending to get more competitive games. Some of these teams were members of the Cheshire Club Conference and there were people who felt this type of cricket should be what we were aiming for.

Off the field there was celebration in the village as they won 'The Best Kept Village' competition in their group with the cricket ground being commended, so to mark this event (I presume it was the Sheriff and his deputies) organised a tree-planting ceremony on the cricket ground. They did not bother to inform the Club who were the tenants and in our opinion should have had a say as to where the tree should go, as it could prove a nuisance when established and be in the way of future plans we may have had. As it turned out the lack of information did nobody in the village any favours as a tree-planting ceremony was arranged for the Sunday morning after the village bonfire which was always a big event with five to six hundred people attending, so with the farm still in use, and all these people going across, the track could be horrendous, with mud over your shoe tops. However, for the bonfire we had made a walkway with old pallets but not knowing anything was taking place, had taken them up and burned them! After completing this operation we had a bit of time to spare and as we had been working on some drains at the far side of the ground, Graham Higginbotham got a spade which had been leaning at the side of the pavilion and off he went down the hole digging. We were then amazed to see the choir with the vicar and all the council and congregation walking through the mud and up to the pavilion, where a tree had appeared from somewhere. I left Graham digging and wandered across to show a bit of interest. The vicar conducted a short service, the choir sang a hymn then the Sheriff took over introducing the chairman, Isaac Cooper, who would remove the first turf. He turned round to give him the spade which he had obviously put at the side of the door for this purpose, but there was Graham with only the top of his head showing digging happily away at the other side of the ground. Panic then set in with the Sheriff running round the back to the shed to find something else but of course the shed was locked. Standing a few yards away I found the whole episode hilarious but did go to their

42

aid, got the key to the shed and produced another spade. A week later Don Hackney dug the tree up and replanted it near the fence which brought the usual threats but the tree still stands there to this day.

1966 saw a year when several new personalities joined the Club. Trevor Hill became chairman even though in some circles it was assumed he wanted his finger in the pie as he was the main push behind getting a village hall and at that time they were obviously looking to build it on the entrance to the cricket ground. Typical of how things worked in Pott the rules could be changed when it suited and as there was no proper track to the ground this would have to be sorted. Looking at the council minutes in 1952 a piece of land known as 'The Village Green' had been offered with an entrance through the stack yard. On several occasions we had asked to put a track to the ground this way, but were told it was a non-starter. Also we had not been allowed to play Sunday cricket. Who made the rules you could only guess but suddenly we were allowed to play a few Sunday games if no one objected.

Having got Trevor, who was a BBC producer, as chairman he was a very thorough organiser and was instrumental in starting the village bonfire and fireworks which we still hold every year. He also found us guest speakers for the annual dinners. The first I believe was Alan Dixon who commentated on the Isle of Man TT races, who was excellent and a young man from BBC North, Stuart Hall. This was before his *It's a Knockout* days. We presented him with a club tie which had a 'Hillman' on with a cricket bat. He obviously wore it on television one day and said we were the cavemen who used the bat to keep their wives in check.

A number of years later I asked Trevor to find us a quizmaster for one night and this turned out to be Graham Taylor's sidekick David Davies who asked the questions in a similar manner to how he appears on the screen today, and then didn't please the treasurer by asking for extra travel expenses.

One of the local characters, farmer Oliver Heathcote, knowing Trevor's obsession for detail was always trying to catch him out on his productions. One of his favourites was *Poldark* in which the cows in the scenes were Friesians which had not been introduced to this country at that time, and also the cows had numbers on their ears for electric milking. To be fair Trevor always took the criticism in good part as Oliver was always right.

Even though I did not live in the village and Trevor had come up from Bollington, he spoke to me on many occasions regarding the future of villages like Pott Shrigley, his big concern being the lack of cheap houses so that young people could live there. He felt the oppor-

43

tunity should have been taken to have had a small council estate erected after the war. Trevor was one of the chief figures in getting the village hall project off the ground. Another event he always played a big part in was 'The Spinners at Shrigley' concert which was held on the superb forecourt of the 'Salesian College' now Shrigley Hall Hotel, which attracted thousands of people to the village. I heard an interview on the radio with Tony Davies of the Spinners who said of the many places in the world they had performed at, Pott Shrigley was his favourite venue and on one occasion gave a large part of the proceeds to the Club.

Don Hackney was Saturday captain and Alan Edworthy Sunday captain. Both adopted a cavalier attitude to the game, Alan's pre-match tactic talks always a bit of a novelty as when we arrived at the middle he appeared to have forgotten all he had said.

Don as Saturday captain learned a sharp lesson on our first visit to Woore (Shropshire). We had been informed they had two big hitting opening batsmen and it was only a small ground. We won the toss, decided to bat and were going quite well at about 85 for 1 when a thunderstorm hit the area. However we took tea and decided we could finish the game on another wicket at the edge of the square so we carried on for about a further half hour taking our total to 120 and when Don declared leaving them the same time, it took them just 18 minutes to reach this total and we had to hang on until the pub opened. Ian Lawton and Derek Bailey were the two batsmen. We always remained great friends and the games with Woore were always something special.

Even though Alan only stayed with the Club about three years he left his mark by designing 'The Hillman' badge. He was also the instigator in providing the Club with a proper set of rules. At the time he perhaps upset one or two people by coming to the AGM, getting the rules passed and then stating it would make no difference to him as he was going to live in Africa – typical Alan but the rules have always held us in good stead. The next time we met Alan was in 1994 when he walked into the village hall as if he had never been away. He had brought his daughter Sally to see the church where she was christened. Sadly when I got to this paragraph I decided to phone him but his son answered and informed me Alan had died of lung cancer in March 1998.

As most of us are aware, and it happened again in 1998, there are the usual prophets of doom stating that cricket is dead. Obviously we had it in 1966 and an article in the *Daily Express* about a Lindow vs. Pott second team match sought to disprove this.

Another big step forward was made in 1966 with the full list of

I wouldn't say that a game like this was doomed

by GEOFFREY NEWSON

THE hillmen from Pott Shrigley troop on to the green turf, a blend of well-seasoned age and fresh-faced youth with a crease in its pants.

Minutes later the home skipper, a hairpin of a man, scoops a catch to mid-wicket, mutters something to his bat and lopes back to the pavilion.

The setting: the village sports green at Lindow, near Wilmslow, in Cheshire.

The game: cricket, which will be dead in 10 years, if we are to believe Mr. Graham Dowson. Talking about Britain's leisure habits in the next decade, he made this forecast to an advertising conference at Brighton.

The visitors' fast bowler, a gentleman called Farrer, who had shoulders as wide as a cart and a heaving chest which threatened to burst after each delivery, showed few signs of fading out.

A fact soon discovered by home batsman Dave Matthews, a man of ample girth, who was hit by a quickie and felled like a ripe oak.

PROTESTING

Said the Pott Shrigley captain: "I don't think we'll need the heavy roller after all."

Matthews was scraped from the wicket, protesting.

When there's sun on your back and a bat in your hand there are only two things that will persuade a cricket addict to leave the field—having to retire hurt or "opening time."

That is why it will take more than a Job-like prophecy from Mr. Dowson or competition from other leisure forms to kill cricket.

Roger Maggs, a huge and healthy lad who had come up from the cider-apple acres of Somerset, took guard and began to thump the bowling with great agricultural swipes.

In half an hour he had hit 45, including seven fours and two sixes—and this was only Lindow's second team.

Which explains why I was batting at the other end at the time, compiling a more leisurely 29 before treading on my wicket just before the ham salads were up.

FEET UP

"Neither of us was built for speed," Maggs had said when our not inconsiderable waists had met during one of those vital mid-wicket conferences. "Let's get the runs in boundaries." Next ball he was out to a catch and minutes later we all were. For 117.

There is nothing dead about a cricket pavilion at teabreak. It's feet up, fags out, mugs of tea, and yarn-spinning.

"Cricket dying, lad?" said skipper Brian Schofield, passing the plate round for the three bobs. "You can believe that when you see me going water ski-ing or go-karting on a Saturday afternoon."

A sad, battered returning Matthews, with suspected broken nose, was prepared to do battle on the cricket field for another 20 years at least. "You can't kill off the sort of cricket we've been seeing here this afternoon," he said.

But there was better to come. A teenage Pott Shriglian, Marshall Worthington, puny in size but prodigious in performance, sent the fielders scampering in an orgy of whining willow and bruised leather.

With five wickets left the hillmen needed only 14 runs to win. Then up strode Harry Davison, a man of 55 with 40 summers in the field behind him, for his second bowling spell.

LAST BALL

On most days a bat to Harry is well-nigh useless. The club's regular No. 11 since Suez, he refers to himself as a batting ferret—"I go in after the rabbits" he says.

But put a ball in his hand and he is capable of making it do anything short of singing Handel's Largo.

He bowled two men out with his first three balls. Then with three men and four minutes left and the Pott needing two runs to win, he took another wicket.

The third last ball of the match left his hand, buzzed like a hornet, and landed at the foot of three shattered stumps. Next ball a run was scored and the visitors needed to score from the last ball to win.

Harry's last fling bamboozled the bat and the match ended with the vicar's son racing the full length of the pitch to run out the stranded survivor.

Back on the pavilion step both teams gathered, applauded, then parted reverently, like the Red Sea, allowing Harry to pass, flushed and beaming, through their ranks.

Fifteen minutes later in the pub, Harry was sitting behind a half-gallon enamel jug of best bitter and talking about playing cricket until he was 65.

In a word, Mr. Dowson, rubbish.

We feature in the *Daily Express*, May 1966.

fixtures for a junior side and with David Rushton as captain and Steve Higginbotham vice-captain, we achieved the remarkable success of played ten, won ten, so with young club members like Graham Hackney now back to fitness and scoring over 1,000 runs and John Pickford always a force to be reckoned with the future looked bright.

1967 saw nearly all games played against Conference sides and it became increasingly obvious we would have to become members as in most games we were equal to the opposition and just playing 'Friendlies' was getting more difficult, the occasional poor fixture turning up. One at Wigan Unionists in 1969 was mercifully finished by a violent thunderstorm but we had to wade through a foot of water to get out of the shed we changed in and back to the cars. The results were quite good but it was now time to reflect on all the good times friendly cricket had given us.

A lot of the people who made it such a good family club have now unfortunately passed on, but memories linger on. People like Shep Broster who won two bats in a day in the 1950s. He treated these bats with such care that when he retired and went to live at Fleetwood and played for ICI there, we went to see him and out came the bats, well-oiled looking almost as good as new. John Vernon, who never held a bat but gave 40 loyal years to the Club despite tragically losing a son in a car accident and himself being in poor health for several years. Philip Hammond also suffered the same fate, losing his only son. May and Ernest Hackney, Ernie had his hip-bone broken whilst umpiring and his ashes are by the side of the pavilion. You could probably fill a few pages with May's misfortunes. I remember going to play cricket one Saturday and seeing someone in the first field by the barbed-wire fence near the gate. It was May who had tried to get through the fence to avoid the horse standing in the gateway and had got her knickers snagged on the fence, so I had to go and free her. Years later, after Ernie had passed away, she had two sons who lived in Macclesfield and a daughter who lived in Australia. She had all their phone numbers in case she needed anything. Realising she needed a loaf, she rang Australia and asked her daughter to bring a loaf on her way home from work.

Another I must mention who left us before old age was Kathleen Higginbotham as for several years we spent many Sundays together with Graham and me often going to work on the ground. They were great years for the club and I am sure if any of them meet up above, it will be one of the first things they talk about.

3

The Conference Years

1968 heralded quite a few changes for the first year of Conference cricket. David Rushton took over as secretary and Fred Wrigley was appointed first team Captain. Off the field of play we were now getting concerned as Brabazon Lowther had now passed away and the estate was being sold off. Pott Hall Farm at the entrance to the ground was up for sale and with no idea what was happening regarding our rights

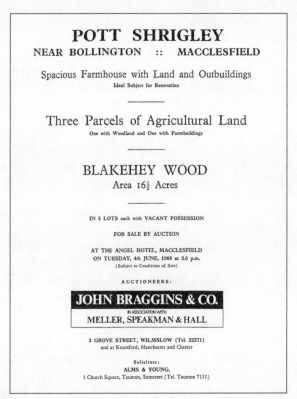

POTT SHRIGLEY
NEAR BOLLINGTON :: MACCLESFIELD

Spacious Farmhouse with Land and Outbuildings
Ideal Subject for Renovation

Three Parcels of Agricultural Land
One with Woodland and One with Farmbuildings

BLAKEHEY WOOD
Area 16½ Acres

IN 5 LOTS each with VACANT POSSESSION

FOR SALE BY AUCTION

AT THE ANGEL HOTEL, MACCLESFIELD
ON TUESDAY, 4th JUNE, 1968 at 3.0 p.m.
(Subject to Conditions of Sale)

AUCTIONEERS:

JOHN BRAGGINS & CO.
IN ASSOCIATION WITH
MELLER, SPEAKMAN & HALL

3 GROVE STREET, WILMSLOW (Tel. 22271)
and at Knutsford, Manchester and Chester

Solicitors:
ALMS & YOUNG,
1 Church Square, Taunton, Somerset (Tel. Taunton 7151)

With the Lowther Estate being sold off, members were concerned about the future of the cricket ground.

of way we were beginning to wonder, yet again, if all our work may be in vain as there was no point in having a ground if you could not get to it. It appeared, as usual, even though we were tenants we always seemed to be kept in the dark. The impact the Lowthers had on village life can be grasped by the following account:

The Lowthers, 1847–1929

Ellen Jane's own marriage is at first sight puzzling if one was expecting her father to make a good marriage in keeping with her (and his) position. The Revd. Brabazon Lowther was a younger son and a poor clergyman, though from a well-to-do family distantly related to the aristocracy. His branch of the Lowthers had been Anglo-Irish gentry since the seventeenth century but his father had sold up in county Meath, moved to a country house near Bath, married a niece of the bishop of Hereford, and indulged a taste for naming his sons after the families of his female forebears, Brabazon being the fourth in line after Ponsonby, St. George, and Beresford. In families like the Lowthers younger sons were expected to make their own careers in the armed forces or the Church, and in 1829, when he was eighteen, Brabazon was sent to Merton College, Oxford, to obtain an education before becoming a clergyman. He took his B.A. in 1834, was ordained, and looked set for a career as a parson. Perhaps his first position was the very humble one as curate at Barton Blount, a tiny village near Derby. He owed his appointment there to a family connection, since the non-resident rector of Barton Blount, who needed a curate to look after the church while he lived rather more grandly in Wiltshire as a prebendary of Salisbury cathedral, was a Lowther.

In 1845 Brabazon Lowther stepped up to a better position, though still hardly a well-appointed one, as perpetual curate at Disley. It was again the result of family influence. Disley church stands immediately outside Lyme Park and had been associated with the Leghs for hundreds of years. Two years earlier Thomas Legh, Ellen Jane's father, had married Brabazon's sister Maud. Appointments to the curacy at Disley were in his gift.

Extensive alterations to the house took place during the early Lowther years to accommodate the growing family and numerous servants. Part of the surviving bit of Old Shrigley Hall at the north end of the house was evidently pulled down and replaced by a new wing over the kitchens, probably for the servants. A matching wing behind the south end of the house was needed for the children's bedrooms and nurseries, and for visitors.

Meanwhile the family was growing up, the boys sent to school at Harrow. The Revd. and Mrs. Lowther's eldest son, named Brabazon after his father, died unmarried in Italy in 1874 before he was thirty. His brother William was the next in line. Since he had not been expected to inherit, he had been sent on from school to Sandhurst and joined the Royal Artillery. In 1873–4, in his early twenties, he took part as a junior officer in one of the more remarkable of Britain's colonial wars, Sir Garnet Wolseley's campaign against the Ashanti in what is now Ghana and was then the hinterland of the Gold Coast colony. In 1874, the year his elder brother died, William married a Lincolnshire clergyman's daughter, but he remained a serving artillery officer, rising slowly to the rank of colonel.

The younger brother, Henry, went to Oxford University and joined the diplomatic service. Like William, he can have had only limited contact with Shrigley as he progressed steadily through the service, with postings in Europe, South America, and Tokyo, eventually serving as British minister in Chile and then Denmark. Almost fifty when he married, he was knighted in 1913 and retired to Kent in 1916.

The only one of the Lowthers' children to remain at home was the boys' sister, Eleanor, who never married and stayed in Shrigley all her life, doing good works with her mother, teaching at the village school and building the corrugated iron reading room which survives as the Coffee Tavern on the road to Poynton. After his brother inherited the Hall she moved out and lived until her death in 1924 at Snape House, barely a mile away.

The Lowthers were squires in the traditional sense, controlling almost every aspect of life in Pott Shrigley beyond the park walls as well as within them. Besides the house and grounds, there was a home farm, estate woods, and a grouse moor in Bakestonedale east of the Hall, with a gamekeeper's cottage. The family owned all the farms in Pott Shrigley but one (of only 40 acres) and almost all the cottages, so that almost every family, from farmers to labourers, were their tenants. They appointed the curates, and later the vicars, of the chapel at Pott and helped pay for repairs and refurbishments when they were needed. Most of the Lowthers were buried in a family vault in the graveyard, and the church itself contains several memorials to them. They supported the village school and owned the village pub, naturally called the

49

Lowther Arms. They owned the brickworks and colliery operated by the Hammond family, and even the vicarage and post office. Some time between 1897 and 1907 they let a large block of land south of the church, together with a cottage, to a committee which set up the Bollington and Pott Shrigley Golf Club, though the course there did not last beyond the First World War.

Ellen Jane Legh's marriage to the Revd. Brabazon Lowther followed in 1847. She was 17, he 33. It might have been a love match, but the suspicion remains that the Leghs were only too relieved to bundle her out of Lyme and into her own inheritance at Shrigley at the earliest opportunity. Thomas Legh might still have hoped for children from his second marriage, and his adolescent daughter was possibly an embarrassment. There were certainly financial complications over Ellen Jane's expectations. When he had married Ellen Turner, Thomas had set aside £20,000 for any younger children. Since Ellen Jane, being a girl, was never going to inherit Lyme, he had then, after his wife's death, assigned that £20,000 specifically to her. Even before he married again he was clearly thinking that he might one day have to provide for younger children from a second marriage, and wondering whether the arrangements in Ellen Jane's favour could be set aside. After he married Maud Lowther there was even talk of making Ellen Jane a ward of court. By then, of course, she had inherited the Shrigley estate from her grandfather William Turner and could be cut out of the Legh money without many qualms of conscience.

The two Legh-Lowther marriages, of a father and daughter to a sister and brother, made for some surreal family relationships: Brabazon was Thomas Legh's brother-in-law as well as his son-in-law; while even more disconcertingly Ellen Jane was her own father's sister-in-law. Whatever the circumstances of the marriage, the Revd. Brabazon and Mrs. Lowther settled down at Shrigley Hall in 1847 into the ordinary domesticities of the minor landed gentry, enjoying thirty years of married life there. Brabazon was doubtless hugely relieved, and perhaps somewhat surprised, to find himself freed from the struggle to make a way for himself in the Church, as two of his less lucky brothers were doing. The marriage produced three sons (Brabazon, William, and Henry) and a daughter (Eleanor) over the first ten years or so. Shrigley Hall was a real family home for all the period of the marriage, the only time in its history that it was home to young children. Until the Revd. Lowther died it seems always to have been full of visitors and servants as well as the growing family.

For much of the time there were a dozen or more servants living in the house, headed in typical Upstairs Downstairs manner by a butler and a housekeeper. The other women servants included Mrs. Lowther's lady's-maid, two or three in the kitchen, and usually two laundrymaids and two housemaids. While the children were little there were also nursemaids. In addition there was a groom or a coachman, and a footman or a page. A few of the servants were from the immediate district, but most came from a distance into service with the Lowthers. There were also gardeners, perhaps sometimes as many as three men and a boy.

Even after her husband died in 1877, Mrs. Lowther's household still ran to six or seven servants, though with no gentleman in the house she could dispense with the services of a butler. The children's Scottish nurse, a middle-aged widow called Jemima McLean, came back to Shrigley probably at about that time as Mrs. Lowther's lady's-maid. Old Mrs. Lowther survived her husband by almost thirty years, dying only in 1906 when her son William, by then Colonel Lowther, was past fifty-five. In her later years she may have become crotchety and wilful, perhaps even eccentric. The ramblers and cyclists who were becoming common in the Peak District around the beginning of the twentieth century were apparently not made at all welcome on the Shrigley estate, and there are stories of a long feud with one of the vicars of Pott Shrigley.

Colonel Lowther left the army when his mother died in 1906 and moved back to Shrigley as a country gentleman. His children, four sons born between 1876 and 1890, were already grown up or virtually so. Alterations to the house in his time seem to have been confined to the interior decorations. The entrance hall and the rooms to its south, for instance, were given lush plasterwork echoing the neoclassical style used by Emett.

The family suffered many tragedies. The colonel's eldest son, William, had been drowned at twenty-one in 1898 while serving in the Royal Navy. A window was put into the church in his memory. The next, Edward, died at twenty-eight in 1907 and was commemorated in a new porch for the church, put up by the tenants. The youngest, Thomas, was killed at Gallipoli in 1915. When the colonel died in 1928 his heir was thus his only surviving son, John Brabazon Lowther, who showed no interest in the lifestyle of the landed gentry. The reasons for that remain obscure. The landed gentry in general found it much more expensive to keep up their way of life after the First World War, and many estates and their country houses were being sold at the time. John Lowther, however, seems to have been something of an unconventional character. It showed mainly in his religious views. Already in 1924 the vicar of Pott Shrigley who admittedly got on very badly with all the Lowthers, wrote disapprovingly that Colonel Lowther's son and heir had severed himself from the Church of England. His religious quest seems to have taken several turns, including an interest in the Christian Science movement, which ended with him founding his own religious order and entitling himself Archbishop of the Ancient Catholic Church and Abbot of the Order of the Cloister of the Holy Presence. Shortly after his mother's death in 1932 he marked a further small breach with the family by changing his surname to Brabazon-Lowther, though by the 1950s he was instead calling himself Monsignor Francis Huntingford, though explaining to perplexed correspondents that he had not abandoned the name Brabazon-Lowther altogether. John apparently did not live at Shrigley and the house stood empty for a year after Colonel Lowther's death before it was sold in 1929.

Once again we tried to make overtures to see if we could purchase the

Lyme Hall, now owned by the National Trust. It is situated in the next parish of Lyme Handley, but has long associations with Shrigley.

ground but got offered a three-year lease which was not very satisfactory and once again we were left wondering what future we may have.

However, we played our cricket in the Cheshire Conference with enthusiasm. I suppose it was a similar competition to the Manchester Association where you arranged your own fixtures but played for points. It seemed to work quite well and revolved around one man called Stanley Briggs. I remember him asking me to get involved. I refused as I had no transport, so he said we could do with having meetings in different areas of Cheshire so could I fix a meeting in this area. I did this at a local pub, organised sandwiches etc. and only Stanley turned up.

We started the season quite well by beating old rivals Prestbury in the first game and completing the double later in the season, but three games in a row were called off for rain in May. The geographical position of the 'Nab Hill', the first high ground the clouds hit when coming through the Cheshire gap, will always be a problem to us in unsettled weather. The Conference did introduce us to 'The Pennant Cup' competition playing 16 eight-ball overs a side and though we beat a strong Hale Barns team in the first round, we went out in the second round.

Once again the season saw some good knocks, Graham Hackneys score of 136 against Toft being a record for the ground at that time and an economical bowler John Walsh had come through the junior ranks and topped the bowling. Our position in the Conference was reasonable. We were still playing five-hour cricket and generally in those days most Clubs seemed to have a few players with the ability to play long innings so there were a lot of draws. We had also abandoned the idea of travelling by coach so there were people who thought some of the fun was missing.

President's Day was a big success with both teams playing against Bollington, and with Geoff Taylor as host, a great evening followed. At this time I again got involved with Bollington looking after their wicket as well as Potts for the next 17 years.

Off the field, reading through the minutes there was a proposition that the Club seek the help of a solicitor to look to our interests, but it appears this was not followed up. There was also discussion regarding light and water. The Water Board quoted 100 yards free, 150 yards at 1/- per foot. Two tilley lamps were to be purchased by Brian Moss for the dressing rooms. A later letter from the Water Board informed us nothing could be done until the supply in the village improved.

1969 saw the start of the local 'Knockout Cup' competition sponsored by the local *Macclesfield Express*. The man behind this was our captain, Bob Fairhall. Although not a local, Bob was always an enthusiastic organiser whatever he gave his mind to. He was always

POTT SHRIGLEY CRICKET CAPTAIN WANTS 20 OVERS KNOCKOUT

A suggestion that clubs in the Macclesfield area should get together to start a 20 overs knockout competition was made by Mr. Bob Fairhall, Captain of Pott Shrigley Cricket Club, at the club's annual dinner at Bollington Conservative Club on Friday.

Officials, players and their wives at Pott Shrigley Cricket Club dinner on Friday.

Mr. Fairhall said he felt the district lacked such a competition, which was run with much success in some other areas. It would help to create interest, and he hoped it would be possible to call a meeting to discuss the matter.

He also suggested that a bigger effort could be made to make a success of the "derby" game between Bollington and Pott Shrigley particularly now that Sunday cricket was played at Bollington. He felt certain that if they had 2,000 tickets printed and gave the match publicity they would get a large crowd, especially if the weather was good.

The dinner was again a big success being largely attended.

FULL OF INTEREST

Mr. G. Taylor, President, was in the chair. He said last season was full of interest even though from a playing point of view it was not as successful as they would have liked. They had a good fixture list for next season and he wished the players every success.

One very pleasing aspect of the past season was the growth of the junior section. The point was that they were regular in their attendance at the ground and their enthusiasm was very good, something which he could commend to some of the older members.

He extended a warm welcome to all their guests and said it was always nice to see them, especially representatives from other clubs.

YOUNG PLAYERS

The toast to the club was submitted by Mr. George Mellor, who in a witty speech congratulated the club on the enthusiasm of its members.

Replying Mr. Fairhall said that of the 42 games played, 14 were won, 19 lost and eight drawn, and one tied. The second eleven won only six of their games, but they had always enjoyed their cricket. During the season they introduced a lot of young players into the side, especially for the Sunday games. Those young players had never let them down. They were looking to the future with confidence.

They were all delighted to see Graham Hackney back among them. The club would like to extend their congratulations to the village of Pott Shrigley on winning their section in the Cheshire best-kept village competition.

FINE PERFORMANCE

The President presented the cup for the best individual performance to Ian Parrar, a member of the second eleven, for his performance at Elworth when he scored 59 not out and took four wickets for 32. This was the first time the cup had been awarded to a member of the second team.

The Secretary thanked the Ladies' Committee for the splendid work they did in providing refreshments, and Mrs. Taylor presented gifts to Mrs. Hackney, senior, Mrs. Higginbotham, Mrs. Hackney, junior, Miss Ann Connor, Miss Heapy, Mrs. C. Williams and Mrs. Jean Wrigley.

Mr. G. Higginbotham was the toastmaster. Afterwards, there was dancing and a fine entertainment provided by the players.

It was stated that the annual meeting of the club would be held at the Turner's Arms on Thursday, February 24.

The *Macclesfield Express* report of our 1966 annual dinner.

54

keen on a successful annual dinner and brought the house down on occasions when a few of us put on some sketches. The first one we had was a 'Miss Pott' competition. Bob's wife Pat had made him a yellow polka-dot bikini and as he was about 6' tall and weighed in around 15 stone, he won first prize hands down and was suitably crowned with a pot of the 'under the bed' variety by John Vernon and at one point Bob was suggesting something and Fred could be heard saying 'Don't forget the vicar will be present' and Bob said 'Bugger the vicar'. The number of times we have made this statement to each other over the years must go into hundreds.

Another year we performed a ballet in which of course once again Bob was the star attraction. Unfortunately this took place in a sports hall where all the pipes were frozen and just a few paraffin heaters placed about the room, so it was not ideal for performing in a ballet frock but they were memorable times which made such a good Club spirit.

Pat and Bob didn't always see eye to eye and on one occasion we had gone to play at Crewe with Pat, Bob, Don Hackney and myself in the car. When we got to Crewe Pat said she was going shopping in the town. At Crewe the changing rooms were on one side of the ground and the clubhouse and bar on the other side. It turned out to be another of those days with a thunderstorm in the middle of the afternoon (match abandoned) so we all got changed and everyone went home: but no Pat. We decided to go into town to see if we could find her. We looked in the bus station and the railway station, no Pat, so we decided to go back to the ground. We drove round to the clubhouse and there she was, sat at the window not looking very pleased. We went inside and typical Bob greeted her with 'Hello love' but Don who was always chirpy said 'We got to Congleton when we remembered you'. Needless to say the air turned blue and Bob was not exactly flavour of the day. Sadly Pat and Bob got divorced about three years ago after 35 years of marriage and I have said to him that it all went downhill after that day.

Back to the cricket, and again bad weather at the start left a lot to be desired. After losing the first game to Prestbury, of the next six matches two were rained off and two drawn. The first win was on 31 May and even though the season ended on a high note, we again didn't make any impact. We did beat Langley in the Pennant Cup and Woodford in the *Macclesfield Express* Cup but progressed no further.

Another new venture appeared in the minutes in October reading 'Stag Night 20th November'. We had always had a hot-pot supper in a local pub but this time it was a bus to a strip club. The hot-pot was not up to much but the entertainment was different. The non-playing members usually the first to put their names down were Nevill Birch and his dad, president Geoff Taylor and Corris Mawer, always out to enjoy themselves. Geoff and Corris at one time going back to the Turners Arms had another drink or two and were obviously still there the following morning. Geoff never remembered how he got to his house about three miles away.

One slip up we did make was not to celebrate the clubs fiftieth anniversary, but it did appear from records that even though the club was formed in 1919 no games were played, so we decided to celebrate it in 1970.

With the farm at the entrance now being bought by Mr and Mrs Casson the Club quickly approached them to see if we could improve the track across to the ground. This they agreed to but asked us to make another entrance so we would not have to go through the farmyard. This we agreed to do and on 7 March started work. Apart from tipping materials from the local foundry we paid a local stone-mason to knock the wall out and rebuild it in a slightly different place but after going to the trouble and expense Mr Casson informed us that he wanted us to knock the old pigsties down and go round the back of the house. We had enquired about this possibility before but it had to go before the parish council and some of them appeared to be under the impression that cars would never get as far as Pott Shrigley so we decided to leave the matter in abeyance.

However, Mr Casson later approached the Club to tell us they were putting in for planning permission to convert the barn into a restaurant and the croft into a car park that we could use if we would support them. This we agreed to do but knowing full well they didn't have much of a chance.

I was again appointed 1st XI captain so I always carried on as I had done before when playing friendly cricket – if I won the toss we batted. With a good batting side and playing five hours cricket we usually got a big score and tried not to close the game up. Two terrific games in that season reflected this policy. Against Chomondeley Graham Hackney and myself put on 119 for the opening stand and we declared at 240 runs for 5 wickets. I then used seven bowlers, I myself going for five sixes in one over, but the visitors finished one run short at 239 runs for 7 wickets.

The second game against Cheadle saw us declare at 246 for 3. I myself finished with 102 and Jim Berry with 82 put on 161 for the opening partnership. We left Cheadle three hours to get the runs. They took up the challenge winning off the last ball with 3 wickets left.

We were now beginning to look one of the better sides playing in the Conference with Graham Hackney and myself regularly opening the

County Captain's tribute
to Pott Shrigley C.C.

Freddie Millett, captain of Macclesfield and Cheshire cricket clubs, was the principal speaker at the annual dinner of Pott Shrigley Cricket Club at the Beehive Restaurant on Friday.

More than 100 members, wives and friends were present to hear Mr. Millett give local cricket clubs like Pott Shrigley a verbal "pat on the back."

He said when there were so many things being changed in this world, it was always refreshing to think of cricket, because here was something which the politicians could not interfere with.

The heart of the game was in clubs like Pott Shrigley, not in Test cricket or county cricket.

He was pleased to see that many more people were playing the game, and this was possible because of the efforts of the Pott Shrigleys of sport. He paid a fine tribute to the hard work of the club's officials and members.

In proposing the toast to the club, he said that the sport could live on without Test matches, but not without clubs like Pott Shrigley.

He was introduced to the large gathering by Mr. E. Hackney, the club Chairman, who outlined Mr. Millett's achievements as an all-round sportsman, making particular mention of his success as a table tennis player. He was the Macclesfield junior champion in 1945-46, and was a member of the town team. Mr. Hackney presented him with a club tie.

The club President, Mr. Geoffrey Taylor, thanked Mr. Millett and said how fortunate the Macclesfield district was to have a cricketer of Freddie's calibre. "He puts more into cricket than he gets out of it."

Mr. Taylor then reviewed the past season, mentioning outstanding performances by Graham Hackney, who scored 1,021 runs in the season. Mr. Bob Fairhall, the M.C., asked the guest speaker to present the awards.

The first team trophy for the player who did most towards winning a match went to Alan Hutton, who scored 67 against the President's XI, enabling Pott Shrigley to win by one wicket.

A trophy for the outstanding performance by a second team player was awarded to Philip Hammond, who took six out of seven wickets against Chelford, and the new trophy for the most promising junior was given to Martin Davies.

Dancing to the Hawaiian-aires and an excellent cabaret, which included songs from the shows by the St. Michael's Players, rounded off a very enjoyable evening. The singers were Lyn Wrigley, Joan Whittaker and Christopher Porter. Roland Longson was the pianist and Richard Porter introduced the programme.

The *Macclesfield Express* reports on the guest speaker at our annual dinner in 1970.

batting and taking wickets also. During the season both finished with over 800 runs and a 50-plus wickets and with John Pickford and Bob Fairhall, both quite quick bowlers taking wickets, we were a force to be reckoned with.

Another newcomer, Alan Hutton, topped the batting with an average of 45.5 He was a left-hander of immense talent but sometimes a pain in the neck, always wanting a bowl which wasn't the best part of his game.

Apart from a strong 1st XI we had a very good 2nd XI with experienced players like Graham Higginbotham, Fred Wrigley and Shep Broster as captain.

Even though everything seemed to be going well at Pott Shrigley I was still looking to the wicket at Bollington who at this time really looked as if they were going places with a large log cabin pavilion built in the wood adjacent to the ground which allowed them to have a bar and was large enough for all types of functions. It did appear they would be the club of the future in the area and we may struggle but we always managed to keep a junior section going so we were not worried about their seemingly excellent progress and tried to help as much as possible and again Bollington were opponents on President's Day.

Another local club who seemed to be having problems was Chelford who had sent a letter round asking clubs to protest about their ground being built on. It is still a cricket ground today so the protest must have worked.

Back to Pott and the plans for the 'Jubilee Train' to London were completed, and although in the first instance we would have been able to make a good profit, several events restricted our early ambitions. Firstly we had chosen the day of the Motor Show and put out adverts regarding the train. This upset a local coach operator who was running buses to the show and insisted any travel like this was for members of the organisation and not the public and he was prepared to take the matter to court, so any advertising was low-key after this.

However, the trip went ahead with British Rail just charging for the passengers who had tickets. A raffle was held on the train so we made a few pounds on the day and everyone enjoyed a superb day out. At the meeting on 22 October a vote of thanks to myself and Mr Barnes of British Rail was proposed. Also the train ran bang on schedule in both directions.

Two more events also mentioned at this meeting were the forming of a table tennis section and the 'Stag Night' at 'Ocean Eleven'. I think it was felt there were more girls there.

1971 saw Eric Burgess return to the club as president with Neville

Members and friends await the special train at Macclesfield station.

Birch as chairman. Again I was appointed 1st XI captain and for the first time I gave the Hackney brothers Don and Graham the chance to open the innings. This proved a big success: Don finished the season with 933 runs and Graham with 991 runs. The feature of their batting was that the running between the wickets sometimes appeared suicidal but most of the time effective, and also putting the other team off.

In a Cheshire Cup match at Hyde, being a man short, we had taken David Goate (Billie) our 2nd XI wicket keeper to play. He duly took five for 35 and won us the game.

Again the season went well with John Pickford and David Rushton taking over 40 wickets and David, whose method of batting was block the first ball then hit everything out of sight but if he stayed in was a terrific match winner, finished with 451 runs. We finished the season in

The advert for our trip to London, which did not please Bostocks.

the top half of the competition but even though we were not involved, rumblings were being made regarding the structure of the competition as some Clubs who could only field one team were only playing the second team of Clubs like ours and were finishing higher in the competition.

In the summer we received a letter from the agents acting for the Lowther Estate offering to sell the ground for £600. Naturally we were happy about this but later got an invitation to a meeting with the parish council and the parochial council. Unfortunately transport in the club in those days was in short supply and a last minute mix up ended with no one getting to the meeting. Shortly after this we received another letter stating the ground had been sold to the parish council for £700. Naturally we were disappointed as we felt, knowing the parish council, it was their obvious dislike for people outside the village trying to improve things. As this could be understood, it seemed to us a very narrow view as the Club would not survive without us.

Again the matter of trying to find an alternative venue was discussed but having built the pavilion ourselves and improved the ground, we decided there was no other place available. Later in the year a sub-committee of John Pickford, D. Rushton, E. Hackney and myself met with members of the parish council. John spoke on our behalf stating that we should be allowed to progress as before, without interference,

60

with the running of the Club. This was agreed and indications of a long lease were made, also help with the fencing of the ground but a lot of this was just 'pie in the sky'. With regard to the fence, it caused us problems for years until eventually in the 1980s we had a 'sponsored post' appeal to re-fence all round the ground. We sent a letter to the council asking them to sponsor a post at £10 but they refused.

1972 saw Graham Hackney appointed 1st XI captain. I suppose some of the players who had played under me for years had now gone down to the 2nd XI and other people had different ideas, particularly the idea of batting first and Clubs paying for points seemed to favour the idea of always putting the opposition in to bat. In most leagues today they have tinkered around with the points system to try and get clubs to bat first but this never seems to work.

Another 'first' happened at the Club and I don't think it has happened in many clubs. A lad called John Houghton was appointed junior captain at the AGM but by the time the first game was played he was a married man. Unfortunately for John and Helen the marriage lasted no time at all.

This year also saw the introduction of 'The National Village Cup' competition sponsored by 'Haig' and we were drawn to play at Rostherne where the outfield was not very well cut so it was not a high scoring game. We won and I won the 'Man of the Match' with 3 wickets and 30 plus runs and was presented with a 'Haig' tie which I still have. Unfortunately we lost a close game with Charlesworth in the next round.

Later in the year I almost made news in the national newspapers. I had given a trophy to Bollington Cricket Club when they started their annual 'Sixes' in memory of my dad so I was asked to go on the platform where the trophies were ready to be presented. Anyway, when the winning captain came up to receive it, the trophy had disappeared. Someone obviously gave the story to the press and several reporters contacted me for a story, but I told them someone had had a pint too many and done it for a joke. Sure enough, when I went to go to work the following morning the trophy was in my back garden. Nobody ever owned up but I had an idea who it was. If they read this, no action will be taken.

Good progress was again made in 'The *Macclesfield Express* Cup' reaching the semi-finals against local rivals Bollington. Once again knowing Bollington had two useful quick bowlers in Brian Jackson and Keith Oliver we used the old ploy of playing on the end wicket where there was only about a six-yard run-up at one end before you went down a big dip. But on this occasion it didn't seem to work as

Pott Shrigley Cricket Club's
fears over ground

Once again the Pott Shrigley Cricket Club annual dinner at the Beehive Restaurant on Friday proved to be a very happy event and the President (Mr. E. R. Burgess) said that every effort should be made to encourage youngsters, who are the life-blood of any club. He also appealed to all who were in any way connected with the club to rally round the officials.

Continuing, the President said it was a credit to the dinner committee that they were there at all for power cuts had made things so uncertain. That, combined with sickness prevented quite a number from being present and they hoped that friends like Mr. George Mellor (Vice-President), Mrs. Mellor, Mr. and Mrs. A. Pickford, Mr. I. Cooper, all Vice-Presidents, amongst others, would soon be well again.

Mr. Burgess said, he and his wife were delighted with the recent success of Presidents' day matches and that so many had been able to enjoy the event. He welcomed Mr. G. Harding (Chairman of the Parish Council), the Rev. C. I. and Mrs. Siviter and Mr. G. Taylor (past President) amongst others.

The Club experienced a difficult season in having to adjust to the rather more competitive play of the Cheshire Club Conference and not a few matches were spoiled by over-zealous gamesmanship, but the Club upheld its tradition of putting the game first.

The matter of renewal of lease of the ground had given rise for concern, but he was happy to say that he now understood that the Club would not only secure a lengthy lease, but that there was every prospect that the amenities would be also improved in the near future. These things have created a certain amount of apathy, but this must be erased and nothing must stand in the way of the Club's future and he hoped everyone concerned would rally round the officials.

The players, said the President, must see that the Club continues to equal the best village club in the competitions. They had proved they had the ability.

In conclusion, Mr. Burgess especially thanked the ladies committee for their wonderful work and said that many clubs had expressed appreciation of their hospitality.

Mr. David Goate, the M.C. called on the President to present the club trophies. The first eleven cup and replica for best match - winning performance event to John Pickford for his 8 for 32 v. Wilmslow, away.

The second eleven recipient was Fred Wrigley for his 59 not out v. Lindow.

The trophy for the outstanding junior of the season went to Chris Martin.

Bouquets were presented to Mrs. E. R. Burgess, Mrs. P. Birch and Mrs. C. I. Siviter by Mrs. D. Brooke, Mrs. D. Goate and Mrs. E. Hackney respectively.

The Chairman Mr. N. Birch said it was a pleasure to present a brief resume of outstanding performances during the past season, a none-too-easy task for as usual there were many noteworthy efforts.

For some seasons now it has been impossible to commence this first eleven review without recalling the ability displayed by the Hackney brothers and it is again no exception to find Graham at the top of the averages in the batting with 991 runs, plus some fine innings in the Bollington six-a-side which saw him once again achieve over 1,000 runs. He was also the only player to hit over a "ton" 104 not out and he showed his versatility by also taking 47 wickets.

Not to be outdone, Donald Hackney had one of his best seasons in hitting up 933 runs. His match-winning knock of 54 not out in the Cup at Toft and his part in a hundred partnership with Graham against ollington was a delight. David Rushton also made his mark with the bat with 451 runs and took 41 wickets. He had quite a few 50's to his credit.

John Pickford was a tower of strength in attack to top the bowling averages. His 7-42 at Davenham and 8 for 32 at Wilmslow were outstanding,

but he often was unlucky to do even better. He also contributed 342 runs in sixteen innings.

A young player to make his mark was Chris Martin who in his 28 wickets had 7 for 40 at Springfield and 6 for 38 at Cholmondley. Skipper Brooke hit up 350 runs. Ken Vare 289 while Brian Moss, David Goate, Harry Lawson and Jeff Newton all turned in some sound performances as did Jim Berry who hit up 292 runs and on one occasion had a great knock of 80.

The Second XI had a moderate season, but Skipper Broster said they all enjoyed themselves. Graham Higginbotham led the batting and his son, Steven the bowling. Well done! Graham hit 302 and had the mortification of being caught behind when on 99 in one match. Fred Wrigley also batted well with 302 runs as also did Peter Chadwick (147), S. Broster (189), Corris Mawer (133) and Jeff Newton (94). Steven Higginbotham topped the bowling and Graham Bailey took most wickets and carried the brunt along with Corris Mawer. Graham had 23 and Corris 18. Brian Warhurst also bowled well with 16 wickets to his credit.

Entertainment was provided by Chris Francis and his band along with Johnny Maxfield and the M.E.P.S. and staff were thanked for their contribution to the success of the event.

The report of our annual dinner in 1972, again from the *Macclesfield Express*.

Dennis Goodwin, a nippy little swing bowler of about six paces, took 5 for 34 out of a total of 143 but this proved enough as Bollington finished on 129 for 9 with only Martin Tute with 75 offering any real threat. Ken Vare as usual in these games was the best bowler with 4 for 16.

In the Pennant Trophy we beat Davenham in Round One. I remember I then had got to the stage of regular mid-on fielder when 'Pancho' their big hitter hit one of the highest vertical drives I ever remember and there seemed a chorus of people shouting my name. By the time it came down 'Pancho' was standing at the side of me. I somehow managed to cling on and he looked at me and said 'You want your bloody hands chopping off' but as always with Davenham it was back to the Turners Arms for a good friendly get-together. After that we surprisingly lost to Hartford in the next round.

Once again in the Conference we finished about halfway, this only after winning the last five out of six games.

At the end of the season there appears to have been a church service when the deeds to the ground were handed over to the parish council. I cannot find any record of the cricket club being invited to this service and cannot recall anybody attending.

At the final meeting of the year, the Sheriff attended and I again, as on many occasions, queried him regarding the state of the right of way onto the ground now it had been purchased by the council. His answer appeared to be with a little diplomacy 'He would sort it out' but as was to be proved in years to come, a proper effort could have been made to help to improve things for the benefit of Club members, spectators and visitors but nothing was ever done and for the next 20 plus years we had to put up with this problem just to please the narrow-minded antiquated ideas of a few.

With little change of officials in 1973, plans were now getting off the ground to improve the playing area and facilities and a sub-committee met the parish council to discuss a longer lease so that grants could be applied for. The council intimated a new lease would be drawn up by a solicitor and submitted to the council. The problems regarding the entrance to the ground and right of way were pointed out.

For the first time a social committee was appointed with Peter Neale as secretary and another useful newcomer on the social side. Brian Clear, who was the chef at the Salesian College. With the village hall now in business and the Club wanting to give as much support as possible, Don Hackney volunteered to be on this social committee and as another token of goodwill, a friendly fixture was arranged. Cricket Club vs. Village Hall. Our president, Eric Burgess, gave a cup to be played for annually.

63

This was generally ignored by members, who were not over-excited about this turn of events.

One unfortunate incident during the season was when Ernie Hackney our umpire and secretary was hit by the ball whilst officiating at square leg and taken to hospital with a broken femur.

From a cricket point of view the season seemed to follow a usual pattern, winning the first round of cups then failing at the next hurdle, the Hackneys again consistent run-getters and David Rushton again with 625 runs and 48 wickets.

The end of the cricket season was somewhat overshadowed by rumours that several Conference Clubs were breaking away to form a league of their own, and this was more or less confirmed when these Clubs wrote to me cancelling fixtures for 1974.

As could only be expected, the forming of the Cheshire league and the way it was done caused friction between old friends and there were several moves to try and outlaw it, but to no avail, plus you got the aggro as to who had been invited before them. We did not see how old Alltrinchamians were made members when they played on someone

64

MACCLESFIELD EXPRESS
August 1973

A rare and unfortunate mishap on the cricket field has robbed Pott Shrigley and grounds for miles around of that personality-plus among umpires — Mr. Ernest Hackney — for the remainder of the season.

Mr. Hackney, who is 67 and lives at 326 Buxton - road, Macclesfield, was one of the umpires in the Pott Shrigley and Macclesfield friendly game on Sunday and while positioned at square leg he suddenly swerved to avoid a ball hit by Steve Foley.

He collapsed, was carried off the field to await an ambulance, and after examination at Macclesfield Infirmary it was stated that he had a fractured femur.

A member of Mr. Hackney's family said he understood his father was to have a metal plate fitted into his injured leg and he would be in hospital for an estimated 10 weeks.

Macclesfield Infirmary stated Mr. Hackey was treated for a fractured femur and that after an operation on Tuesday he was "doing fine".

■ Mr. Hackney has two sons playing for Pott Shrigley — Graham, who is team captain, and Don.

Umpire Hackney breaks leg on field

The *Macclesfield Express* reports umpire Ernest Hackney's unfortunate injury in August 1973.

else's ground and I think our feelings were later justified when they folded and joined Ashley.

However, after a lot of hard work rearranging fixtures with Clubs in the Conference and one or two wishing to join, plus a few friendlies, a full fixture list was completed from 20 April to 21 September.

Even though at the time the mood of the Club was one of annoyance it did concentrate our mind on the fact that our ground and facilities were not up to standard so a small sub-committee led by John Pickford was formed to look into this matter. After laying our plans John wrote to the parish council, obviously knowing that some of the people we were dealing with thought progress and change were dirty words.

Sure to form I was working on the ground one night when across came the Sheriff with a gentleman I had not met before. We got talking about the weather. It happened to be a lovely night and the man complimented me on the state of the ground. However, the Sheriff turned to me and said 'Yes, but they have a Mr Pickford who wants to make it into the "Lords" of the North'. This remark didn't surprise me but I suspected he felt I was going to agree with him but in fact John, apart from his negotiating ability, would spend hours helping to keep the ground tidy so I gave them a conducted tour of our poor facilities. I pointed out that we had only basic toilets, no electricity and no running water for people to wash their hands. The Sheriff remarked 'Lad, in the trenches in the Great War, all we had was a stick over a hole'. I informed him he was talking a lot of rubbish as it was now 1974 but he didn't seem to see the funny side of this and we continued to face opposition despite John Pickford's best efforts. We had the jibes of people from out of the village but at the end of the day they were improvements that in normal circumstances benefited everyone, including the schoolchildren who used the ground.

Although we had been concerned by not getting invited to join the Cheshire league, and had feared Bollington with their new pavilion may attract some members away, the reverse seemed to happen with Alan Beckett (a superb player), Martin Tute and Alan Sherrat joining us.

Ken Vare, a very steady medium-pace bowler was vice-captain with Steve Higginbotham captain. Steve certainly had an impact on the game at Woore: when playing for a draw he never let fielders crowd him by the simple tactic of trying to hit everything out of the ground. On this occasion with two balls left, he hit a huge skyer into the deep and three Woore players in their eagerness all collided. Two were taken to hospital, one with a huge gash in his forehead, the other with both wrists broken. The third lost two teeth which only goes to prove that you must always call.

In the first round of the Village Cup at Moore and Daresbury we were not impressed by the look of the wicket. When the home team

19 Coniston Drive, Handforth,
Wilmslow, Cheshire, SK9 3NN

Mr W.H. Bennett,
Pott Shrigley Parish Council,
'Woodside Cottage',
Pott Shrigley.   27th April, 1974

Dear Sir,

Alterations to Cricket Ground

In compliance with the Town & Country Planning Act, 1971, I enclose Notice
No. 1 in respect of planning permission for the levelling of the Cricket
Ground, Pott Shrigley.

As you have possibly heard, the Cricket Club Committee has elected a sub
committee which has discussed the improvements necessary to maintain the
Pavilion and Ground in good order. I feel that it is both appropriate and
courteous at this stage to appraise you and the Parish Council of the
conclusions we have reached and the changes we are planning.

It has been agreed that priority should be given to the provision of water
and electricity to the Pavilion and that a degree of ground levelling should
take place. We are attempting to achieve these aims in the autumn of this
year, 1974.

The second phase of the work will entail an extension to the rear of the
present Pavilion to provide new toilets, a new kitchen and a larger equipment
shed. It is also our intention to construct a sewage disposal unit and it is
hoped that this second phase will be completed in 1975. Request for planning
permission will be submitted at a later date.

I am sure you will appreciate that the completion of this work is dependant
on our ability to provide the necessary finance. To this end, it is our
intention to apply for grants and itn is one of the conditions for the receipt
of Playing Fields Association grants, that the club has a lease of at least
28 years. It is now over twelve months since we discussed with you the question
of the lease and it would assist the Cricket Club if this matter could be
finalised as soon as possible.

In the past I feel that a lack of communication between the Cricket Club
and the Council has caused many difficulties. I hope that this letter explains
clearly what our intentions are and will enable you to consider our plans and
raise any objections at an early stage. We would, of course, be delighted to
receive your blessing on this scheme as such encouragement would be helpful to
the Club.

Thank you for your attention in this matter.

                                        Yours faithfully,

                                        J.A. Pickford

Correspondence regarding the new lease and ground improvement.

67

were five wickets down without a run on the board with Ken Vare and Steven bowling, I honestly thought at one time I was going to play on a team that dismissed the opposition without scoring but they eventually managed 43. We went out in the third round in a totally different game at Pott with the home side scoring 201 for 9 and Tintwistle eventually won with five balls to spare. We always felt this game was lost because their bowler ran Ken Vare out when backing up off the last ball (or as our umpire Harry Lawson said, 'Did him for ufting'). Ken was determined to get his own back and did, eventually, but at the cost of bowling badly by his standards.

In the Cheshire Cup we once again got the better of Bollington who scored 188 for 9, Pott winning with overs to spare. Graham Hackney was 'Man of the Match' with 80 not out and 3 for 23.

Obviously with so many clubs in the league the standard was not quite as good and I am sure most people would agree we were the strongest club in the Conference. With a powerful batting side we were finding a lot of teams playing for a draw so with a few rained-off matches and eight drawn games, only one lost by 3 runs, we could end the season winning the Aggregate Trophy once again, Graham Hackney winning the batting with an average of 55. I myself topped the bowling with 43 wickets so it was nice to see the 'Old Faithfuls' still doing well amongst the talented newcomers. The second team captained by Fred Wrigley also did well with Jim Berry starring with bat and ball.

During the year at most of the meetings, questions were asked regarding the proposed ground improvements but one felt sorry for John as nothing further could be done until we had a new lease from the parish council but nothing seemed to happen and people were getting annoyed with their attitude towards this matter.

With the Village Hall open and a good social committee, apart from having a 'Hundred Club' and more social events, we started collecting waste paper in the area on the last Friday of each month – never missing a collection for 26 years.

By the November meeting we had received a letter from the newly formed Cheshire league stating that they were considering extending in the near future. We were also awarded £5 for making progress in the 'Watney Cup'.

At the AGM in 1975 Bob Fairhall was appointed chairman and Alan Sherratt 1st XI captain. Both were outgoing personalities. Alan was a stocky small person whose size sometimes belied his ability, apart from being able to hit the ball very hard. He was a useful bowler, quick between the wickets and a good fielder. One amazing catch at Old Altrinchamians didn't count but was quite outstanding, fielding at long off a skyer was struck straight into the deep. He scurried after it when he got to the sight screen realising it was going over, did a chase round the screen and came out at the other side with the ball in his hands.

On looking back on the minutes of the 1975 AGM it was obviously a bit of a turning point in the Club's history with us having to find a new chairman, treasurer, 1st XI captain and vice-captain. Fortunately all the new officials were in for a busy year if our plans went ahead. The new treasurer, Brian Warhurst, a chartered accountant and long-standing member of the club, found it very hectic.

One new member of the committee was Mr Hedley Patrick, a local businessman who probably gave the club its biggest boost in its history. John and myself had been to see him, as he owned a plant hire firm, for his advice and help and over the next few years he was to have work done for us at the cost of thousands of pounds. Hedley was probably one of the last generous big spenders in the area, not only helping us but many other organisations in the area. He was president of the Bowling Club and choirmaster at Bollington parish church from where he brought one of his choiristers, Jack Archer, to join us and come and score. I think if you asked the older members who was the personality they remembered most, it would be Jack – a big booming voice which could be heard miles away but also a superb bass singer who was always sought after to perform at local functions. His most requested masterpiece was 'Sylvest' and the picture of Jack with his jacket off and braces showing on his chest, the line in the song of 'Silver medals on his chest – big chest' will always stay in the memory.

Another thing Jack became known for was finding nicknames for people, his first one christening Alan Sherratt 'Captain Mainwaring' a name that suited his personality. I always felt Alan thought it to be a compliment. Another one was Andy Smith who was christened the 'Chocolate Lion' because he drove a van for Lyons cakes.

Jack also took immense pride in the score book with different coloured pens for sixes and fours and after the games Ernie Hackney used to go in to the village hall and borrow the scorebook for details for match reports for the local paper. One night he went home and took the book with him. All hell broke loose with Jack and when he got the book back he had the corner drilled and fastened it with a lock and chain to his briefcase.

About this time the *Manchester Evening News* ran the 'Panama Sixes' competition and Alan Sherratt was in second place for most of the season so every time he hit another six Jack, who was supposed to be neutral, would jump up and shout 'Panama' and frighten the life out of the opposition's scorer.

The Frustrated Scorer: by the Bard of Harrop Wood
There was hell up early on in the season.
Caused by a strike at the Macclesfield Times
He'll have to let have the score book.
So I can get my report in on time
He'd written his proverbs and Gospels.
Like a Psalmist he quoted big words
His Pontifications should be preserved for posterity
And placed in the Archives at Lords
Jack Archer then opened his scorebook
And said I'me certainly not standing for that
There were numerouse funerial inscriptions
Of players who'd lost there desireabilaly to Bat

Jack's expression of annoyance with Ernie for taking the score book home.

Jack was never afraid to say what he felt. I remember one evening waiting in the schoolyard for the village hall to open, when up comes the Sheriff with the keys. Jack saw him coming and boomed, 'They will never do any good in this village until there has been a lynching'. He would also make up poetry, particularly of events inside the Club.

At the committee meeting in March, Mr Birch stated he had been informed that the lease would be completed by 31 March but most people were prepared to wait and see.

Once again, we were a very strong Club in the Conference, unbeaten all season but once. Again the first team finished runners-up and the second team joint leaders, so again we won the Aggregate Trophy but in the 'Cups' went out in the early rounds. Alan Beckett broke the record for the most runs scoring 1,380 runs, but top of the averages on his return to the club was Keith Arnold, averaging 55–75. He could make batting look easy by the simple technique of stopping the good ones and hitting the bad ones.

In general we all felt it was a good year for Pott with both the playing side and village hall. Together we had a few social nights, dances etc. and at these events were a couple, Dot and Cyril, who lived down the road and supported the village hall. Cyril was a quiet chap who didn't say very much and Dot, to put it mildly, just the opposite.

What happened in the bike shed we will never know but shortly after Dot and Brian, our social secretary, took off together. Dot returned a few months later but we never heard from Brian again.

On 26 September we got to sign the lease which of course contained one or two petty restrictions but at least they had overlooked the silly 'Sunday terms'. A few years later as more junior teams came into operation I did get rumbles about the under 13s playing on Sunday mornings, but again we were a Cricket Club and to have a future we had to encourage juniors.

Another condition was that 50 per cent of the committee must reside in Pott Shrigley. Whilst we always adhered to this, it meant half the committee were just names who never attended meetings and even those who were obviously keen to have their names on would prefer to snipe from a distance and not even attend the AGM.

With the season over it was now time for the contractor to move in. I had insisted the turf to be cut up and put back rather than re-seeding as it is a moorland grass which we didn't want to lose so this did make it a slower job. With this completed, Hedley got the heavy machinery onto the ground and for the next three weeks they were working non-stop but this was only the beginning of Hedley's generosity.

One interesting event took place on Sunday 14 September when the villagers organised an Old Tyme Cricket Match. Naturally we supported this as much as possible but on the lease we were still governed by their petty restriction on the number of games to be played on Sundays.

With the unexpected disappearance of the social secretary it does appear that one of the old faithful members of the Club was left with the problem of sorting out the financial situation regarding the social committee. Graham Higginbotham who was the auditor at the time asked for details of each individual effort to be produced. Although no accusations of any wrongdoing were ever made the bank account had been frozen so members who had won the '100 Club' had to wait a while for their winnings, as we were a Club who liked to do things in a proper manner.

At the following meeting Don Hackney gave a report regarding the social committee and most aspects he had found answers to so after more discussion it was unanimously decided the matter be closed as a float had been supplied.

With the AGM of the Conference coming up, John Smith our representative was asking for views to be expressed as there seemed to be an increasing view that something a bit more disciplined was required as some of the Clubs started when they felt like it and some of the grounds were in poor condition. The captains and vice-captains proposed a strong letter be sent to the Conference AGM.

With the ground now beginning to take shape one or two new problems arose with drains and culverts getting damaged so new

71

drains had to be laid. Unfortunately the plastic ones we use today had not been invented. Also, the pavilion which had been at the edge of the undulating outfield was now about two feet above it, so once again Hedley paid for steps to be built. Admittedly at first sight these appeared to protrude a way out and some wag called them 'The Pott Pier' but once you got used to them it was difficult to see how else it could have been done.

Also other people seemed to think we would finish with a perfectly flat ground, which was never the idea as we had agreed with the Peak Park planning people to keep basically to the existing contours. I think most people think the hill at the Bollington end is part of the attraction of Pott Shrigley Cricket Club. Obviously it occasionally saves a few runs particularly when it is wet when the opposition batsman play a glorious shot and stand back to admire it only to find it gets about two inches from the boundary and then rolls back. Also it can be a disaster to start running in for a skyer, find you can't stop and then the ball drops over your head.

Unfortunately for the contractor winter set in early that year, before all the turf was re-laid and when he returned in early spring a lot of the turf that had been left had rotted away so he had to seed again. The conditions were not favourable as older people will remember. The first part of 1976 was cold, snow even stopped play between Derbyshire and Lancashire in June. Poor Clive Lloyd wondered what he had let himself in for then this was followed by one of the hottest driest summers in memory so the seeded part, which had been rolled a lot, hardly grew. This side also has quite a slope on it and the ball ran so quick and also made such a noise we called it 'The Floorboards'. An inch either side of you and it was a boundary. However, later in the year Oliver came with his tractor and sprayed it with feed so we eventually finished up with an outfield to be proud of.

At the AGM in 1976 most of the officials stayed on and we managed to talk Hedley in to being chairman of the social committee, a job he carried out with his usual enthusiasm. One event of the year being a garden party on his lawn, a large house about a quarter of a mile from the ground with glorious views of the countryside around Pott Shrigley. Hedley had organised a big marquee for food, a bar, and marvellous buffet supplied by local butchers, Heathcotes. Music was played by Bollington Brass Band and there were side shows and stalls. Jack Archer was dressed up like a Mississippi gambler and making good use of his booming bass voice to get custom. We couldn't guess how much it cost to put this event on but at the next meeting Hedley turned up with all the takings in a biscuit tin – there was over £500 mostly in small cash which was quite handy in those days. Obviously he could just as easily have written a cheque but preferred to do it this way. Most people associated with the Club will always remember the event.

Another first the Club undertook was to try and get advertising for the fixture cards and in 1976 we managed six adverts. Also, to try and encourage very young members, practice for 7–11 years olds was arranged.

With the work carried out on the ground we had also had a new practice area laid but with the weather we had encountered this was not fit for use and even though most people had been to the indoor nets, it was nice to have a go on grass before you started. The real magic for most people was being able to turn the tap on or flush the toilet and to switch the light on after night matches. It was 1976 but it had been a hell of a fight to get these basic necessities. It also meant that for the first time we would be able to use a proper sprinkler on the ground, but sods law saw to it that due to the long hot summer we had a water ban. However, Bob Fairhall fixed a pump in a well situated adjoining field and this did the trick. A number of years later when our neighbours threatened to cut off our water supply we almost had to resort to this again.

The season started with a fixture against Endon followed by three games against Rode Park. This is one of the strange things you find in sport from time to time. We played them in the Conference and two cup matches in eight days, but with probably the strongest batting side in the Conference we turned out to be too strong for them, beating them on each occasion. However, we enjoyed playing on their beautiful ground and got on well together. We had three great nights in their local which when we arrived found 'Mine Host' to be a local Kerridge man – Alan Snape, well-known in the Bollington area as a keen sportsman, both at cricket and football, a game he played being semi-professional for both Macclesfield and Congleton. He knew most of us, particularly Jack, so it wasn't long before he had him with his jacket off, leading a sing-song which the locals seemed to enjoy and join in. When we played midweek in the cup, there appeared to be more people in the pub and when we went the following Sunday, Alan had spread the word around and the pub was full. As most people have agreed, Jack's rendering of 'Sylvest' was as good as you could hear anywhere.

Alan Snape later came back to live in Bollington and was instrumental in helping to make the local firm of 'Gradus' a big success and a company always prepared to help local clubs and organisations with donations and sponsorship. He was also a local councillor who worked tirelessly for Bollington and the area, always prepared to help at Pott Shrigley. He was also mayor of Bollington.

With good hard wickets in 1976, the Pott Shrigley batsmen came into their own and a record eight centuries were scored by them. Once again Alan Beckett led the way with 1,223 runs and it was now becoming apparent that the bigger clubs in the area were doing their best to prise him away from Pott. Martin Tute also scored over 1,000 runs. Alan Sherratt, apart from captaining the team, showed what a useful player he was taking 39 wickets and scoring over 500 runs. After not being defeated in 1974 and 1975 we lost our first game for two and a half years early in July, and again with a lot of drawn games, did not do as well as expected. The success that year came from winning the Pennant Cup, beating Mere in the final at the end of the season with Pott being 109 for 6, then restricting Mere to 74 for 8.

The President's Day at the end of the season was a bit unusual with us deciding to help bolster club funds by holding a 20-mile sponsored walk. One memory of this was of Ernie Hackney, always willing to help, given the job of steward on the canal bridge at Whiteley Green. Bob Fairhall and myself had arranged to be the final entrants through so we could inform the steward but could not see Ernie when we got back to the Club and we were told he was not there. We got in the car and went looking for him and found him stood at the old railway bridge about 30 yards down the road complaining he had not seen a soul. One strange remark in the minutes after the walk was when John Smith, who had organised the walk, was asked to give his report and he stated 'Financially it was well worth running'. In the evening dancing and entertainment took place in the village hall with Hedley again supplying the buffet but Jack provided the entertainment. On this occasion it was the 2nd XI wicket keeper, Geoff Newton, who was the butt of his prank.

Geoff, who had come up through the junior ranks, was not very tall and a bit on the tubby side but a great trier whatever he did. He always took a lot of getting out and never seemed to care about getting hit with the ball. He would not let you down behind the stumps but was a bit ponderous and Jack had given him the name of 'Moon Boots'. Jack, who was a storeman at the Gas Board, had a habit of bringing items and presenting them on these occasions and typical of him usually made it into a one-act play and after a few funny remarks opened a box with the biggest pair of Gas Board boots painted silver and presented them to Geoff, who will always be known to most of us as 'Moon Boots'.

With the season over it was now time to start with the second part of our improvements, this time extending the pavilion. Again what had looked like a big task was made easy. I was now working for Henry and Leigh Slater, looking after their bowling green and social

74

club. Most afternoons local pensioners would come and play bowls, snooker and dominoes. One of these gentlemen was Sam Hill who had just returned after a life in the building trade. Another was Harry Needham who was probably the best part of 70 years old but always on the lookout for some work to do. As strong as a horse, Harry had done a bit of boxing in his younger days and even at that age if any pub landlord wanted anyone throwing out, Harry was your man. These two saw to the building of the extension. Hedley must have kept the money flowing because I never got any complaints. Unfortunately all three have now departed, so it is no use the taxman getting excited, the only thing it cost the Club was a load of tea bags, a few broken pots and a burnt-out boiler.

At the end of the 1976 season the option arose of the Cheshire league forming a second division and we were invited to join. Thus we tendered our resignation to the Conference, obeying the rules by giving one year's notice.

1977 saw little change in officials but I was elected chairman. With the pavilion extension now completed John Vernon and his team of ladies now had a decent-sized kitchen to work in and Geoff Newton gave a lot of his time and money tiling and decorating it and for the first two games we had tea at the village hall.

We had now lost the services of Alan Beckett who had moved to Macclesfield where he opened the batting for several years. He would be missed, not only for his playing ability, but for the fact that he was always prepared, together with his father-in-law, to help with the running of the Club.

I found myself being dropped into the second team for the first time and the standard was pretty poor on occasions and sometimes not that enjoyable. In fact the Club in general had a poor start to the season. However, I did get back onto the first team in time to see Alan lose his temper. One day he called everyone to him in the middle of the ground and gave them a piece of his mind. This obviously had an effect as after a mediocre start in Conference matches, the last 12 games were all won in a tremendous run of success to take the 1st XI title. Don Hackney's 84 vs. Rylands was completely overshadowed by John Pickford. His 8 wickets for 8 runs off 14 overs was magnificent. Only four scoring shots came off his bowling, the first being a four in his eighth over. He repeated the medicine in the last game of the season against Heavily. This time his 8 wickets cost 19 runs but to make up for that he threw in a 'Hat Trick'. His 46 wickets at an average of 75 topped the bowling though Derrick Brooke (59) Alan Sherratt (50) and Bob Fairhall (49) all took more wickets. Bob had an exceptional year taking wickets for both 1st and 2nd XIs. In all matches his haul was a mammoth 102 wickets. Barry Patrick's contribution throughout the season was also invaluable, his fielding ability being of exceptional quality.

Martin Tute scored 846 runs but was pushed down to fourth in the averages by Keith Arnold (574), Graham Hackney (549) and Don Hackney (649), Skipper Sherratt totalling 606.

Winning the *Macclesfield Express* Cup in 1977 was no mean achievement as it was done the hard way by beating the top three major clubs in the area, Poynton being the first in round one. Bob Fairhall's 2 for 16 was the best return of a fine all-round bowling performance, backed up by top-class fielding. Pott inflicted four run-outs in restricting Poynton to 93. Keith Arnold saw Pott home with a controlled 48 not out.

It was Keith again in the second round against mighty Macclesfield who steered Pott to a fine win. Despite Alan Sherratt's 3 for 19 Macclesfield totalled 161–6 but a fine opening stand of 98 between Martin Tute (50 including 3 huge sixes) and Keith Arnold with a superb 80 gave Don Hackney the chance to hit three boundaries to win the game with two overs to spare.

The final against Bollington, played in front of several hundred spectators at Macclesfield, was totally one-sided. This time batting first it was Martin Tute who showed all his attacking strokeplay in a dashing knock of 73. This was backed up by Graham Hackney's 35 and Bob Fairhall's hard hit 32 not out, two sixes and three fours. This took the 'Hillmen' to a commanding 192 for 5. Bollington were on the rack immediately with Steven Higginbotham bowling Frank Gosling first ball then centre stage was taken over by Tony Hutter who proceeded to run through the Bollington batsmen, mainly with his inswinging yorker. Along with Bob Fairhall (2 for 15) Tony's five wickets for 24 runs ensured victory and a thrilling climax to a successful season.

We then said goodbye to Conference cricket although some members probably had reservations but it was a move we felt had to be made to try and keep up standards. Naturally the Conference dinner was well supported by members as tends to happen when the Club is presented with trophies and with President's Day again a big success, the year had probably been one of the most successful in the Club's history. The 'Conference Trophies' were presented by Ron Hedley (Dean's dad).

4

Members of the Cheshire League

1978 saw us for the first time since before the war playing league cricket although there was still a feeling with some members that this maybe was not the best for Pott Shrigley, but as time was later to prove this was best for the Club in the long run.

The season started with a bang, beating Chester Deaf Hospital in the first game in the Cheshire Cup. In this game Don Hackney caused a bit of a commotion by hitting a six through one of the hospital windows and upsetting one of the patients. Unfortunately Ernie must have made some lighthearted remark about this in the local paper and an irate member of the public sent a letter to the paper criticising us, so we had to apologise the following week.

We also got off to a good start in the Village Cup with Martin Tute hitting 129 in the first round against Aston on a bitterly cold day at Pott with the easterly wind coming straight off the Pennines and Martin hitting the ball with plenty of power. It wasn't the best conditions to be fielding in. I was pleased to be put on to bowl to get warmed up and finished with 5 for 26 in an easy win.

In the league with everyone playing each other once we were not finding things easy. With quite a few close games going against us we were unlucky in our first league encounter against Prestbury, in which Martin again got 'a ton', we looked on our way to victory when the rain came. Even though in general it was a poor league season with both first and second teams finishing third from bottom we did boast two of the highest team totals: 259 for 7 against Bredbury and 228 for 5 against Alsager. In the league cup we had wins against Prestbury, Ashley and Christleton before losing to the eventual winners: Holmes Chapel.

The 1978 season saw us once again improving the junior section with teams playing for the first time at under 13s, under 15s and under 18s, and with Fred Wrigley and Tony Hutter organising and coaching them and Hedley providing a mini-bus for them, we were hoping to provide players for the future.

We did still have quite a good social side to the Club with John

Smith as social secretary, Tuesday nights being very popular for meeting on social occasions. Dot and Cyril were back together, both working for Hedley, Dot in the office and Cyril as the gardener. However, Cyril was taken ill and passed away a few months later.

On reflection at the end of the season it was probably felt that finishing in the second division was not the end of the world, and we hoped we would be able to improve from there on and after the problems of getting the lease from the parish council and carrying through the improvements to the ground, it was a pleasure just to get on and play cricket.

1979 saw Keith Arnold as 1st XI captain and John Smith 2nd XI captain. Both were committed to the Club being match secretary and social secretary respectively. Alan Sherratt took over as secretary from John Pickford who, having carried most of the burden for the improvements to the ground, had to move to Yorkshire to carry on his career in Customs and Excise. John who had come along with his dad in 1957 when we built the pavilion, later to score and then play for many years, was along with Graham Hackney, who also came as a lad at the same time, a model Club man. At a young age he was always prepared to help the Club and take on responsibilities, but unfortunately for Pott, John only played a handful of games after this, but his devotion to the Club never faltered, always sending a subscription and when I informed him I was writing this account, I was going through old fixture cards and one appeared to be missing, so John said 'give me a ring, I will have it'.

Another problem that was beginning to crop up was the state of the outfield mower, although we had a 28" Acto sit-on model, it was getting a lot of wear and tear. The idea of having a rota system for cutting the outfield was OK but the playing area was now a lot bigger and players were tending to cut corners and were usually struggling to complete the job properly, and if they did, it was getting dark by the time they had finished so they didn't bother to look after the machine properly. As I was now looking after the bowling green as well as two cricket squares I usually went to the Institute of Groundsmen exhibitions, so I called in to see Mr Allett and have a look at their outfield mower. I was naturally impressed but at close on £2,000 it seemed a bit beyond us. When I came back I spoke to Alan, the secretary, to see if we should see if Hedley would be interested in buying it through his plant hire business and renting it to us. Alan, who didn't let the grass grow under his feet said 'I'll go and have a word'. Back he came about half-an-hour later to say it had been ordered and a few days later Mr Allett delivered it personally.

We did arrange to pay Hedley back on a monthly basis, but when

Graham Hackney, who was treasurer used to give him the cash in the village hall, he would pay for all his shares in 'The 100 Club', usually buy everyone a drink, and more often than not, the monthly payment had all gone.

The season turned out to be a successful one with big scores by a number of teams, Pott Shrigley being amongst them with:

259 for 7 against Bredbury
250 for 3 against Oakmere
234 for 4 against Weaverham
225 for 2 against Middlewich
218 for 8 against Alsager

Most of these scores produced a century opening stand featuring the captain. However, we did feel what it was like when we were on the receiving end against Mobberley who scored 217 for 3 with 100 each for the two Blackburn brothers.

One strange game I personally remember during that year was against Old Altrinchamians at the end of June.

With the outfield now running quick and a good hard wicket, the visitors won the toss and batted scoring two boundaries off the first three balls and another big score looked on the cards. Keith wasted no time in changing the bowling, threw the ball to me and I finished with 5 for 16 bowling them out for just above 100, so with batting like we had been doing getting the runs looked a formality, however, I found myself going to the wicket with our score at 53 for 7, but with the help of Graham Hackney and Bob Fairhall I finished on 28 not out and the game was won. I got my name again on the first team trophy. After this we played quite consistently in the league winning the final game by ten wickets finishing third in the league and winning promotion.

The juniors had now joined the High Peak Junior Cricket League and after a poor start had improved as the season went on with Andy Smith replacing Tony Hutter as coach and Fred still junior secretary, the season finished on a high note. One thing that is disappointing is 16 teams entered the 'Colts Cup' in 1979 – in 1998 there were only five teams.

At the July meeting Keith Arnold proposed we try a new format so that more members could be involved, so a 'Trios' competition was arranged with food and entertainment again provided by Hedley, this as usual to be held at the village hall. However, there appeared to be some misunderstanding regarding this, and Hedley, who was probably the biggest spending customer, was not pleased, but Jack, who always saw the amusing side of things wrote one of his famous odes.

79

Presidents Day 1979.

It was President's day at Pott Shrigley
When Hedley payed us a call
Just to say He'd give us party
In the top room of the Old Village Hall
Allan Heathcote will see to the Catering
Their Oll', he'll look after the Bar
Brian Buffey will play records for dancing
"I've got a Bionic Cabaret star"
Then into the proceedings came Geof Hardm
A regular profit of doom
"You can't go up there next Saturday.
Bollington's Light Opera have hired the room
Bob Fairhall trembled with temper
Ernie Hackney transfixed in a trance
"I could have told you this last December
They'd booked this room for a dance"
Allan Sherratt stood there speechless
Derek Brooke cried out in dismay
"They couldn't run booze up in a Brewery,
We'd better call it a day"
Then Hedley came to the rescue
Among rioting CRaos and Hub bub
Politely But firmly said ——— "Blow them
We'll go to the Conservative Club."

Jack's ode at not being able to use the village hall for President's Night.

The day and evening proved a big success and included a 'Race Night' but not everyone was happy. Hedley as usual, being generous, gave the winners £10 each for being on the winning team. There was also quite a bit of money on the last race and one lad who probably only played two games for the Club brought his mum and dad (both who liked their drink), so with the food and drink on Hedley they won on the last race, so they had a very profitable night out.

With the start of a new decade prospects looked excellent for Pott Shrigley, especially as we had just won promotion. But it never seemed to materialise, in fact of the five decades I have been associated with the club I think it was the one with the least stability with old members retiring, some going to the pavilion in the sky and new people coming and going at frequent intervals.

One new member, Martin Perry, looked likely to make himself public enemy number one with the natives by suggesting we have a fruit machine installed in the village hall. Our minute reads: 'it was felt it would not be looked on in good light' and in any event we did not have the authority to install one ourselves. At the next meeting the minutes read: 'Martin Perry repeated the request made at the last meeting that we explore the possibility of a fruit machine being installed in the village hall'. A short discussion on this resulted in the matter not being pursued. The Club also received a letter from the social secretary John Smith resigning his position.

Two musical events were to take place, a coachload of members going to the James Last Concert in March and later on in the summer 'The Spinners at Shrigley' concert was to be held at the Salesian College which is now Shrigley Hall Hotel, Golf and Country Club. Still financially helping the club in any way he could, Hedley asked for the accounts to be sent to him when Tony Hutter booked Poynton Sports Centre for junior coaching.

Obviously a lot of planning had to be done before the Spinners Concert in June, but with Trevor Hill in control with his experience in radio and television, no stone was left unturned.

Donald Hackney now constructed a new steel sightscreen with most of the material given by his works, E.R. Burgess & Son, so with the ground being on a slope, it had to be fairly high, so when we eventually got it in place the usual complaints came from the locals who wanted the back painted the colour of grass, so we had paint specially mixed, which always looked an eyesore – when the sun was shining it looked black. Later we painted it white which made it look a sightscreen on a cricket ground, a sight you see all over the country.

On the cricket side we were not finding life as easy in the first division and had not made much progress in cup matches. One match at Irby was best forgotten, when they opened with a good leg spinner and were soon in trouble at 28 for 5. Another record was broken at Pott in the season when Alvanley scored 276 for none. I then opened for Pott on a wicket made for runs, got a short one outside the off stump off the second ball, hit it right off the meat of the bat only to see backward point stick his hand out and make a stunning catch.

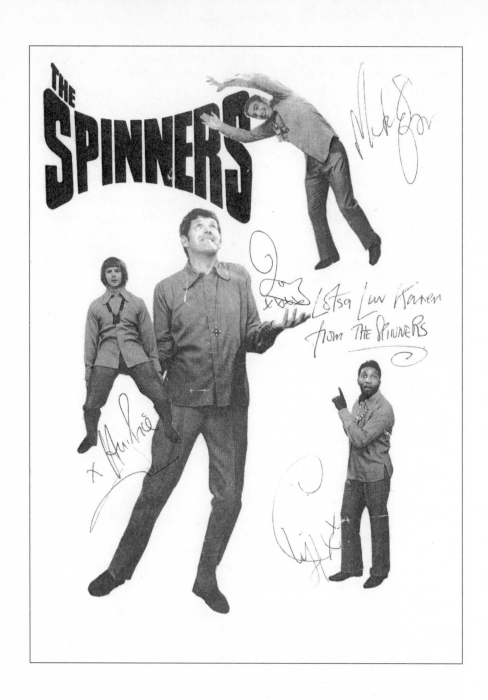

Shrigley was a popular venue for the Spinners for several years.

However, our batsmen played well and at one time it looked as though we were in with a chance, but we finished on 220 for 4.

Another incident in the season happened when Keith turned up at Cholmondeley in a new car, another of Jack's odes can describe it best.

Once again relations with the parish council were not enhanced when I was informed by Brian Stewart that they were having a large number of trees planted round the cricket ground. I informed him that there are places on a cricket ground where you don't need trees, particularly as they start maturing, plus the fact it would make the cutting of the grass outside the boundary more difficult. However he insisted the council had agreed to plant them, but we could move them afterwards, and before it could be discussed by our members the trees arrived and were planted.

Some of the councillors got upset when Bob Fairham wrote to the local paper criticising them, but he was quite right to do so – the matter should have been put to us and debated in committee properly as the terms of the lease stated clearly that 'the Cricket Club shall peaceably hold and enjoy the demised premises during the said term without any interruption by the landlords or any person rightfully claiming to be under or in trust for them'.

Also at the time the village hall was getting well supported and there were people coming along who felt maybe some of the spare land may someday be used for a bowling green, but trees were very important to some who I think would plant a tree in the middle of each road at the Pott Shrigley boundary.

However, none of these distractions could be blamed for the dismal performance of the teams and when the 1st XI were bowled out for 47 on the penultimate game of the season, admittedly on a bad wicket, at Hale Barns it was down to the second division. The tables at the end of the season made sorry reading with the first team second from bottom, the second team bottom, aggregate trophy bottom and the worrying part of this was that people were threatening to pack it in and play golf, so you did begin to wonder if all the work over the last few years had been in vain. Socially it had been a good year and ended with a very successful fashion show in November.

The first event of 1981 was the Shrigley Ball at the Salesian College which we had decided to help with even though we would be making no money out of the effort. The general feeling was the more the organisations helped each other, the better relations would be. Also as another stage along this process, the Club asked the chairman of the parish council, Mr Martin Collins, to propose the toast to the Cricket Club at the annual dinner on 12 march. In an eloquent speech as you would expect for a man in his profession, he began by saying he had a

The Steamrollering of Pott Shrigley 24th June 1980

It was quite a pleasant day at Cholmondeley
Outside the castle wall
A little fox nodded his head at Shoestring
Who promptly shouted "No Ball"
Then Arnie and the Cholmondley captain
A man named Morgan Wynne
Tossed up and Arnie won it
And decided to put them in.
Martin Perry bowled well and got 5 wickets
With speed, penetration and force.
At the Interval they said "Well done Martin me old fruit drop
You've bowled like an old ten bob Horse"
We were all eating our butties
And drinking cups of boiling hot tea
When suddenly a loud chugging engine
Desturbed the peaceful scerenity
Everyone rose to their feet in hurry
The pavilion was cleared in a flash
The chugging of the engine was silenced
At the sound of a bloody great crash.
Poor Arnie stood dumfounded
He muttered and He hummed and He ARh'd.
"I can't just go Rome and tell Sandra
A Steamrollers run into the car"
The game once again got into motion
Full incidents it got keen and tense
When Brookie called for a quick run from Mannering
Who remarked he should have more Bloody sense
When the match was over and we were all having drinks round the bar
T Burton produced his analisis 8overs 5Runs 5wickets 1car.

Another ode from Jack.

84

dream that he passed away, and came back a few years later and at the entrance to the ground there were huge gates like the 'Grace Gates' at Lord's, but these were the Patrick Gates, and when he got on to the ground there was a match on, but it was a strange game with trees planted all over the ground and the match being played between them.

Keith Arnold was again captain of the 1st XI. But with four of them out of the seven players who had featured in the league averages having departed, obviously all with still a lot of cricket in them, I myself had taken on captaining the second team, so another struggle looked on the cards, although we did get a few new players – John Walsh returning from Macclesfield, plus Geoff Dawson who had played for Northants minor county side and Peter Harper who had come to live in the area. Those who had called it a day were Don Hackney and Ken Barlow. Both had been members from a very tender age and worked hard for the Club. Ken stayed on the committee for many years running a successful junior side and even though we didn't see much of Don, he as always, answered the call if needed.

New officials were Fred Wrigley, chairman, and Martin Perry as secretary, and as we expected Martin would once again be putting the idea of a fruit machine over.

Also before the season started we had held a successful quiz and a 'Good as New' sale.

Although we started the season quite well in cup matches, again both teams struggled in the league and at the end of the season it looked as if only the captains had been playing, Keith finishing with 548 runs, third in the league averages. I took the league second division record with 577 runs and was top wicket-taker with 22 wickets. Unfortunately, Keith followed the trend which was happening in the club at that time, by retiring.

Another loss for the club was Hedley resigning as president. Unfortunately Hedley, like Brian Clear before him, had fallen for the charms of Dot, who was now his secretary, and a while after was to go and live with her on the Isle of Man, where sadly a few years later he passed away. Unfortunately all the three lads (two of whom played for us) seemed to finish up with broken marriages, and what had appeared to be one of the most successful wealthy families in the area deteriorated. Sadly one of the sons was found dead fairly recently. I suppose you may always find people who like to see the fall of families who appeared to have everything, but from a Cricket Club point of view or any of the other organisations, not only was his generosity appreciated, but also his manner; never a snob, nearly always turning up at club functions, and always one of the lads.

The new president elected for 1982 was Mrs Daphne Collins who lived at Pott Hall across the road from the ground. Her father, George Swindells, who owned cotton mills in Bollington, had also been president from 1937 to 1948.

Graham Hackney was appointed first team captain even though he made everyone aware there would be difficulties in playing in cup matches because of working commitments. I myself carried on as 2nd XI captain.

With all the comings and goings of members and the Club going through one of those difficult periods which most clubs have, the last thing we needed was more problems with the parish council. However, this looked on the cards when in January a letter was received from Martin Collins, the chairman of the parish council, stating there would be an increase in the rent from April. Even though it was only £30, there was always a lot of bitterness about the fact that on buying the ground statements had been made about helping with the upkeep, plus all the petty restrictions, so we wrote back offering £50 but this saga was to go on for a while yet. The usual jibe about outsiders again cropped up and club members, after trying to do their best for the Club, left disillusioned.

Also at the AGM, Andy Smith had resigned as junior secretary. Andy, one of the clubs personalities, who had started as a junior, was very popular but always seemed to lead a bit of a tangled existence both in his cricket and private life. So that year I attended the High Peak junior league meeting for the first time and quite frankly I was surprised at the lack of interest, even though the chairman, R. Harrop, and the secretary, Eddie Lindsey, worked hard for the league. Eddie, one of the best administrators in the area, was also secretary of the newly-formed 'Cheshire Competition', and his wife not enjoying good health was trying to get him to resign from the position. However, he was talked into taking it on for another year.

At Pott Shrigley we did have plans passed to extend the pavilion again but with other distractions and a huge increase in the rent threatened we never got around to carrying out this project.

A new idea was for the junior section to hold their own AGM which proved successful. Geoff Dawson chaired the meeting at which Dominic Lisle was appointed captain and Andy Hart vice-captain, and in 1999 both of them still hold office, Dominic as 1st XI captain and Andy as social secretary. Also at the meeting Tony Hutter offered to do some coaching. He was always keen on this side of the game and with an ability to organise the lads he was respected in this area.

One funny remark he made one evening when he told a boy to get padded up, the boy turned and asked how many pads should I wear, and Tony asked 'How many legs have you got?' The boy looked a bit gone out, and said two, so Tony responded by telling him he needed two pads. However, he did bring the Sheriff into action by trying to keep the lads together in the winter by doing a bit of training and having a kick about, but the terms of the lease were not being adhered to, so their names and addresses were put in a notebook.

Even though the Club seemed to have lost a lot of good players over the last couple of years, we seemed to have gained quite a few older experienced players, Peter Harper and John Leach from Cheadle Hulme, and Mike Smith from High Lane, who became the first player to take over 50 wickets in a league season, but even with a lot of good individual performances, Geoff Dawson scoring over 500 runs, the fielding and running between the wickets left a lot to be desired and neither team looked like winning any honours. Also the second team were finding it difficult to get sides out and I was finding out what a difficult job it can be in a Club.

One incident which nearly drove me to distraction was in a game against Styal who wanted 6 runs to win off the last ball. I was bowling the last over myself and the last ball was hit to deep mid-off which probably should only have been one run, however the fielder decided to underarm the ball back to me and with the ball about a couple of yards from me and the game virtually over, mid-off suddenly dashed across almost took the ball from my hands and hurled it at the wicket-keeper at the far end who was in the process of taking his gloves off. Fine leg managed to stop the ball going for 4 runs and hurled the ball back from the other end missing the keeper by a mile, so 5 runs were scored and the match ended in a tie.

Another couple who could drive you to distraction were Arthurs one and two, brothers-in-law who had been given the names by Alan Sherratt. Being fair to them they had come as Sunday players, but were always prepared to help out. Arthur one was a bit on the deaf side and could never catch on. If you were at third man when there was a left- and a right-hander batting you should move across and you usually finished up hoarse by the end of the match. Both of them used to practise, Arthur two (a big strong lad) was a fearsome prospect to face in the nets but when he opened the bowling in the second team, he would just stand there and lob the ball up. At the annual village match in July when both teams had got a number of ladies to play, we were all surprised when our lady president turned out for the opposition. She had obviously played at college and performed quite well. We always tried to get the game as close as possible and usually finished a tie so by dropping dollies, silly over throws etc., managed this result again. Martin Collins spoke many times later about this extraordinary result. I myself felt that a lot of the newer members were

87

showing a bit of initiative in helping the Club and Yvette and Peter Harper and Ann and John Leach put on a splendid hotpot supper in the village hall. Peter felt we could improve the club and that people in the village would help in doing this, but I did warn him that this was not usually the way things worked at Pott Shrigley, and you generally had to have a big fight to get what you wanted.

At the next committee meeting our minutes read, Peter Harper expressed concern that the village hall should have received half of the profits from the hotpot supper. Members felt the wording on the tickets left this in doubt.

Also at this meeting a letter was received from Martin Collins, suggesting the parish council would be seeking to raise the rent from £30 to £300 per annum. Naturally the older members, who only a few years earlier had been offered a chance to purchase the ground for £600, were not impressed and once again some people felt it would be better if the Club engaged a solicitor to look to our interests. Geoff Harding, who had a foot in both camps, stated he felt this was only a figure for discussion. At this meeting changes to the league rules were discussed and this led to a proposition that 20 points be awarded for a win – this was passed. I personally was against it but finished up at the league AGM putting our case for it. I was obviously not very convincing and the proposition was defeated, at the league AGM. At the league dinner that year, the speaker was Colin Milburn, and having seen him bat a couple of times it makes you wonder what an asset he would have been for English cricket had he been able to carry on.

The season came to a close with quite a bit of activity: A fancy dress six-a-side competition on President's day, a sponsored walk in October and a treasure hunt in November plus the usual annual bonfire. The club also received £17 plus 48 pints of Wilsons Beer for winning two rounds of the Cheshire Cup.

As usual relations were beginning to get strained with first the council over the rent increase and also the village hall who informed us no junior members would be allowed in. With regard to the rent three officials of the Club had again met the council and a figure of £140 was now being mentioned.

At the start of the 1983 season I felt confident that the club in general was getting in good shape again. Daphne Collins had informed us they would be leaving the area so a new president was elected, this being Peter Harper, the first time in the Clubs history that a playing member had taken the office. Mike Smith, a very enthusiastic cricketer and committee member was appointed chairman and a local school-teacher, Barry Carney, was a superb secretary for the next few years. Tony Hutter had taken on the position of social secretary and formed a small hard-working committee. I myself had volunteered to be junior secretary and to manage the under 17s, so one of my first jobs was to attend the High Peak junior league AGM. I turned up at Norbury Sunday School and the only two people there were the chairman and secretary and one other person. Even though there was not enough for a quorum, we went to a dingy little room upstairs, sat down and had a talk. Eddie Lindsey stated he was not prepared to carry on any longer. Unfortunately the league, that at one time had been very strong, had been decimated by the forming of the Cheshire County League, who had formed their own junior section. I myself could not stand by and see a league like this go out of existence, as apart from being the lifeblood of Clubs like ours it had provided at least four players who made county cricket, plus one Test player in Frank Hayes, so I told the multitude if I could talk my wife into doing the typing etc., I would do the job. So with Ron Harrop as chairman (his wife always leading the way) and Gordon Potter as president we started to pull things around.

The annual dinner of Pott Shrigley CC was again held at The Whisper, this being a big success with Oliver Heathcote bringing all his family along to celebrate his and Beulah's Ruby Wedding. At the same time, Tony had raffled a television on the night and made a profit of £150.

A sub-committee had been appointed to meet the parish council on 9 March to discuss the rent increase. Mike Smith had enquired why such a huge increase was necessary, and the council replied they had been accused of bad housekeeping. Mike stated that an increase could well put the Club in jeopardy but the not surprising reply was if the Pott Shrigley Club folded, someone else would probably play on the ground, so what with the negotiations regarding the rent and the refusing of older juniors who were playing more and more in the teams to even go into the hallway at the village hall, and incessant complaints about the sightscreen once again members, particularly new ones who thought they were coming to play at a nice village club, were getting disillusioned, and together with the new lease, it was again becoming a pain in the backside for both the old and new officials of the club.

Another strange minute in the March meeting stated that we had problems with moles on the outfield, but Derrick said he thought he could stamp this out.

At the April meeting with the new president (Peter Harper) in the chair, a letter was read out from the chairman of three months, tending his resignation. Mike, a go-ahead sort of person, had got himself very involved with the rent situation, and found it difficult to

89

understand the attitude towards the Cricket Club, who after all spent hundreds of pounds, plus people giving their time to give the village a ground they ought to be proud of. Peter Harper in his remarks highlighted the almost forgotten fact that we exist to play cricket happily, but supported the fact that some areas caused grief.

As I was already vice-chairman, it was decided that I carry on as chairman, so I proposed that I personally meet both the chairman of the parish council and the chairman of the village hall to try and get some common sense talking done. However, the situation did provoke Jack to produce another of his famous odes and bring a smile back to people's faces.

Just to add to my problem at the meeting we had plans passed for a proposed extension to the pavilion and we had appointed a sub-committee, chaired by Geoff Dawson, to look into the ways of financing this extension. Geoff made a statement that someone had seriously questioned the competence and integrity of this committee in a manner which could be deemed to be fraudulent and invited the person to retract the comments, there was no reaction and nobody, myself included ever found out the reason for these remarks.

As promised at the last meeting I had been to see the Reverend Wigram who had been appointed chairman of the village hall regarding younger members of the teams being allowed in after games, but he virtually finished with a sermon highlighting the sins of playing cricket at Pott on Sundays, and also stating that he had been informed that at one time, there had been a paragraph in the lease not allowing Sunday games, and he was looking into this matter, to see if it could be reinstated as he felt juniors should not be playing on Sundays. I did not see the point in any further discussion with him, so I thanked him for his time and left. Hence we made a complete break from the village hall and took our custom elsewhere.

After my discussions with the vicar, I then met Jack Challiner, the chairman of the parish council, thinking that he may be more sympathetic to junior cricket as Tony Hutter, the junior coach, was his son-in-law. However apart from the problems with the rent it was felt there was too much cricket going on. I informed him that as a Cricket Club we could not live in the past as it appeared the parish council wished, and over the years we hoped the junior section would increase. Also the policy of not allowing us to hire the ground was not only losing us revenue but also the village hall bar takings would be down as some of the firms used the bar after the games. However, before I left the £140 ground rent was again mentioned and as Jack was criticising the newcomers who wanted it for nothing I pointed out to him that it was the council that had asked for £300 and a review every

Mr Bennett as Pott Shrigley Adolf Hitler
Put the Gestapo on our scent
But forget the rate of inflation
When they wanted to raise the rent
One crept into a cricket club meeting
drinking whiskey and Bottles of Bor
When he got his required information
disapeared like a snake in the grass.
Mayor Stuart in his portrayal of Shylock
Just wondered wether he could
With the pound of flesh he demanded
Take a bucket to catch all the blood
Brian Buffey in satorial alire of Fagin
Said its not quite as bad as it sounds
And confronted the plump Pete Harper
With a figure of £200
These wolves dressed up in sheeps clothing
Are always wandering around
Like the clock in Bell Tower at Pott Shrigley
The Gestapo are faced all the way round
Mike Smith the cricket club chairman
Couldn't take all this Hassal and made it quite plain
Shook his head stroke his chin and said
I'll go back and play for High Lane.

Jack's light-hearted view of the rent dispute.

three years to increase with inflation, so it was obvious we could not agree with that amount and now they were asking half the amount, so I considered most of the problems were not of our making but forced upon us.

At the June meeting I reported to the committee the outcome of these two meetings and Peter Harper had an assessment by Brocklehursts, estate agents, of £60 per annum for the rent but felt that we should go to arbitration. I personally was concerned that, as they had asked £300 and we had offered £60, we may spend time and money and finish up paying the £140 or even more, and I proposed we cease further opposition, agree to pay the £140, but we would expect them to keep the grass tidy round the outer outfield which they had promised when they had purchased the ground. So it was agreed a further meeting with the parish council should be arranged.

As I had started the year thinking I would have a quiet time and devote most of my energies towards the juniors, I was hoping that taking over as chairman there would be no more problems and I could get 100 percent support, but this was not to be, as on the Sunday previous, the 1st XI had played in the Cheshire Cup at Birkenhead Park, and as Graham Hackney the captain had to work a lot of Sundays, and Mike Smith the appointed vice-captain had now left the club, the selection committee had appointed Mike Lisle (the 2nd XI captain) as captain for the day. Geoff Dawson made a remark stating that a more experienced player may have given better guidance and Steve Higginbotham had sent a letter remarking that only three first team players had turned up and they had taken the field with ten men. While having a certain amount of sympathy with people, I am sure most Clubs have experienced problems with cup matches, and if we have played against a scratched team we have usually considered it our good fortune.

I think Barry Carney in his first year as secretary began to wonder what he had let himself in for as his minute suggests, i.e. the discussion that followed was rather suspicious and charged with emotive irrelevances, so the chairman closed the meeting. The following morning I received a letter from Tony Hutter tendering his resignation as social secretary, so with the season only a few weeks old we had lost the chairman and 1st XI vice-captain, the social secretary and most of the social committee, as well as help with the juniors, so it did appear we were on a downward spiral of our own making.

At the July meeting which was virtually the end of the junior season I reported the under 17s had finished fourth in the league and Geoff Dawson, who had been with the new under 13s side stated he was impressed with the exuberance and commitment of these youngsters.

Both senior teams in the league failed to make any real impact which wasn't surprising after the comings and goings which did no one any favours.

The highlight or lowlight of the season was yet to come when we travelled to Woodford, who always had a lad called Gerrard supporting them. He was obviously a bit 'backward' but everyone got on with him. Woodford had a rota system for teas which held each player responsible for providing the tea and it was the turn of 'Maz', a lad who had given Gerrard a sum of money to get the food and prepare it. I think he bought one tin of meat and a sack of lettuce and all we got was one slice of meat submerged in water, and lettuce. We had always been on superb relations with Woodford so the whole episode finished as a joke.

Relations with our friends from Pott Shrigley did not improve any, and we were informed we had been withdrawn from the area of benefit at the village hall but we did keep the social side going with a trio competition and a barbecue at Slaters Bowling Club. This was always a popular event which only came to an end in 1997.

A hotpot supper was provided by Patti Dawson and Janet Smith for the juniors plus an excellent evening at The Whisper with David Davies who was at this time political correspondent for the BBC hosting a quiz. Although he was a very good question master, there was not a lot of humour to it. He then asked for extra expenses for travelling from Blackpool where he was covering the Labour conference. However, it turned out to be a financial success as we had managed to get the event sponsored by Mr David Ash who owned a local petfood suppliers. At the following meeting in social matters, Ken Barlow opened the discussion on the quiz by commenting on the smoothness of the operation, but stated some of the questions were obscure. Whether that was because he didn't know the answers, we weren't sure, but I am sure Offerton were the winners with the Gas Board taking the booby prize.

At the final meeting of the year my remarks as stated in the minutes read: 'We began in a blaze of glory but the flames dwindled to a spark, due to the number of resignations'. I pleaded for a more consistent pattern the following season. The problem of not having a social committee did not help us to maintain a good social calendar.

One of the last events of the season was President's Day. A match between club members was followed by an evening at Peter Harpers home. This was enjoyed by everyone. Geoff Dawson, who turned up in a green suit which George Melly would have been proud of, was the butt of most people's jokes, so Jack, christened him 'The Jolly Green Giant' after an advertisement being shown on the television for peas, and as usual one of his odes followed. Unfortunately this was his last contribution, as he had suffered heart problems for some time and passed away shortly afterwards. Jack's ashes were later scattered on the cricket field by the pavilion. The service was conducted by the vicar of Bollington. It was well attended and a moving ceremony. I think he would have enjoyed the three standing performances during the season which appeared in the league handbook. These were: Geoff Dawson 103 against Chelford, Ian

> It was a pleasent night at Baxendale
> The summertime at its brilliant best
> The sun was bright and dazeling
> Like the salorial attire of one of the guests
> It wasn't Joseph in his wonderful dreamcoat
> Or a wiseman studying the stars
> But the Jolly Green Giant from Bollington
> Dressed up like E Ts Brother from Mars

IN MEMORY OF:

JACK ARCHER

The plaque on the wall in the pavilion reads Jack Archer, Singer, Poet, Scorer.

This in no way covers the amount that Jack gave to Pott Shrigley Cricket Club. His first and greatest love was that of chorister at St. John's Church, Bollington which often led to him being made centre of attraction in many rousing sing songs in cricket clubs and hostelries wherever the Club travelled. His rendition of 'Sylvest' becoming the Club signature tune, to which we would all love to join in. His exuberant sense of humour showed in the many poems he wrote of the people and the happenings around the Club, which when read out by Jack with his descriptive lilt would bring tears of laughter to our eyes.

Another talent Jack had was that of christening many of the players with humorous nicknames that stuck with you for the rest of your career, such as The Chocolate Lion (Andy Smith), Captain Mainwaring (Allan Sherratt), The Run Machine (Martin Tute), Weetabix the Builder (George Gleave) and many more.

He helped wherever he could from cutting the grass and digging the drains to his official position of Club Scorer, where once again his humour would creep in. He could never understand why he had to keep repeating *Did Not Bat* so many times when he could write *Excess to Requirements* or *Redundant*.

Jack Archer was well respected and a good friend to all, who gave so much by just being himself, asking only for companionship in return.

94

Mrs. L. Archer.
7, Arundel Close,
Macclesfield,
Cheshire.
                                        15th November 1983.

Dear Lillian,
            On behalf of Pott Shrigley Cricket Club may I express
our deepest sympathies upon your bereavement.

Jack was a particularly popular member of the Club, forever cheerful
and unselfish in his thoughts and consequently creating a most
pleasant and enjoyable atmosphere.

His contribution as 'scorer' for our 1st eleven was invaluable as
he dutifully attended games both away and at home, producing neat
and accurate score sheets. After a game, Jack would always have the
right words to offer to our players whether in victory or defeat and
very often, his great wit and sense of humour would produce some of
the funniest collections of words, or odes, I have ever heard.

Jack's odes,one of which I am proud to be the subject of, are part of
the folk-lore of Pott Shrigley Cricket Club; they also demonstrate
quite clearly his commitment and involvement with the Club over the
years.

Jack was a reliable and conscientious member of the Club and the type
of man who stamped his genial and caring personality on everyone he

met; it is a great pity that Jack was one of a rare breed of men.

He will be sorely missed by everyone at Pott Shrigley Cricket Club.

                        Kind regards,
                        yours sincerely

                        B. KEARNEY
                        HON. SEC.

Sadly we lost Jack, who passed away only in his 50s. When our battle over the right of
way was going on, Jack would have had a ball.

95

Brooke 2nd XI best performance, 8 for 41 against Lindow, and Steve Higginbotham top 2nd XI wicket-taker with 41 wickets. It was also Bob Fairhall's first season as league chairman, so with this and I myself taking on the HPJCL, Pott Shrigley were doing their fair share in maintaining cricket in the area.

With all the traumas of 1983 and the rent situation still not settled, we moved our meetings to Henry and Leigh Slaters social club, so with still having to keep the 50 percent rule on the committee, none of them bothered to come down to meetings, so in essence we could vote in what we wanted, so now nearly half of the names on the committee were, from running a club point of view, just a waste of time.

However, three new names from Pott Shrigley did appear: Andy Hart, Penny Hart and dad (Michael Hart) who together with Jamie and mum (Margaret) were to serve the Club for many years. With the reluctance of people to stand for office, I myself finished up as chairman, junior secretary and 1st XI captain.

At the AGM of the High Peak junior league an under 13s section was formed which meant most of the games were held on Sunday mornings, so it was agreed we would play our home games on Sundays as there was nothing in the terms of the lease barring this, so if people wanted to object it was up to them. Ken Barlow took charge of the boys and we got together a very useful team.

At the AGM of the Cheshire league five clubs (Oakmere, Alsager, Old Alts, Davenham and Bredbury), received a formal warning from the ground inspection committee, so even though playing-wise we were struggling, we hadn't got this problem.

At the Club's January meeting, as usual, the rent was again on the agenda, with the council now refusing to cut the grass outside the playing area and now asking £120. There were two propositions, one to accept this, but I proposed that if we had to maintain all the area which is 4¾ acres, we should only pay £100, and after a long debate the £100 was voted on.

The annual dinner was again held at The Whisper, but after the successes of the previous years, this was poorly attended and obviously the treasury department were not pleased when a substantial financial loss occurred. However it was a good event with one of our friends from Prestbury making one of his amusing speeches.

At the meeting on 2 April 1984 the meeting was informed that the rent dispute had reached a settlement of £110 per annum. The chairman said emphatically that the matter was now closed and for information the following points were made.

The rent would be linked to inflation, and would be reviewed at three-yearly intervals. The Cricket Club would be responsible for all the ground. So ended another saga which again emphasised that as long as the parish council had control of the ground, any progress the Club wanted to make would be extremely difficult.

Probably the most encouraging section of the club in this season was the junior team. Andy Smith proved to be an excellent captain of the under 17s, who in a normal season would have won trophies, but as it turned out, Stockport Georgians were exceptionally strong and swept the board. A lot of the older juniors were happy to play Sundays and with two Sunday captains, Barry Carney and Ian Brooke always encouraging, and some of the dads turning out, this area of the Club seemed to flourish.

In the league the one highlight was Bob Fairhall scoring his maiden ton 103 against Bredbury 2nd XI. In July I received a letter from our president, resigning from all positions and membership of the Club. I was personally sorry to lose both Evette and himself because I think his intentions with the cricket club were genuine, but he had got himself embroiled in the rent dispute and seemed to feel it had become a personal issue with some parishioners.

Another first was a musical evening after the game with the BBC Philharmonic Orchestra who had quite a useful cricket team organised by percussionist Ray Lomax; a very keen outgoing personality who later gained fame by being drunk in charge of his drums and falling off his seat. This event was held at the home of Pattie and Geoff Dawson. Pattie was an accomplished pianist so with food and wine laid on it was expected we may make a bob or two, but instead of charging a price it was suggested that a dish was left on the way out for you to put your money in. To say the takings were a disappointment was an understatement so with the loss on this event and the annual dinner, the treasurer was not very happy.

However, one event that was a big success was the HPJL 'Sixes' competition, which was sponsored by Cogram Reclamation. With Norbury backing out at the last minute we managed to field two teams, the 'A' team doing extremely well before losing in the final to Stockport Georgians, however with Cogran kindly supplying the trophies and all the food we did make a nice profit, and the juniors did get 'runners up' medals in three competitions.

About this time Pott Hall Farm at the entrance to the ground had been sold to Chesney Orme who had started Cogram up a few years earlier. Ches always had an eye for business and making money. I remember him as a child when I had the sports and cycle shop, he was always buying spares to do old bikes up and sell them. From there he went to buying and selling cars then to plastic reclamation which went under the name Cogram. It was apparent that he had his eye on

Evette & Peter R. Harper
Fine Arts

Bakestonedale Farm, Pott Shrigley, Bollington, Nr. Macclesfield.
Telephone Bollington 72487

date 29th July 1984   ref.

Dear Derek,

    I do not think this letter will be a surprise to you but for some weeks it has been on my mind. I have not been enjoying my cricket at Pott Shrigley and have decided to resign all positions and memberships of the club as from to-day.

    I have given this a great deal of thought and my continuing to hold offices with Pott Cricket Club cannot be of any benefit to the club. As president I am an embarrassment with regards to any negociations with the Parish Council as I hold views far removed from that body. Similarly, if talks with the Village Hall Committee are to be restarted it may be easier if I am not in either organisation.

    May I thank the club for the last few seasons and the experiences it has given me. I am only sorry my performances both on and off the field were not better. However, the club has turned a number of corners and is improving. May this improvement continue and you go from strength to strength.

    Please wish everyone in the club — plenty of runs and wickets for the rest of the season.

Yours most sincerely,
Peter R. Harper.

The Chairman,
Pott Shrigley Cricket Club,

VAT number 158 317651
Registered number 1727917 England

Oil Paintings, Watercolours, Etchings, Drawings,
Framing, Restoration and Valuations.

The letter from President Peter Harper informing us he wished to resign from this office.

98

renovating the old outbuilding to the farm and knowing the Pott Shrigley attitude to any improvement or progress, how things would turn out? However, Ches was always prepared to help, particularly with the annual bonfire and for the first time we built it on his field which we crossed to get to the cricket ground, but we built the fire on the top of one of the culverts that crossed our ground and even though we knew it could flood in extreme conditions, we had always been lucky with the weather, but on this occasion the rain was torrential and when we went in the evening all the centre of the fire had been washed away and what remained looked like a wigwam which eventually we managed to set light to, and the end result was quite spectacular with water pouring in at one side and steam bellowing out at the other. So, in keeping with a lot of money-making efforts that year the weather kept the crowds away and another money-making effort finished with us losing out. One amusing incident: we put a notice up saying 'Anyone throwing fireworks will be ejected': Two boys were looking at this, and one said 'If you throw bangers, you are executed'.

I think most people who have played and helped at Pott Shrigley always seem to have some affection for the Club, and 1985 seemed to prove the point with a lot of old stalwarts in office: Ernie Hackney was appointed president, the Hackney's between them had put more than 100 years into helping the Club. Fred was again treasurer. We had given him a rest after giving nearly 20 years to this important position. As someone stated, we had better not show losses on events now, as Fred treats each hard-earned pound as an antique that would rise in value if only we could hang onto it long enough.

Another bonus was the return of the two Alans: Sherratt as captain, and Beckett returning as one of the most successful batsmen the Club has had. With John Walsh vice-captain and Bob Fairhall 2nd XI captain, most people were looking forward to the new season.

Also during the closed season Barry Carney had taken charge of improving the pavilion board and the walls with tongue and groove. Also with the help of old friend Bryon Holmes and 'Jack of all trades' John Jackson, we had installed showers, so the Sunday before the season started Ian organised another treasure hunt followed by a buffet in the refurbished pavilion, and as at the time we were getting a good price for the wastepaper and all the labour provided free, a superb job was carried out with hardly any drain on the Club funds.

With the Club always prepared to make progress with the junior section and the Cheshire League now running an under 15s competition for which we had entered, we were now one of the few Clubs in the area with teams at under 13s, under 15s and under 17s. All this took a lot of organising, with transport etc.

99

Also in 1985 our juniors joined Chelford, who had run a successful junior festival, to take part in the BBC *Blue Peter* programme, so Bob and myself went down to London with the boys and girls. We were a bit past *Blue Peter* but it was an enjoyable day out and I am sure a good way to get cricket over to the youngsters.

Chelford and Pott Shrigley juniors in the *Blue Peter* studios. (Photo courtesy of *Blue Peter*)

As a Club we always seemed to be coming up with good ideas, but never quite making the most of them, one being a golf competition off the top of The Nab, but to do this we had to get permission from the local farmer, Geoff Barber. This he gave, providing he was given a couple of bottles of scotch, so the event took place, and even though the weather was poor there was quite a good entry and a lot of them hoped we would make it an annual event, but Bob Fairhall did not give the farmer his whisky which annoyed him, so he would not agree to this. He has helped the Club in many ways since but was never happy with the promise of his whisky not being kept. Cogram also allowed us to hold a car boot sale in Nab Quarry on the same day which attracted quite a crowd so we did make a profit. Also to try and improve match ball sponsorship we agreed to give a £200 prize.

Once again with a wet spring and Ches using the way in more, the entrance to the ground was appalling, not helped by the fact that a couple of ponies had taken up residence in the field. This was always a source of aggravation with members as in the terms of the lease it

100

Guide to NAB HEAD (285m), Bollington
with Panoramic Views.

Nab Head beyond Bollington Town seen from White Nancy.

The Triangulation Pillar in centre of remains of barrow on summit.

Nab Head has been significant since prehistoric times for on the top are still the remains of a circular barrow, scheduled as an ancient monument, where some great local chief was buried, on a suitable eminence. Much later, in the days when Ordnance Survey was setting up its points for the triangulation and measurement of distances for its first large scale maps from the 1870s in Cheshire, such a point was set with its concrete pillar in the centre of the barrow thus giving their theodolites clear views of other pillars and landmarks. When tourism and enjoyment of the countryside became more popular in the 50s and 60s Nab Head was included as an accessible viewpoint on the Peak District 1: 10560 Tourist map; the Landranger sheet 118, 2nd Ed; Outdoor Leisure Map, the Peak District, White Peak Area, and OS Road Atlases. In 1978 the paths were closed by the landowners, but in the 90s the Ramblers' Association and the Bollington Town Council were able to find sufficient historical evidence and 44 witnesses who testified their enjoyment of the paths and the view for many years before 1978. Cheshire County Council's Rights of Way Committee agreed to make a modification order to restore the paths to the definitive map. After a public inquiry in February 1996 the Department of the Environment Inspector decided to approve the order and both paths are well signed and joyfully in use again.

This leaflet was printed after the long dispute and court case to reopen the footpath to Nab Head.

stated we were responsible for the track but we must only use it as a footpath, so it was agreed we make representation to the new owner.

At the April meeting I reported that Geoff Harding had approached me about the Club using the village hall for our after-match drinking. I personally was always in favour of all the various groups, in a small village like Pott Shrigley, working together, but emphasised that the Cricket Club had to be fully committed to bringing juniors on if the Club were to progress. It appeared they were leaving the matter of who to allow in with the bar steward, George Parker, who we always got on with, even if his adding up sometimes left a lot to be desired, so we decided to get the views of all members before making a decision.

At the same meeting John Walsh was appointed 'Ball Doctor' and did an excellent job renovating second-hand balls.

On the field we once again had probably the best batting side in the league, but our bowling lacked anybody with pace, and particularly at Pott Shrigley, which was always a bit of a feather bed, we found it difficult to bowl teams out, so with a large number of drawn games, it never looked like pushing for honours.

Once again the game at Prestbury provided a bit of a nail-biter. On a good wicket, and Prestbury usually a quick scoring ground, being on the small side, we bowled them out for 126, so with a strong batting side a win looked a formality. But at 36 for 8 it seemed extremely unlikely. However, a young Andy Hart started stroking the ball around (I had been relegated to number 11), so John Walsh joined Andy. How he got in before me, I will never know, but he stayed at the other end until only 4 was needed when Andy got out. I suppose this is what makes cricket such an enthralling game even if you've played for over 40 years as I had then. I still practised a lot and opened the batting on Sundays. The tension is still there, so after getting a single each I managed to push one out to mid-wicket and sensed John had made his mind up. There were two runs, but with me now well in my fifties, I screamed at him only one run, and as so often happens in these situations we got a leg bye off the next ball.

At the July meeting I had to announce that I could no longer look after the wicket without a small remuneration, as like a number of people at the time, 'Slaters' were cutting back and I had been made redundant. But I was still looking after the bowling green on a contract and had to look for work elsewhere. I only asked for £10 per week so it was decided to put a bit extra on the match fee to pay this. I never asked for any more so it stayed the same figure until I went on the pension some ten years later, and then with events that were taking place at the time I again gave my time free so the Club could progress and throw off the shackles that had held us back for years.

Also at this meeting applications from Mike Smith and Martin Tute were passed for a return to the Club, so with the junior section getting stronger the overall outlook and strength in number of playing members was improving all the time. Once again the matter of using the village hall was discussed. Bob Fairhall this time had been approached with the promise of making some provision for juniors and families. Ken Barlow enquired if the rules had been altered and the answer was 'No', so Ken in his usual forthright manner demanded to know how come these people were not allowed in before, but were now. But really it was back to the fact that there was a nucleus of people who were on the parish council and most other committees, and the general impression was they tended to use the rules to suit their own shortsighted policies.

Our secretary stated he had received a visitor from Hawarden who had returned the jug stolen from the Turners Arms earlier in the season.

I think most people felt it was a reasonable season even though no trophies had been won, but with two Saturday and two Sunday teams, plus under 17s, 15s and 13s it was beginning to be a much larger club with more work for officials. Alan Beckett had shown he had lost none of his ability, winning the league averages scoring 657 runs, an average of 54.75 with 119 not out against Sandbach.

The season ended with another successful President's Day. We had chosen Ernie to be president for services he had rendered to the Club, and Ann and Graham put on a superb buffet in their usual efficient manner. Also at this event a race night was included and the first appearance of Pott Shrigley's own pop group 'No Parking' which included A. Hart, G. Lisle and S. White. The evening went down well, although I think most people felt the lads should not give up the day job. It was a fine night for the bonfire which was one of the best ever with 600-plus turning up.

1986 began with a disastrous race night. We seemed pretty well organised with race cards etc., and secretary Barry Carney had ordered the films from a London firm, giving my address for delivering them. On the Friday before the event, at that time we had sold all the front of our business premises to an insurance broker, but we were still living at the back and upstairs so naturally all the staff knew us and any parcels left there were passed on right away. As night arrived nothing had been received, so we managed to contact the firm who informed us that the films had been taken to our address and no one knew of us. It transpired they had sent the films to a Mr B. Carney – of course no one did know him at that address, so the driver had taken them back to London. Rather than let our customers down I

103

Our own pop group, No Parking, since disbanded.

arranged to go on the early train to London Euston where they promised to meet me with the films. To make matters worse we had a heavy snowfall which tends to frighten a lot of people from venturing to Pott including the person who was going to run the projector. However, a volunteer came forward who seemed to think it was no problem, but after the films of the first two races finished in a big pile in the middle of the floor we began to have doubts. Someone suggested a chap who used to work the projector at the local cinema might be able to help. After making enquiries as to where he lived we eventually tracked him down playing snooker at Bollington Conservative Club and persuaded him to help. He had problems to start with and another film finished the same way, however he did manage to get the last three of four races shown. I suppose people got more laughs out of the evening than if it had run smoothly.

February minutes stated the race night was a disaster.

Officials for 1986 showed few changes and with Bob Fairhall resigning from the committee a newcomer to the Club, Stuart Burrows, was appointed 2nd XI vice-captain.

104

Bob's influence on the Club had been tremendous, always a competitor on the field he had captained both 1st and 2nd teams, been chairman of the Club, league rep and village hall rep. He had been league chairman for the last two years which he was very committed to, so a lot of his time was spent on league business, which he dealt with for the next ten years. He was always prepared to attend other Club functions, particularly their annual dinners where he was always in demand and having seen him at the last Cheshire League dinner he looks as though he still enjoys these dinners at Notts. Forest FC where he was made a director.

We once again appeared to have a good strength playing membership, even though we were beginning to realise the problems associated with juniors who would probably strengthen the sides but were away at colleges and universities until midway through the season. There was not much joy in the cup games, losing to Hale in the Village Cup and Alderley in the Cheshire Cup.

Once again the season began with the way across to the ground in a terrible state and at the May meeting Graham Hackney complained strongly about this matter but with the barn in process of renovation and all sorts of plant being moved about, if you mentioned it to the parish council, who had as usual opposed some aspects of the development, the answer was that some of the work was being carried out without planning permission and would have to be demolished.

Greg Lisle had taken on the office of social secretary and we decided to hold a 'Superstars' competition followed by a barbecue in place of the 'Trios'. We again played the village hall match. This had been a tradition over the years and we liked to keep it going in an effort to help relations with the community but with an ageing population and interest in the village hall at a low level, it began to look if this was a function we may have to call a halt to.

The 'Superstars' competition turned out to be a big success with an assault course, crazy golf, pistol shooting, wellie throwing, bowls, etc., and our industrious junior captain 'Woollie' White turned up in his oilskins to run a fishing competition in a cast-iron trough borrowed from his dad's farm. After the event Stuart and the oilskins disappeared but the trough remained waiting to be taken back for the next 12 years, and with the grass growing through it was taken by the scrapman.

The barbecue after was run and all the food provided by Ches Orme, who was always easy to get along with and helped the Club so it was not worth complaining too much about the state of the way in at this time and the £100-plus was very welcome.

There turned out to be a lot of good individual performances during the season with five batsmen and four bowlers all appearing in the league handbook, Martin Tute excelling behind the stumps with 18 victims and scoring 625. Another feat worth mentioning was Nobby Houston being third in the league catching table. Nobby was not the most athletic of fielder's and his eyesight not the best, but he was a good Club man to have on your side. Always a bit of a grumpy character (I don't think Kay, his wife, will sue me for writing this) and if he had been shedded and didn't feel he was out you were advised not to enter the shower area until he had finished taking his shower. He will always be remembered for the occasion Nigel Reeves borrowed his bat. Nigel, a completely different character, always on the quiet side, did have a panache for coming up with corny jokes, a bit of a failed Frank Carson (it's the way I tell 'em), but even though he was not a big chap he was probably one of the hardest hitters of the ball the Club has had. He was batting well one Saturday using Nobby's bat but going for another big hit the ball finished up about two yards away and a lump of Nobby's bat half way down the track. It was a lovely day so we were all sat on the hill at the far side of the ground. Nobby jumped up and the air went blue for a few seconds before he set off across the ground like he had been shot from a cannon, and we were all pleased not to be in Nigel's boots at that time. However, Nigel is still playing, last year spending most of his time on the 2nd XI, where he was one of the top run-scorers in the league, and he still comes along with a new joke. Nobby has taken up the rich man's game of golf and Kay says she gets him wound-up by calling his clubs sticks.

Not only did the 1st XI have a good year, but also the 2nd XI with Paul Wrigley setting a new 2nd XI league record of 647, so the record I had held for six years went to another Pott player. Stuart Burrows also had an excellent season behind the stumps with 24 victims. Probably from my own point of view the highlight of the season was the under 17s winning the Kirk Cup, beating Norbury on August bank holiday Monday, with typical bank holiday weather. By the time the game finished you could hardly stand up and the rain was coming at you sideways.

With an improvement in virtually every department of the Club as chairman I chaired the player's meeting in October fully expecting a happy meeting with nearly all the captains and vice-captains being prepared to carry on but came away a couple of hours later totally disillusioned with people niggling and even some nastiness creeping in. I abandoned the meeting and rearranged it for the week after in the hope that some sense may return. The meeting took place the week after and was a quieter affair, but it was apparent some damage had been done and several members were departing, one being Alan Beckett who joined rivals Lindow and formed the best opening partnership in the league with Steve Beckett (no relation) and Lindow went on to be one of the best teams in the league for a couple of years.

Another minor irritation at this time was the growing number of people ringing up saying they could not contact the secretary, Barry Carney. Barry, who had been a good secretary for the last few years had become a bit of a 'Scarlet Pimpernel', so in desperation I contacted Peter Chadwick who had introduced Barry to the Club as he taught at the same school. He informed me that he had got a lady friend and as far as he knew spent all his time at 30 Queen Street, Bollington which was virtually at the end of our back garden. Peter said Barry had only gone to put a shelf up in the kitchen, but he thought it was a bit more serious than that which proved correct, as they later got married and had a family.

We went into 1987 on a very downward spiral, with meetings poorly attended, on occasions not even getting a quorum and this was always made worse with the rule of 50 percent parishioners, you could usually rely on Geoff Harding turning up but he had taken a liking to the whisky bottle and you couldn't always expect him to attend. For the first time since the 1970s no one had bothered to book the indoor nets which usually tends to bring members together. The annual dinner, again held at Macclesfield Golf Club was a reasonable success.

Early in the year one of the most extraordinary incidents happened. Mr Bennett, 'The Sheriff' passed away: he had been clerk to the council for over 50 years and obviously there had been many times people had not seen eye to eye with him, but you had to admit he and his family had given most of their lives to keeping village life going even thought it was their way, always the attitude that nothing should progress and naturally as a thriving Cricket Club if we had gone down that road it would have led to oblivion.

Naturally with his long association with all forms of public life the church was full and as the door was opened and the coffin was carried through there was a huge crack of thunder which put the church in darkness and interrupted the organ for a few minutes. It was an eerie experience which ensured The Sheriff would always be remembered.

The first competitive game was in the Cheshire Cup against Cheadle, and even though Nigel Reeves produced one of his vintage knocks, we lost. We then won in the Village Cup at Ashton Hayes, a game I remember. By then I didn't play regularly in cup matches but played there and got 3 wickets and 3 catches, but Dominic Bull, a superb catcher, managed to drop 3.

Once again the way onto the ground and parking in the village reared their ugly heads. Chesney Orme had sold Pott Hall Farm to a Mr Ian Luckhurst. Shortly after he came to live there I was on the ground with the juniors when Ian, who I had not met before, came across in a bit of a tantrum as he could not get his car out of the garage. I informed him I would ask around but told him the area in front of the church had always been used for parking and the Cricket Club had neither the authority or the inclination to ask people not to park there. Being fair to Ian a few days later he invited me in and said he had discussed the parking problem with Ches Orme and felt there may be a possibility of making the top of the field a place to park and perhaps find a way round their field. Naturally we were interested but could do nothing without parish council permission so a letter was sent to the council, but we received a reply stating they felt there was no problem.

Most of the Cheshire League business that year seemed to be concerning the Cheshire County League which apparently had been formed by a nucleus of clubs who they felt fit to enter, and the county league were banned from voting in the league cricket conference. Personally I did not think it much different how the Cheshire league was formed but in those days there was talk of putting Cheshire cricket under one umbrella.

At the July meeting of the league, Prestbury made a name for themselves in the disciplinary records by getting fined for drunkenness on the field. Apparently the game had been rained off for a while and the batsmen had been in the bar. When the game was about to resume, one batsman came out, took guard and fell over – typical Prestbury but always good opponents.

Cheshire Association of Cricket Clubs were running a coaching course at Poynton, so Barry Carney and myself took the course and with Ken Ingram in charge found it hard work but well worth the effort. Once again the playing highlight of the season was provided by the juniors who again won the Kirk Cup and finished third in the league, Mark Dean scoring a record 670 runs. 'Deano' has got runs at all A-levels and still regularly tops the 1st XI batting averages in the present team.

Away from the cricket it looked as though the Gods had it in for Pott Shrigley that year, when during a violent thunderstorm in August both the schoolyard and the main road collapsed into a culvert. It so happened that a few days after this we had hired the ground to National Chemicals who were bringing players from various parts of the country to play at Pott and with all the wet weather and work still going on at the barn it was difficult to get to the entrance and then going across to the ground it was like a quagmire. However, I met

COACHING THE COACHES

By
Simon Carter

● AN AMBITIOUS plan to improve the standard of local cricket has been masterminded by Poynton Cricket Club.

★

They have brought in ex-Cheshire player and fully qualified coach Ken Ingham to give advice on how to coach. This will give some of the village's players a chance to give something back to the game they have enjoyed themselves and hopefully help to eiradicate the technical errors of our youngsters.

★

The coaching scheme is held on a Sunday morning at the Leisure Centre and dads looking for a few tips are welcome.

● Back to basics: Ken shows them how to hold the bat properly.

The *Macclesfield Express* supporting Cheshire in their plan to improve cricket in the area.

David Layfield, the managing director, and Sheila, his secretary, who had got all the food to carry across and as other players started to arrive. I thought with most of the road missing and the way in like the Klondyke, this is the last time these people will come to Pott. The day itself was horrendous, the ground was virtually under water to start with and large black clouds were coming over the Nab at regular intervals with more deluges, but with a lot of mopping up and the rain easing in the afternoon, they managed eight overs a side before retiring to The Cheshire Hunt. David invited Kit and myself to the evening meal and videos of the day were shown, mainly consisting of me mopping up plus Beauty, our dog, chasing birds. I was certainly wrong about not seeing them again, as they have been several times since, and on most occasions picked a pleasant day. They always remember their first introduction to Pott Shrigley.

The end of a fairly gloomy year finished with both the secretary and his assistant resigning. The Club was also informed that former president and benefactor, Hedley Patrick, had passed away in the Isle of Man. It was agreed to send a donation to the church he had attended there.

With the previous year finishing on a low note and several officials departing we had to get some reliable officials to get the Club back on even keel, so Mike Hart was appointed chairman and I was made secretary. Other people voted into office who were to have a major influence on the Club were Dominic Lisle as 1st XI captain, and his brother Greg as social secretary. Things had gone quite well in the closed season with a race night, a quiz, and the Christmas draw, as usual held at the Turners Arms where Bernard and Brenda Dingle were now 'mine hosts', always making us welcome and helping the Club in many ways. Unfortunately, this Christmas one of the juniors had kept coming back for more tickets to sell, but did not bring many counterfoils back which made us a bit suspicious, even more so when someone found some of the sold counterfoils in the canal. As far as I recall he became the first member we had to ban from the Club.

In the winter months we did get a trophy, winning the second division of the Macclesfield indoor league.

The dinner in April was again held at Macclesfield Golf Club and a success, but marred a little bit when one of our guests was asked to leave or put a jacket and tie on. He was not one of the younger members and as he did not live very far away, could have soon got himself properly attired, but appeared to take offence, so his party of four departed. It was proposed at the next meeting that we have 'lounge suits' printed on the tickets.

By a strange coincidence the idea of purchasing a new batch of club ties was on the agenda, plus a letter from a local resident who had met a gentleman working in France who was at one time a junior with the club, asking if we had any club ties – if so he would like to purchase some.

Another nice innovation at the start of the season was the production of a club newsletter which Greg Lisle and Andy Hart have produced over the years, sometimes criticising people but often amusing and these have become an integral part of the Club.

With work still being carried out on the barn at the entrance to the ground I issued my first warning of problems which could arise when I stated that as our right of way had been altered, it had left our water-pipes and electricity cables under new gardens, about seven feet under-ground.

By the July meeting both teams were well placed in the league. I myself was doing a bit of umpiring for the second team and still playing on Sundays, and in many cases called up to play on a Saturday.

We also did get a letter from Bob Fairhall as chairman of the league for criticising the umpires in the local paper which was quite correct even though when he opened the bowling for us I have heard him come out with a few remarks.

Also at this meeting a tour of Devon was proposed for the 1989 season. The indoor nets at Macclesfield Leisure Centre had been booked for January. Playing results during the second half of the season took a bit of a downward slide and both teams finished again round the halfway position in the league, but a newcomer, Richard Hollinshead, proved to be an assett to the Club by topping the batting, bowling and fielding. He was top scorer with 103 at Cholmondeley.

We had at last an improvement to the track across to the ground when Ches Orme repaired the culvert at the gateway to the field, but despite more complaints to the parish council no progress was made on diverting the services round the enlarged garden.

Yet another sad end to the season when our popular president passed away in November and Ernie's ashes were scattered with Jack's by the pavilion, but at May's request only the immediate family were there on this occasion.

The bonfire was again a success with over £500 profit being shared by the Cricket Club and village hall. A joint venture with a race night also took place, but as usual the village hall were behind getting sponsors in, so programmes were not ready to sell in advance.

There was at this time a proposal sent to myself as secretary of the HPJCL that an under 15s section be formed for the 1989 season. We agreed to back this proposition and with A. Hart, D. Lisle and D. Bull offering to take charge of the under 17s I stated I would take charge of the under 15s.

At the last meeting of the year I stated that I had written to the parish council stating we must shortly replace the fence round the ground and hoped they might give some financial assistance. As usual I

Ernest Hackney, our President from 1985–88.

did not think any help would be forthcoming but felt it was worth a try.

1989, saw Jim Lisle made president. Jim's three sons were all playing for the Club and all held official positions at some time: Dominic 1st XI captain, Michael 2nd XI captain and Greg social secretary and assistant treasurer. For the last few years he had been excellent treasurer, following in Fred's footsteps – life has not altered much in that department.

At the first committee meeting of the season the predictable reply came from the parish council, stating that they would not help with the erection of a new fence, so with the sum of £800 required for materials, we would have to erect it ourselves. A sub-committee consisting of John Walsh, Stuart Burrows and Rod Wakelin were appointed in an effort to raise the money to finance this urgent matter.

Good attendances were reported at the indoor nets plus a team in the indoor league and Steven Higginbotham reported progress on the tour to Devon with an approximate cost of £85. It was also announced that Meller Braggins, estate agents had agreed to sponsor the Cheshire League.

Our own match ball sponsorship had been placed in the hands of assistant treasurer Rod Wakelin, with spectacular results and the best returns ever. Rod was a very useful batsman but a bit on the slow side for the limited overs cricket that now rules most competitions.

During the years Pott Shrigley had always had a good reputation for providing excellent teas, with Margaret Hart organising the Saturday teas, so when she was recovering from a stay in hospital the Club had sent her some flowers and this was appreciated in a letter which was received by the Club.

The annual dinner was again held at Macclesfield Golf Club when the toast to the Club was proposed by Reg Carlisle, a legendary figure in local cricket for several years. He was always renowned for his big hitting and was also quite a useful quick bowler, first at Kerridge where he lived and later at Bollington.

Again the Club in general had an excellent start to the season with all the teams doing reasonably well and progress made in both cups. I had managed to get together enough under 15s and made Sam Jackson the captain. Sam was always a bit wild but was a great competitor who would be prepared to take anybody on, probably taking after John – his dad.

A new event on the social calendar was a night out at Chester Races which everyone enjoyed but we didn't finish up with any rich benefactors. However, we did manage to lose the president who arrived home early the following morning after getting the train to Crewe, then on to Stockport, and Macclesfield, then a taxi to home. The village match was again a big success with Sarah and Penny Hart amongst the ladies who starred.

We were doing well on the field and also socially, as we now had a good working committee. At the July meeting John Walsh stated the fence committee had now £700 in the bank so it was obvious work could start on this urgent job in the closed season.

The under 17s had another successful season finishing third in the league and being beaten in the finals of the Kirk Cup, and the Cheshire league Colts Cup, so once again we were proving that even though we were regarded as a small village Club we kept producing good junior players, even though we didn't always hang on to them.

Another job I got involved with, and later was to regret, was when Ian Luckhurst, who owned Pott Hall Farm, asked if I could help him with the problem he had been left with after the road had collapsed the previous year. The footpath had originally gone right to the front of the farm, but after repairing the road they had raised the footpath and only made it a normal width so it was left with just a path to the front door with two quite big craters on either side. So now, apart from our water pipe going under someone's garden, the water meter was no longer on the footpath as it was originally. There was quite a lot of work entailed, so I asked Oliver Heathcote, who was now no longer farming, to help me with this job. Oliver always had a dry sense of humour. Even though he had worked up in the hills he was always very observant and ready to spin a yarn. We had a ten-ton load of soil dumped and started to fill the crater in. I realised we would need a wheelbarrow and knew there was one just through the gate in the churchyard, so I casually said 'I don't think anyone will mind if we use the barrow': Oliver replied, 'well no bugger in there will say very much'.

A little later while we were working, a Telecom van drew up and parked in the square close to us. When it did not move for a while, Oliver said 'I wonder what is wrong with that', I looked at him wondering what he was going on about, and he said, 'if they hang around for long they start breeding', and sure enough we looked up a minute or so later and there were three of them.

Apart from Oliver the rest of the family have all followed their father in the butchery business with several shops in the area and a slaughterhouse at the top of Shrigley Road, and more or less attached to this is a bungalow where Fred Allaby and his wife, Margaret (née Heathcote) live. I was chatting to Fred a while ago about things in general like you do as you get older, bemoaning how things are now what they used to be and he got on to the subject of television programmes which, I am sure a lot of people will agree, are poor. He

113

said he was watching one night when there was a hospital operation going on, pathologists inspecting bodies and all sorts of gruesome murders, so he said he switched the telly off and said 'we would have more fun carrying our chairs in the slaughter house'. However, Oliver and myself got the job finished, grassed over and an improvement to the centre of the village.

There were a lot of good things reported at the August meeting and one felt we were getting the Club back on the right footing. John Walsh reported the fence fund had now reached £1,000. Andy Hart's 'Crazy Ape' day had made over £100. A party of 16 players had now paid for the tour to Devon and also all Club records had gone when Warren Barlow and Paul Wrigley scored 294 for the opening partnership in a Sunday game at Hale Barns.

However, we did get a rocket from the league for playing Mathew Palmer in the Colts Cup final but we felt justified in doing this as even though Mathew had informed us he was going to play at Macclesfield, he had been playing for his school and not yet had a game with the Macclesfield Club. He had been with us since he was 11 years old, so until he played at Macclesfield we were still claiming him.

Both teams had performed well during the season but with still probably the youngest team in the league, we lacked a couple of older experienced players, but after being in with a chance of honours for most of the season, we had to settle for fifth in the league for the first team and fourth for the seconds. With two teams turning out on most Sundays and three junior sides it was becoming a big Club to organise.

Richard Hollinshead was again star of the 1st XI, topping the bowling and batting. In the 2nd XI Ian Brooke was the leagues top wicket-taker with 52 wickets. Two more from the juniors made a name: Mark Dean finished third in the league batting averages and Warren Barlow achieved the league's top score of 128.

Another character who also scored a few fifties for the 2nd XI was Jim Isherwood who had played his cricket in the Bolton league, a bit past his best, but he could hit the ball very hard particularly on the leg side and for a couple of seasons travelled regularly from Bolton to play for us.

With another successful President's Day at the end of the season we then had to turn our attention to erecting the fence with John Walsh reporting that the fence appeal fund had now been closed at the figure of £1,123, a marvellous effort by any standards. It was decided any surplus would go to pavilion improvements. Now it was time to fix a date to start work. As usual for any project of this size the key is pegging John Jackson down to a date. John is a well-known local farmer whose family had farmed in Pott Shrigley for many years. His

114

dad Doug had provided the Club with milk for years. John had also qualified as an electrician with the Electricity Board but like most farmers worked a seven-day week and hard work seemed to be a big part of his life. Not only is John a terrific worker, but with the equipment and tools he can produce, I always say he could start World War Three, so a start was made on Sunday 8 October and John came down on his JCB to dig in the corner posts which would take him almost all day, but he had brought a big iron post 'knocker-in' so the rest of us cold set to work on the other posts. I think by lunchtime we had managed about nine posts. The following week most people turned up again, John had now finished the corners so he picked up the 'knocker-in' and proceeded to bang the other hundred posts in, virtually single-handed and then helped us to put the wire on. If he had not been around I am sure it would have taken us all winter. What had been quite a good year all round ended with another successful bonfire, race night and Christmas draw.

So we moved into the nineties with a good crop of young players. A lot of Clubs find this can be frustrating at times with the more ambitious ones trying to improve by joining bigger Clubs and while one cannot blame them for this, it always seems a pity when things don't work as expected and they stop playing, or in some cases prefer tennis or lacrosse. I would think that all the time I was associated with juniors, Doug Martin was one of the most talented natural batsmen, but he preferred lacrosse and went on to play for England.

The parish council came to life in April asking for the increase in rent. They had just realised we had agreed to a review and an increase linked to inflation every three years but they had forgotten to expedite this. We did not agree with their assessment, so asked our auditor and he worked it out at £142 so this amount was sent and accepted.

We had again sent out letters for match ball sponsorship and had a pleasant surprise when Effluent Services sent a cheque for £150 to sponsor the junior section. One thing that came to an end this year was the waste paper collection. I had allowed the Club to use my garage for storage which was on the Pool Bank car park in Bollington, which was handy for people to come to, and with a skip coming every month we had made quite a bit of money over the years, but in June I found the entire area around the garage swamped with paper as the firm who collected it had gone bankrupt. I did eventually get rid of it but received no money, so after something like 20 years of collecting we had to abandon the scheme.

With the fence completed and a bit of money to spare, attention was now turned to the pavilion. Even though we had done a lot of improvements inside, the roof which was asbestos and had received a

115

few direct hits, so it was leaking, plus when we had built the extension the Peak Park had insisted on a flat roof, so we now had to look to ways of getting this problem sorted and funded.

On the playing side it was turning out to be a pretty ordinary season, again we were bringing juniors into the teams and even though there was ability and consistency there, to organise themselves left a lot to be desired and this was getting proved with the downward slide of the junior section which had been generally left in the hands of the 18–20 year-old members.

This sloppy organisation caused conflict when they asked me to enter a team in the under 21s Cheshire cup. It is always a problem entering too many competitions as they have always wanted the first round to be played by the end of May. However the lad organised the game to be played in the first week of June. This Sunday turned out to be one of those cricket days I'm sure most people in the game dread, all the food bought and about 1.30 p.m. it starts to rain and you are 99 per cent certain it is not going to stop. This is always worse for junior games as they play in anything without any consideration for the ground. By the time I arrived the ground was virtually waterlogged and I was far from pleased to see the Sale players plus the manager playing football on the ground. Naturally I blew my top and told them to clear off back to where they came from. The manager was talking about trying to get a few overs in, and at one point about claiming the game. However I would have none of this, told him I was not happy with their attitude and would phone the CACC to complain and let them sort the matter out. In the evening I phoned the competition secretary and started to make our complaint in a firm manner but he stopped me in my tracks and said Sale had complained about Pott because they had arranged the game for the week before with our contact and had arrived at Pott to find no one there and he had sent a letter to our contact who had not let me know. With the same people in charge of the under 17s, it wasn't surprising they had a poor season.

All these matters were discussed at the July meeting and it was felt improvements would be needed in the junior administration for next year. I had again been with the under 15s who had won 50 per cent of their games and Nigel Reeves was with the under 13s.

The village match and family fun day were held on a Sunday late in the season and was enjoyed by quite a large gathering.

The season again ended with President's Day which was run in conjunction with a flower festival in the church and an exhibition entitled 'The History of Pott Shrigley'. In the village hall some of the photographs on view caused a bit of a laugh with Graham Hackneys 'Englebert Humperdinck' hairstyle and John Walsh wearing one of his

116

'cardigans' which Andy Hart claimed was the same one as in one of the photos some 30 years past.

The only two players in the Club to appear in the league averages were Richard Hollinshead, both batting and bowling which was getting him selected for the league XI, and Tony Hutter who topped both batting and bowling in the 2nd XI.

Graham Hackney was again 1st XI captain in 1991 but Rod Wakelin who had done an excellent job as assistant treasurer particularly with the match ball sponsorship, resigned to go and play at Chelford, as he was unable to get regular Saturday cricket at Pott. In exchange we had got back David Rushton and his son Paul to play with the juniors as David had done some 30 years previously. This also brought us two more supporters in Christine and Michelle, and also some more help with the teas.

I personally was getting concerned about the barn at the entrance. This was now getting to the stage of completion, and there seemed to be no apparent endeavour by the parish council to consider the problems which might occur regarding the right of way and our services, and when prior to the season we had a burst water pipe it meant digging up Mr Luckhurst's new lawn to repair it. As it happened it was lucky that it burst in that place as it was only about three feet down but another few feet towards the cricket ground it was about eight feet below the surface of the new garden. I appeared to be the only one concerned with this particular when Ian Hughes, who was the Water Board inspector informed me he was having a lot of problems with this type of pipe in Pott Shrigley because of the high water pressure.

With expected expense for a new roof we decided to hold a car boot sale in the schoolyard again on spring Bank Holiday Monday with Denise running a stall for the Club and making a profit on top of the car booter's fees. Denise's efforts for the Club have been immense, running stalls, providing teas, and scoring, and she is usually one of the bankers on race nights.

The cricket in the nineties seemed to follow more or less the same pattern with a mixture of good results and poor performances. We seemed to be getting a reputation for being a good family Club with no desire to win matches.

Another blow hit the Club in May when the president, Jim Lisle, passed away only a few months after his wife, so it was obviously a sad time for the Club, as their three boys, Mike, Greg, and Dominic had all come through the junior ranks at Pott. Jim had always supported the juniors, taking them to most grounds in the area where he always managed to find a local pub for a couple of whiskies during the interval. They also had a daughter, Caroline, who attended functions with the family. At the July meeting it was decided in the circumstances there would not be a President's Night at the end of the season but a game between two Club sides with Andy Hart and his 'End of the pier' concert party putting on a performance.

Some discussion also took place regarding the purchase of 'all weather' practice wickets, but it was felt the new roof should take priority, and also that we would have to get the three main officials and captains to a meeting to think about a new president for 1992.

At the October meeting which was also the players meeting Andy Hart stated that the end of the season evening had been a big success and thanked Rick Mattock, a Yorkshire import who had come to work as a chef at Shrigley Hall for the excellent food he had prepared.

Rick soon got the name of 'Boycsie', how I don't know. Just as Geoff guards his wicket jealously, Rick tends to start like a world-beater and then throws his wicket away. I don't think his dad was overpleased with him, when one day coming all the way from Yorkshire to Woore in Shropshire to watch him bat, Rick opened the batting and dad got his video camera out but the second ball was about a yard and a half outside the off stump and the umpire was all ready, getting his arms outstretched and Rick decided to have a go at it. He got a toe end, which just dollied to gulley, so the camera was quickly returned to its case.

I also reported on a meeting Mike Hart and myself had with Ian Lyckhurst of Pott Hall Farm once again regarding parking and the possibility of trying to get a new way into the ground. Again we had to inform him that where we were prepared to help but if possible should be left in the hands of the parish council as owners. Mike Hart had also been approached by Chesney Orme to see if I would have a key if they locked the gate. I had been approached myself but as adamant I was not going to get involved as I very much suspected the properties were going up for sale and they probably felt the way across to the cricket ground over the land may take some of the value off. My suspicions were confirmed shortly after. I met councillor Brian Stewart who informed me that Pott Hall Farm was being sold by Bridgefords and they had supplied incorrect details regarding the right of way to the cricket ground. The Club did make representation to the estate agents and Mr C. Bourne, chairman of the parish council wrote to them stating clearly that they had purchased the cricket ground in 1970 together with the right of way. Shortly after the barn was on offer at Gascoigne Halmans estate agents.

As a Club we were prepared to back Mr Bourne and the parish council in any way possible, realising the problem that could arise should we finish up with neighbours who were not cricket lovers, even though the estate agents' jargon stated 'an *en suite*' cricket ground. At the same time we had for many years complained about the way across to the ground and even though the terms of our lease stated we should keep the track in good order, any application to do this and make some sensible parking arrangements were always treated with disdain, and with more and more traffic through the village, this policy caused one or two minor accidents, but luckily nothing serious.

1992 saw the beginning of the reign of Mrs Lily Tute as president, the third lady to hold this office. At the time she was also Mayor of Bollington. All the family at one time had been stalwarts of Bollington Cricket Club. Lewis, her husband, died in 1982 and Lily had taken over his mantle on the council, never afraid to make her views heard, a procedure she followed in her years with the Cricket Club.

I was still the secretary of the HPJCL and had managed to get Tony Hutter to take on the job of treasurer. I had now been associated with the league for ten years and had never met the treasurer, so it was nice to have someone you knew would take an interest for a while and would make an impact on trying to improve things even more.

At the February meeting some discussion took place regarding some money being spent on new practice facilities but it was decided a new roof for the pavilion must take priority, and we must now get some estimates. As secretary I would see if any grants or loans were available. Following on from this we did have several quotations, and decided on giving the work to John Drabble, not just because he was our president's son-in-law, but because his idea to do away with the flat roof seemed the best proposition, and he did live locally and had a good reputation. I had also obtained an interest-free loan of £2,000 from Macclesfield Borough Council, who we found extremely helpful, so we were now able to tell John to get on with the work, at a cost of £4,365 as soon as possible.

I had also filled in an application form for the Foundation for Sport and the Arts who had shown a willingness to help and had asked for an estimate, and as they had informed us to carry on with the work, I hoped we may get the other £2,000 from them, so I sent a copy of the bill and received a cheque for £4,365 plus a plaque for inside the pavilion.

Prior to the season quite a bit of activity had taken place, with a successful dinner again at Macclesfield Golf Club. Mike Hart had got a friend to run a '60s night' in the village hall and with a good crowd from Mike's local The Boar's Head at Higher Poynton turning up, the place was full, and we made a profit of £200, so with Rod Wakelin back in the Club and organising the match ball sponsorship, bringing

119

in approximately £700, it was felt we could now start looking at the possibility of installing a new practice area for which a cost of £8,000 was estimated. As one who has worked as a groundsman for many years, I do sometimes think if you had £8,000 to spare, you could make a good grass practice area, as I have found most people would prefer to practise on grass, and if given half a chance, would be on last weekend's used wicket as soon as possible.

With all our money still intact from the roof project it was time to press on with getting funds for the practice area. Once again Macclesfield Borough Council were prepared to help by allowing the £2,000 interest-free loan to be used for this and Tony Hutter as assistant treasurer was trying for money elsewhere. The juniors themselves helped by having a sponsored cricket match together with a car boot sale on spring Bank Holiday Monday.

The season was eagerly awaited with a few new members. Two in particular, Terry Hill and Gary Wood, had both played as professionals for Bollington in the Lancashire and Cheshire league. Gary was, as far as I remember, the first Bollington player to score over 1,000 runs in this competition, and Terry, who played at Pott in the fifties when Macclesfield hospitals had a team, was always useful but with one of the longest runs and slowest walk back in the area. However, being well-known as a cricketing nomad around the area he later played at Parkside and got himself well respected as a professional with various clubs in the Lancashire and Cheshire league and the North Staffs league. He was always a strong lad. He had cut out the long run and was very consistently and deadly accurate and would keep one end going all afternoon.

However, playing-wise things did not go to expectations. We were knocked out of both cups in the first round, and only won one of the first four league games. Once again, batting-wise no one seemed capable of producing a big score, and at the end of May Gary decided to return to Bollington. As we had registered him in the Cheshire league there was, and still is, a lot of concern about people registering and then moving to other clubs whose leagues are not as strict regarding this matter, and with Bob Fairhall, chairman of the league, having very high principles, particularly in regard to keeping league procedures, we insisted a subscription must be paid to us, as both clubs were playing in leagues under the jurisdiction of the league cricket conference. Bob and the officials were getting concerned at some of the poor disciplinary records of some of the league clubs.

At the league AGM problems had occurred regarding the final league game of the 1991 season between Alsager and Davenham when Alsager required 20-plus points to be certain of winning the league and when they looked like getting Davenham out cheaply they had started chucking a bit of rubbish up to give them a few runs. But the Davenham captain took exception to this and declared the innings. However, the umpires obviously displeased at the antics of both captains, reported them to the league disciplinary committee who promptly banned them both for the first four games of the 1992 season.

It appeared that Davenham took exception to this and sent a letter which cast doubts on the integrity of the officials of the league who promptly all resigned and walked out of the room. Anyhow someone had the sense to get the show back on the road, and at the next league meeting Davenham sent a letter of apology. It also appeared that the Styal captain had been banned for two weeks during August, so obviously the disciplinary committee were being kept busy.

Mrs Tute, as President, with the help of Martin, who recruited a number of old members to play, provided everyone with a lovely President's Day, with superb food, nice weather, and a pleasant evening at the bowling club to follow.

Another plus that year was that the village hall had recruited a new steward, Basil Brierley, who was not always on call to open the bar if we had an early finish, but would regularly come to the game and stand at the wall with a glass in his hand, and a bottle of wine by his side. He always seemed to enjoy working behind the bar and all our members seemed keener to use the club than at any times before.

Playing-wise the season was again a mixed one as far as results were concerned. There were a few good individual performances but again, no real consistency, apart from Terry Hill who showed everyone what consistency meant by setting a new league record with 75 wickets, his best return being 9 for 22 against High Lane during the last game of the season. Skipper Graham Hackney at almost 50 years old was the league top catcher with 19, only two short of the league record. Rick Hollinshead, again the most successful batsman with two not out hundreds, finished third in the league averages.

Nathan Bull scored 100 for the 2nd XI against Chelford on the same day as the Woodford Air Show, and his last 50 runs came in 21 balls, almost overshadowing 'The Red Arrows'.

Both Sunday teams did well in an enjoyable season but the icing on the cake was when a photographer turned up to take a photo of the ground for inclusion in the *Rothmans Book of Village Cricket Grounds*, and in doing so got a marvellous shot of our chairman playing an exquisite square cut. This picture provided the front cover picture for this publication. The only XI to meet with any success were the under 15s, who reached the play-offs.

At the September meeting the Club received a letter regarding a donation to the F.W. Millet Memorial Fund. This was approved, as most people who knew him had a lot of respect, not only for his playing ability and captaincy of Macclesfield but also Cheshire and the minor counties. He always treated the lesser Clubs and players with respect. Over a few years Macclesfield were to lose quite a number of good players and clubmen at a young age: apart from Fred, people like Keith Belfield, Maurice Pickford, and John Higginson.

At this meeting I stated it was time we tried to get some sort of covering for the wicket, and Graham Hackney, Richard Hollinshead, and myself were asked to look into this matter. I asked John Jackson to come along knowing his capability for work and the equipment he had for making jobs possible.

As both properties were now for sale at the entrance, I was still concerned as to the problems that may arise, and during the season we received another letter from Ches Orme regarding locking the gate. This we ignored, as it was the council's property and hopefully they could sort it out. They had informed the selling agents of the terms on which they had purchased the ground.

Going up to the cricket ground virtually every day I did see a few people looking round the properties and an elderly couple who seemed very interested in the barn asked me to have a chat with them over a cup of tea. They said how much they liked the place but they were not sure how people going across to the cricket may affect them, but they had been assured that not much went on. I informed them that someone had been telling them lies, as it was a thriving Club with a good membership and four junior teams. However, towards the end of the season the barn was bought by a Mr and Mrs Trevor West. Shortly after they moved in, as secretary of the Club, I called to see them and they seemed quite sociable and asked if I was pleased to see the place at last occupied. My answer was 'yes and no', as I could well see problems arising regarding the access. At the same time I hinted that Ches at one time had offered us a piece of land at the entrance. If there was any possibility of getting another access, and if at any time they may be interested in this idea, and would be prepared to sell a piece of the land, it may prove to be beneficial to both parties. Unfortunately, this was the last friendly conversation we had, and my concerns about the problems that could arise were justified over the next three years, problems which cost the Club thousands, the officials and officers of the parish council a load of worry, caused divisions in the village, a wrongful arrest, and worst of all a near tragedy.

An aerial photo taken in 1990 clearly showing the track across to the ground.

5

Is This the End or Just the Beginning?

This chapter is my personal account of some of the problems which occurred.

Just prior to the end of the 1992 season I had a discussion with the chairman of the parish council regarding the parking of cars on the cricket field as there is about two acres not used. He started mentioning numbers but I informed him that was a non-starter, as who was going to stand there counting cars every time there was a game on? So we agreed to limit them to an area as you come in, which was surrounded by trees so during summer they could hardly be seen. To me, this was a long overdue move. Even so, some of the old guard would object.

However, on 5 November I received a letter from the parish council intended to eliminate any doubts about the Cricket Club's right of way to the cricket field: 'This letter confirms that the parish council as owners of the field have no objections to members of the Club and their guests using the access granted when the field was purchased from the executors of the Lowther Estate'. The precise wording regarding the access recorded in the deeds is as follows: 'Together with the benefit of a right of way at all times and for all purposes over and along the track or path across Ordnance Survey Nos. part 235 and part 236'.

On the same day that I received this letter I had been on the ground in the morning when I was accosted by Mr and Mrs West who informed me that if I needed to transport anything across to the ground, I would have to get their permission. I told them not to talk a load of rubbish, and left. I was going back after lunch, as I had arranged to meet John Walsh to carry out some work, knowing John would arrive more or less on time. When John arrived I had the letter from the council in my hands and was showing it to Mr and Mrs West, who I was telling in no uncertain manner that the letter stated the track was for all purposes at all times and that the estate agents had been informed of this, and that I would be using the track, as and when I needed, as I had done for over 40 years. I was well aware that the lease to the cricket ground did say 'footpath and service road', but the letter in my hand stated clearly that the council had now given us permission to use the track and park cars on the corner of the ground. It was clearly obvious there was a track across when they bought the place.

During the confrontation John came walking across, punctual to time, and; proceeded to take on the 'Henry Kissinger' role. He said that we should be able to come to some sort of compromise, but I was adamant that the ground and right of way were in the deeds of the parish council, so they should sort it out. While I was not impressed by the attitude of the Wests, as I had stated for years once development took place at the entrance we would have to stand our ground or we would finish up flying supplies in like the 'Berlin Airlift'.

However, things went quiet for a while as we were busy manufacturing covers up at John's farm at Moorside and finding out how the term 'living in a barn' originated. A couple of times the clouds were coming in to keep us company, but Ann kept us well supplied with hot drinks. Like most things we had done at Pott, we always seemed to find people to help in various ways, so with a friend of John's supplying the timber and Don Hackney making all the brackets, and John's never ending store of equipment and odds and ends, things soon started to take shape.

At the November meeting Mike Hart gave an up-to-date report on matters regarding the right of way, stating that the parish council had received a letter from solicitors representing the Wests, disputing their claim to a right of way, and as the council had very little funds, would we be prepared to pay 50 per cent of the cost if a solicitor had to be appointed. Naturally a lot of people were concerned, being well aware of the escalating costs of litigation. However, Tony Hutter proposed we agree to help with initial proceedings and then review the situation. We also had insurance with the NCA, which, according to their leaflet, included help with legal matters.

The Cricket Club also received a letter from the same solicitors stating that any vehicle would only be allowed across their land at the discretion of Mr and Mrs West.

Personally I was not going to be bullied like that, but was not going to the ground that much during the winter, so chose to ignore their threats.

The next function was the Christmas draw when a lot of members attended so the letter was shown round and the general opinion was that we would have to stand up and be counted, and fight for our rights.

At the AGM in January 1993 I commented on one of the failings in

125

the Club: a shortage of a good wicket-keeper. Fred gave an excellent report on the finance but president Lily Tute queried the £10 paid to an umpire at a second team game. Lily was a superb president and in her last few years just lived for the Club, and during her reign as president came to every AGM and usually had a complaint regarding some matter! Graham Hackney said she did it to keep people on their toes, but on this occasion it was on their feet, as Steve Higginbotham, the 2nd XI captain, stood up and offered to pay the £10 himself.

There was not much change in officials apart from Richard Hollinshead as 1st XI captain. Richard had been the Club's most consistent player for a few years. Also still on the committee was Ches Orme even though he had never attended a meeting. Under the 50 percent rule if people did not resign, their name was put on to make things legal and to keep to the terms of the lease.

Also in January we held a junior evening and a large number of them came to watch the NCA coaching video.

Comment was made at the February meeting regarding the NCA membership fee which was now £700 per annum, but it was decided we must carry on with this. A few month's later we were to ask ourselves if it was money well spent with the problems we were to encounter.

Nobody likes to see a Cricket Club disappear but early in the year we had a letter stating that Crispinians were to join with Rostherne. We had a fixture against Crispinians who used to play on Platt Fields in Manchester before I joined the Club in 1950, and had had a fixture against them every year since. In later years always on August Bank Holiday Monday, at one time they all used to arrive in the morning and have a picnic by the stream in the field next to the ground.

With Tony Hutter now in control of the juniors, this section was one of the best in the area, and Albert Hall was presented with an award from the Canada Life national under 15s competition. Tony was holding coaching courses at Poynton Leisure Centre on Saturday afternoons.

At the end of January I did peruse a letter of advice from an eminent member of the legal profession which gave me even more confidence in our fight over our rights to go to the ground without being harassed by our neighbours.

Mr Bourne was invited to the March meeting and my minutes read: 'To bring us up to date with this long lasting saga', never thinking it was really just beginning.

From a village Cricket Club's point of view we would have expected some support from the cricket authorities, but though we did get a bit of sympathy from various people, nobody seemed interested in any way, but simply informed us that if you have any queries please do not hesitate to contact the Legal Protection Group, which was a complete shambles. Following this we put our insurance business in the hands of brokers. We did eventually receive a letter from the Legal Protection Group in September asking us for our solicitor's name but by then we felt our strong stance against the Wests had paid off. However, in March we were informed the farm had been sold to a Mr and Mrs M. Mosley who had been informed of the letter sent to the estate agents on 5 December 1991, and even though they had replied, this information had never been passed on.

Even though we had promised the parish council we would help with 50 per cent of the costs towards legal fees and were certain of our rights that the parish council had passed on to us, several of the older members were not convinced. Even though we were 100 per cent behind the council, there were some who had been councillors since what appeared to be the year dot and had over the years been instrumental in not allowing us a proper access, and had friends and relations who were always moaning about seeing a few cars about a quarter of a mile away, and with the 50 per cent rule for committee members having to be obeyed they had been on the committee for years but never came to meetings so did not understand the problems facing small Clubs in areas like Pott, who nowadays could not run a successful Club just with local people, so we had to attract both juniors and seniors from outside the village, and they would be turning up in cars.

Even though we were going through a period of uncertainty we were beginning to make plans for 1994 which was the 75th anniversary of the Club, and we were determined to celebrate this so a sub-committee of T. Hutter, G. Hackney, P. Fletcher, myself and my son Ian was formed.

In March we had the first stand-off at the gate Mr West had erected when one of our members, a motor engineer went to service the mower. I had warned him there may be problems, and when he stopped to open the gate, Mrs West came out with a camera and Mike was the first to go into her selection of mug shots and car numbers which must have eventually numbered hundreds. So having posed for his photo, Mike got into his Land Rover and drove round the gate, which had no fence or anything attached to it, and onto the ground.

Confrontation like this only made people more determined to not let them get their way and probably ruin the Club, and if we were not careful, people who were good enough to give their time to come and help the Club would soon get fed up. One felt a bit embarrassed as

Mike was not a regular player and had only walked onto the ground one Sunday, and as usual at Pott, someone had a word with him and though he had not played cricket before decided to give it a go. One Sunday he produced a magic moment, when one of the opposition bowled him a slow Donkey Drop which he wound himself up to thrash to leg and missed. But his impetuous nature made him pivot and somehow he got some bat to it, and hit it down to third man. Being fair to him, he tried very hard to improve and became a good fielder and improved his batting until family ties and work curtailed him, but he tells me he now runs a pub team who call themselves 'The Gnomes'.

With the frames of the covers now completed, the following week it was agreed to take them across to the ground. John as usual being able to supply the right equipment for every situation. He had a low-loader hitched to his Land Rover. We did suggest to him that it might be a good idea to bring his shotgun just in case, or maybe to scare them a bit, but decided against this, as we were beginning to see they were very serious people we were dealing with, and to have a photo of someone with a shotgun on their lap would not help our cause. As it happened, even though we made a bit of a racket going across, nobody tried to stop us.

The worst confrontation came on the first full practice on 15 April as I arrived at the ground followed by one of our members, C. Hall. The following is my account of what transpired. Copies were sent to the parish council and the police.

I wish to report an incident on Thursday night the 15th April 1993. I was driving across onto the cricket ground followed by a committee member, Mr Christopher Hall, when Mrs West who appeared to be on gate duty, informed us that I would be allowed across, but that Mr Hall would not. I informed Chris that he was entitled to follow me, when we were confronted by Mr West, who at one period forcibly held my car door open, and I was unable to close it. I twice told him to allow me to close the door so he then proceeded to put his head inside the car, lifted his arm and threatened to strike me. I obviously did not attempt to retaliate in any manner, and then proceeded along the track to the ground. Mr Hall, who was a witness to this incident, was not allowed across.

I have this morning spoken to the police who told me that behaviour of this type can be considered as a breach of the peace, and asked me to inform them if this type of behaviour happens again.

With the first game only two days away the chairman of the council arranged for several members of the parish council, plus the police, to stand guard. I cannot think of many cricket teams playing in small hamlets like Pott Shrigley that have had an escort of parish councillors to get onto their ground.

However, it did not deter the Wests from making it extremely unpleasant for everyone going across to the ground and at times when they knew people would be turning up, they would make sure they were around with the camera and pen and paper for taking car numbers. But one section of the club who seemed to stand up to them was the junior's mothers, several whom were prepared to give as good as they got when it came to confrontation.

I did try to talk to the Wests on various occasions but the only answer I got was they knew what they had bought, and would not listen to any talk that there had been a right of way reserved in 1968, so I told them as they had threatened to take an injunction out on anyone going to the ground, they should go ahead and do it, and sort the matter out.

With this sort of thing going on, the cricket, which should always be the prime event in any Cricket Club, seemed to be taking second place and it was an embarrassment having visiting teams arriving at the ground and having their car numbers and photos taken. On occasions, spectators getting their chairs out to enjoy the sunshine, scenery and cricket had a head pop up from the adjoining field with a camera.

However, this procedure did die down after a week or two as the Wests owned a boat in Wales somewhere and started to go away most weekends, so the ladies with the juniors on Friday nights seemed to take the brunt of their wrath.

In the month of May we received a call from the Foundation for Sport and the Arts stating we had been awarded a 50 per cent grant towards new practice facilities so with the loan from Macclesfield borough and the money from junior section events, we were able to get this work started as soon as possible. We had informed the chairman of the parish council what we were doing, knowing full well once anyone saw contractor's vehicles on the ground, someone would be snooping round trying to find out what was going on. Rumours abounded that we were making a car park! Personally I don't know how anyone could reach that conclusion as we were siting the nets at the furthest corner of the ground which would have meant all the cars either having to go up the hill or across the playing area.

However, these rumours must have been taken seriously, as I went for a chat with the workers and the chap in charge said, 'You must have a strange council here'. I asked him what was wrong, and he said a lot of these jobs are usually carried out for councils to improve things for young people in the area, and we expected the odd councillor to have a look at the progress being made, but they had just had a couple of councillors across who informed them they could not lay a car park without planning permission.

Once again we hit the headlines when Alan Sherratt captained a 'Pott Past and Present' team against a rugby league team which included several well-known rugby celebrities.

At the August meeting we were informed that the Cheshire league were in discussion to expand the league to four or five divisions and promotion and relegation, and as we were near the bottom of the league some people were getting concerned. But I stated that if clubs were performing badly, they should risk being relegated. At the end of the season the 1st XI finished second from the bottom but the 2nd XI did quite well. Once again the only team with any success were the under 15s, who won every game in their group only to lose to Cheadle Hulme in the final play-off in a game that should really have been postponed, the square being under water when we arrived. So as not to disappoint, the lads played the game on the outfield with a very small boundary behind the wicket. Cheadle Hulme won because they possessed a better keeper than us.

Back at Pott we received yet another solicitor's letter informing us that their clients were putting sheep on their field. It seemed an expensive way of notifying us but we were getting used to this. When the sheep arrived they looked a right tatty foursome and there was not much danger of them being rustled for a bit of mutton, but they could be a nuisance as the state of the field meant there was not a lot to eat, so every time you walked past with a bag, they followed you, and even if you said 'mint sauce' they would not go away, and how they survived the winter no one knows.

Early the following season a couple of farmers who brought their boys for cricket practice said one sheep was expiring, but of course when it was found dead, they blamed us, but no more solicitor's letters were received, and the remaining sheep were removed.

Towards the end of the season the new owners, Mr and Mrs Mosley, moved into Pott Hall Farm, so on the Saturday Fred and myself took Colin Bourne's advice and called to see them. It seemed we were able to get on with them, and we certainly did not think that three years later we would be receiving a writ to appear in the High Court of Justice, Queens Bench Division. After nearly 100 years service between us to Pott Shrigley and a lifetime of not getting involved with the law, it was a bit of a worrying time.

Prior to this we had received the application form for NCA insurance. But with the shambles with the problem regarding the legal expenses we had encountered the previous year and the instructions they required the Club to follow, which would probably have cost a small Club like ours, hundreds of pounds, we decided to look elsewhere. Looking at the Cheshire league minutes, a few of the smaller clubs with no bar etc. were in the same frame of mind.

A sad end to 1993 came when our old stalwart John Vernon passed away.

JOHN VERNON

Sadly, last year saw the passing of John Vernon.

John served the Club in many ways for over forty years. Many is the time he would be working late but still found time to walk up to the ground to clean out the pavilion. He was one of the mainstays of our monthly waste paper collections, which provided much needed revenue over many years.

John was also Club Secretary for five years, as well as helping to provide teas. Throughout his long association with the Club his delicious scones must have numbered in the thousands.

His contribution to helping swell Club funds seemed endless, each year he looked forward to joining battle with Martin Perry and John Tute in trying to sell the most raffle tickets, this was all the more remarkable when you realise that he never held a bat or bowled a ball.

People like John Vernon, who give so much, for so little in return, are so very hard to find and an object lesson to us all. His cheeky laugh will be sadly missed around the pavilion.

The article about John Vernon from our 75th anniversary brochure.

With Tony Hutter in charge of the juniors section, next season's managers were already in place: David Rushton (under 17s), Nigel Reeves (under 15s) and Tony Hutter (under 13s).

Ivy and Mike Mosley and myself had a little chat, however a little later I was invited into their home and Mike informed me that he was not very well, and how helpful he had found Trevor West. He told him that at times he felt he had gone over the top in his attempt to get the message across about the row and they had decided to approach the problem together using just one solicitor, and mention was made regarding insurance and their ability to engage legal advice on an insurance basis. I told him that both the Cricket Club and the parish

131

council had evidence regarding this matter and while we were prepared to discuss things, we would help the parish council with anything which was beneficial to the Club.

We then talked about the matter for a while regarding the state of the right of way when the ground belonged to the estate. It had been obvious to me that some of the locals who were only looking to their own self interest, had told both Trevor and themselves that there was a wall with no gate and everything was carried to the ground. I informed him to be careful in taking notice of these people, as we built the pavilion ourselves in 1957. This was built with concrete blocks, it was 36' × 20' with a concrete floor 9" deep and an asbestos roof attached to steel girders, plus concrete paths all the way round, and as the pavilion was 300 yards plus from the road, we were sensible people, not ancient Egyptians building the pyramids. But he insisted the mystery man, whoever he was had helped to carry all the material across. I told him most of the material had been taken across by a tractor and trailer belonging to Walter Wainwright and even though Walter was dead and buried, his son had helped him, and there was a letter stating this in the hands of Colin Bourne. I also called at Fred's home, certain he would have in his possession the balance sheet for 1957, which he had, and this clearly showed the item for payment to Mr Wainwright. So I borrowed this from him and returned to Mr and Mrs Mosley, and made sure they were aware of this balance sheet.

At the AGM little change took place in committee, so once again to accommodate the 50 per cent residents terms, all we did was send out notification, which stated 'A cordial invitation is extended to you to attend. Please note that all committee members will be reconsidered for election unless the secretary is informed to the contrary'. It was a pointless gesture as some people's names had been on the committee for 20 years or so without them ever attending a meeting or even replying to the notification. As such Chesney Orme's name had been put forward but he never attended a meeting, but his name was again included, and as he had sold the barn to the Wests, and informed them it was only a footpath to the ground in any reasonable conversation you tried to have with the Wests, they would turn round and inform you they had bought the property from a member of the committee.

With the 75th Anniversary now with us, we were determined to celebrate it in a manner befitting a thriving Cricket Club and if our neighbours again made life difficult we would stand up and fight for our rights.

However, at the February meeting we received a letter from the parish council stating it had been proposed that a new way in be

132

considered, and we agreed this could perhaps help us, but we were not prepared to finance this to any great amount. Nothing seemed to materialise regarding this for the next couple of months and our first big event of the 75-year celebrations was a dinner at 'Shrigley Hall' in the evening on the opening day of the season. So, as one would expect, everyone was looking forward to the season, and for once it was quite a nice day. I had been up and got the ground ready, and sat having my lunch when I got a call from club captain Richard Hollinshead informing me that both the Wests and the Mosleys were at the gate with a copy of our lease to the council which stated it was a footpath except for service vehicles. I told him not to allow the players to be influenced by this as the Cricket Club had permission from the council to use the access as a right of way for all purposes at all times as that was the right of way in the agreement when the Lowther Estate was sold in 1968 and both the council and Cricket Club had been legally advised that the terms of the lease between landlord and tenant had nothing to do with them. I also spoke to the chairman of the parish council, who together with our chairman, Mike Hart, and several councillors also informed the police, and went to the ground to ensure our members and guests were not impeded. So, as in 1993, the season once again began, to say the least, in unusual circumstances.

Mr and Mrs Mosley were coming along to the celebration dinner at Shrigley Hall, so as they were fairly new to the village the last thing we wanted was any controversy, but as we had Bob as chairman of the league and Dave Lawson as fixture and results secretary both speaking. As league officials they would not condone members of other league clubs being challenged at the entrance to the ground, so in his opening speech, Bob, in his usual forthright way, stated that if problems like this were to continue, we would risk being expelled from the league. After the various speeches and tributes were over, Bob came to me and said Mrs Mosley had asked if she could help to get the problems sorted out, but he had informed her it was none of her business. However Mrs Mosley came and had a conversation with me. The object seemed to be to get us to support them in their battle with the parish council!

However, I did have a bit of a chat with her, even though it was the last thing I felt like, as most cricketers are aware at a dinner like this that you go to enjoy yourself, talk cricket, meet people you have not seen for a good while, and some you may never see again, and certainly not argue about getting onto the ground. I suggested to her that I was now nearing retirement and had given over 40 years service to Pott Shrigley and I would not be prepared to spend my leisure hours being dictated to by anyone at the entrance to the ground. Just what a ridiculous situation could develop from the point of view of competitive cricket was shown when the second team were at home the following week. I went to the ground early to see that everything was OK and sat watching the match when someone came up to me and said Mrs Mosley had asked him to tell the captain to go and see her. I had a few words occasionally with people when I was captain but I had never been asked to leave the field to speak to someone like that and considered it interference with both the individual and the Club which we were not prepared to tolerate. A while after our chairman Mike Hart arrived and went and had a friendly chat.

Plans were now being finalised for events during the year, most of them to take place during the spring Bank Holiday, so we had asked the parish council's permission to hire a marquee and arranged with Bernard at The Turner's Arms to run a bar for the weekend. We were prepared for a few problems, but were determined to see our plans were not disrupted.

With the help of our former secretary, John Pickford, we had been negotiating to try and arrange a game with an England ladies team to provide the opposition for a celebrity game on Bank Holiday Sunday. However, I did get a letter from Norma Izard of the Women's Cricket Association stating they would not be coming. Peter Fletcher suggested he could arrange a celebrity team from Piccadilly Radio to come along, so with most of the matches and activities being in the Bank Holiday week, plans were now well advanced with the village match being played on the Friday followed by a hoedown in the marquee. On the Saturday to look towards the juniors we had a disco and fun night. Sunday saw a superb night's entertainment by the talented Merseysippi Jazz Band, so for the weekend Pott Shrigley really came alive, and with a Junior Festival and a High Peak junior league under 13s representative match, life was certainly hectic for a week. However, obviously not everyone was happy about all this celebrating, as most of the posters advertising these events at the entrance to the ground kept getting spirited away during the twilight hours.

Another shock was received on the Friday when with everything ready, the marquee in place, plus portable toilets, I had a visit from a bureaucrat from Macclesfield borough council saying we had been reported for having entertainment in the pavilion for which we had no music licence. I informed him that we had no bar in the pavilion and all the licensing had been done through Bernard at the Turners Arms, and that the music etc. would be in the marquee. I took him down to see Bernard and after several phone calls to various people we were allowed to carry on with our festivities. Everyone seemed to enjoy the

Our 75th anniversary celebration match.

events, it had been a lot of hard work for many people, and Graham Hackney and Ian Brooke produced a brochure which everyone could be proud of.

One big disappointment was the Sunday game against Piccadilly Radio XI. They had given us a team including quite a few celebrities and we had got a good write up in the local paper regarding this event. However, as can happen on these occasions some of them cried off and quite frankly it really was a damp squib. Letters appeared in the following week's paper complaining. The following Sunday the Old Stagers of the seventies took on the 1st XI and although a bit limited in the fielding managed to put them in their place and won easily.

In league business there was still a lot of talk about expansion of the league, but we were against it at this stage, as the county league appeared to only be interested, providing their clubs could not be relegated.

The next big event which drew a large crowd to the ground was the Cheshire League Colts Cup final against Bredbury, and with good all-round performances by M. Tarr and M. Fletcher, and also by A. Hall, we won this cup for the first time, so the village hall takings were up

the party at Pott

BLACKBURN Rovers and England footballer Graham Le Saux and former England opening batsman Graeme "Foxy" Fowler are among the stars lined up for Pott Shrigley's 75th anniversary celebration cricket match this Sunday, 2 p.m., writes **DAVID ALLABY.**

They have also picked someone called Inspiral Carpets. A famous pop band, I am told, and not a bunch of lads from Bollington who can fit you a tasteful line in twistpile at £2-99 a yard.

Despite inadvertently being overlooked by the selectors of Sunday's teams, I wish Pott Shrigley every success on their big day.

I can remember the cricket club when it was little more than a hut on the side of a hill where sheep grazed contentedly. It's still like that, you say? Well, things change slowly out in the countryside, and thank goodness for that.

The setting has always been important to cricket, and this has been especially so for those who have played up at Pott.

In recent history, the club have attracted some of the area's genuine cricket talents and characters: Graham and Don Hackney, Alan Beckett, Allan Sherratt, Keith Arnold, Martin Tute among them.

There were times when other clubs would wonder why such players should chose to play on what was once a somewhat rough-cut wedge of the original Pott Shrigley golf course rather than at a club which seemed to offer more status or prestige.

Having known many of the players down the years - even vintage club stalwarts such as Geoff Harding, Ernie Hackney, Frank Hulme, Jack Archer and Arthur Shepley - and even miss-hit the odd six over the pavilion myself, I know there is an endearing and enduring quality about the place and the people.

Derrick Brooke first played for Pott in 1950, captained the first team for 14 years, broke most of the batting and bowling records and was the first Hillman to record two centuries in a season, back in '57.

I can recall writing a profile of Derrick for the Express back in the 60s, and he still looking after the ground after 40-odd years.

Fred Wrigley, of the deft late cut and agonisingly slow leg-breaks, joined the club 45 years ago and must recall the arrival of the infant Hackneys who set standards in the modern era that were to bring the club widespread respect and success.

Reading through the anniversary brochure has brought back a kit-bag full of memories.

I can remember young King's School boy John Barrow taking 5 for 0 against Ashburton in the early '60s. Although, John soon had to devote more time to beef cuts, it was great fun to turn out with John every so often for the church youth club to give the cricket club a going over.

There is an indefinable quality about this wonderful game played Shrigley-style. Corris Mawer, landlord of the Turners Arms, once took eight wickets against Toft despite Bob Fairhall moving Corris's marker to a new spot at the end of each over.

Long may such stories grow in the telling and Pott Shrigley cricket, led by president Lily Tute and chairman Michael Hart, prosper . . . especially this Sunday.

Pott Shrigley C.C. first team who step up the club's anniversary celebrations this week (478 GH)

David Allaby – of the *Macclesfield Express* and ex-Pott Church youth club member – helps to publicise our 75th anniversary.

that week. I do not know whether the neighbours were impressed but when a passing car hit one of the cars parked on the road, a young lady had to be taken to hospital. As it happened she was not seriously injured but it should have proved to people that parking on the road could be a safety hazard.

With the under 13s team also reaching the semi-final of the Cheshire cup and the H.P.J.C.L. cup final and the league play-offs once again, the juniors were bringing most of the glory to the Club. Again from a senior point of view there was nothing to write home about. There were several good performances but no real threat of winning any honours. Performances were: R. Hollinshead 578 runs and M. Dean 516 runs, M. Tarr 42 wickets and R. Mattock 30 wickets.

With no sign of any progress with the right of way and legal costs escalating as some of our older members had feared, the division in the council was coming to light with the old guard who always appeared to be hostile to the Cricket Club making any progress having other ideas. The solicitor called on the Wests and we then were asked to agree with what they called 'A fair deal' which was what we had refused in the first place, as who was going to stand all weekend counting the number of cars going onto the ground? Knowing the people we were dealing with, we would have had them disrupting games once any aspect of this 'deal' had been broken, including terms regarding parking outside the church, which was not our problem.

At our next meeting we refused to have anything to do with this and as were now, nearly £500 in debt to the council's solicitors and had only finished up with ideas we had refused in the first place, we informed the parish council to send us the account for what we owed and that we were withdrawing from our agreement regarding their solicitor. We also informed them we would be prepared to buy the ground. Even though we were well aware of the problems we may encounter, at least the future of the ground and Club would be in our own hands instead of having different parties involved. My own personal view was that we may as well start afresh somewhere else as try and run a Club in a manner some people seemed to expect. The one thing in our favour was that most of the councillors were at retiring age and like myself, getting sick and tired at the bad feeling they were having to put up with.

As usual the season ended with Greg and Andy organising what Greg always called 'The end of season bash', which usually finished as a version of one of the television game shows, but the prizes were not as good. Still, it was good for the Club spirit.

With the season over and all of the closed season renovations to be completed, I was busy doing this on the Saturday morning when Mrs

Mosley and Mrs West came across to tell me that from that day on they would be putting a padlock on the gate and they were being good enough to offer me a key to this for my personal use. I was not impressed with what was being said in terms of how kind they had been not to do this during the season and disrupt the cricket and events. However, I refused the key at that time and informed them that I would think the matter over and let them know. Well I did think it over as at that time it seemed you could not get it off your mind and it would have been easy to say I would accept the key, just do the ground, and leave the official posts to someone else not so involved, but deep down I would not have felt happy if I had done this, plus the further issues of safety etc. which could have been a problem with people playing sport behind a locked gate. I had just been to a sport first-aid meeting where the case of a footballer hurting his neck in a park with the gates locked had been discussed but as luck had it, there was a doctor on hand who diagnosed the seriousness of the injury. If he had not been on hand and someone had tried to move the man, results could have been fatal.

On the Sunday afternoon I went to inform them of my decision not to accept a key. My chat with Mrs Mosley was on a friendly basis but it was clearly obvious she was putting pressure on for me to comply but my mind was made up, and it was going to take more than these two ladies to alter it. I was getting the usual patter regarding the fact that legal proceedings would cost them nothing as they were insured, a threat that both the parish council and ourselves were beginning to query, so I suggested if they were so certain of their rights, then they should take the matter to court. Most of us were now aware that Mike Mosley was a sick man with lung problems and while people were sympathetic and did not wish to do anything to worsen his condition, one got the impression that this was the reason for not going to court.

Another thing which I kept getting told was what a lot of respect they had for the Cricket Club, and the way we encouraged juniors, but their public enemy number one appeared to be the chairman of the parish council, Mr C. Bourne. I informed Mrs Mosley I would not take part in any attack against Colin, as in all the time I had been at Pott he was the first member of the parish council to show any desire to help the Cricket Club to improve, and with regard to the right of way, the matter could have been sorted out in a proper manner 20 years back, as nobody wanted to be in possession of a land-locked piece of ground. Before I left, still on friendly terms, I made my position quite clear that as secretary of the Cricket Club they should not lock the gate as the 1968 agreement stated 'A right of way for all purposes at all times' and the parish council's solicitors had informed

138

me it should be removed causing as little damage as possible, and if the gate was locked as secretary of the Club, I would remove it. I asked if the West's were at home, as they usually went to Wales at the weekend. She informed me they were not at home but she would inform them of my decision. I told her not to, as I would personally see them and ensure there was no mistaking my stance on this matter.

I walked up to see them during the same evening. They had obviously only just arrived back and were unloading a trailer. On the way up to Pott I had wondered if I should have felt more comfortable with a bit of support as I was the one most affected by their attitude, and Pott Shrigley was becoming an unpleasant place to be. However, I managed to get them both to listen to me and I informed them I would not be having the key off them, and told them the same as I had said to Mrs Mosley. They should not lock the gate, and if they obstructed us in any way, the lock would be removed. I also reminded them there was 'A right of way for all purposes at all times' which went back to 1968. Their attitude was that this was a load of nonsense as once they had bought the barn, this was all invalid, and what was more they were now in a position where council could be appointed without any cost to them, to which I informed them to go ahead and then everyone could get on with their lives without all the problems.

The parish council gave us notice of a letter stating that the right of way was inherited when they purchased the property and confirmed by the solicitors as being private right of way for pedestrians *only*, with maintenance equipment being allowed across only with the consent and goodwill of the landowners of the day. As we had to hand the letter the parish council had sent to the estate agents, it was obvious this information had not been passed on, or they had not accepted it. Neither would they accept the conditions as stated in the Land Registry. Also in the letter it stated that negotiations seemed not to have progressed since the council's solicitor had attended a meeting at their home on 8 July. I asked why the Cricket Club officials had not been invited to this meeting, particularly as we had agreed to meet half of the costs, and all it did was to increase costs.

When the lock did go on I had to get the machines (slitter and scarifier) back to the bowling green so I cut the small lock off with a hacksaw to allow me to get them across, but a couple of days later, when I went to collect some equipment, a new, much stronger, lock had been put on, so I lifted the gate off its hinges. When I went back, Trevor was busy putting the top hinge on upside-down, so this procedure could not be repeated.

With the village bonfire already well organised and the fireworks paid for it was essential that we got all the equipment for the

139

Lockout stumps club

By PAT HILLS

CRICKETERS were stumped when they turned up at their club-house last week to discover they had been locked out of their own ground!

Committee members of Pott Shrigley Cricket Club found themselves on a sticky wicket when they were greeted on arrival at the gate by a heavy padlock and chain.

They cried "Howzat?" For the unwelcome shackles hadn't been there the night before.

The exile from the site on Shrigley Road was the final straw in a two-year clash which has raged between the club's landlords, the parish council, and neighbours who barricaded the gate in order to keep traffic off their property.

Simply isn't cricket

Now players have to dump their cars and walk 150 yards up the track just to play or get into the pavilion. And that, they say, simply isn't cricket.

"We are the piggies in the middle," wailed groundsman Derrick Brooke. "The council changed the access rules to accommodate us. They own the land after all."

But neighbours Trevor and Bernadette West, who claim up to 200 cars a week drive over their land outside their magnificent barn-converted home, maintain they bought their property with "pedestrian access only" and never expected the volume of traffic foisted upon them.

"We came to live in the countryside expecting peace and quiet," said Trevor West. "But we have had nothing but aggravation for two years. We didn't know what country life was

●E-LBW-ed off their ground are Cricket Club committee members, left to right, Fred Wrigley, treasurer, Michael Hart, chairman, and Derrick Brooke, groundsman, and Parish Council chairman Colin Bourne.

like until we got here. It's like the Ku Klux Klan.

"We have had every bit of skullduggery thrown at us."

He added: "The lease to the deeds states categorically that the right of way for lessees is on foot only. Suddenly the rules changed when we moved in."

His wife, Bernadette added: "We don't mind a bit of traffic going down the track but in the height of the season there are 200 cars driving over our property in one week. We're not the ones changing the rules."

Outraged Parish Council chairman Colin Bourne said: "Solicitors have got involved and I am rather saddened that the present owners can't wait for the outcome of discussions between lawyers.

"This action is both provocative and illegal. It does nothing to foster good relationships."

He said the precise working recorded in the deeds was "a right of way at all times and for all purposes over and along the track or path."

Threat of violence

Derrick Brooke, who has been a member of the cricket club for 45 years and a groundsman for 40 said: "I have been threatened with violence. I've only been trying to do my job. The Wests did offer me a key to the padlock but I declined. One is all in, or everyone out.

"We need vehicular access. Every night someone is here and locking us out is going to deprive members, including 90 juniors whose parents like to drop them off at the pavilion, of playing cricket.

He said there could be fireworks - or none at all - on Bonfire Night next week when the village holds its annual bash on a site nearby, for electricity cables and tables for the stalls needed to be picked up from the cricket club pavilion.

"If we can't get access we may have to call it off," said Derrick.

And that, he said, was not fair play.

Locked out at the end of 1994.

sideshows etc. from the cricket ground to the field about half a mile away, so once again we relied on John with his Land Rover and trailer. John and myself arrived at the gate which was locked, so we just sat with John's hand on the car horn until Mrs West came to unlock it. As always happens on occasions like this you forget something and a while after we realised we had not brought the boiler and teapots, so Ann and Roger Moore, two old stalwarts of the Club and also regular attenders and workers for the church, went to get these from the pavilion. They came back a while later and Ann was not pleased when she had to give her name to Mrs West in order to get onto the ground. As one of the parish councillors was on hand, we expressed our disgust to her.

Another incident occurred in late November which showed what someone was prepared to do to make life difficult for us. I always had the top dressing for the cricket pitch delivered with the top dressing for the bowling green which was delivered to the factory and put in

140

the stores to keep it dry until it was used. As I was under pressure to move the last dozen or so bags, I took them to the ground and left them by the gate until such time that it might be opened. However, a couple of days later I called at the ground and there were only about four bags left. As I stood wondering what had happened, Trevor came out and informed me that the other eight bags had been thrown into the stream by the entrance to the ground. He assured me they had nothing to do with it, and went and put wellingtons on and fished them out.

Strangely enough this incident led to the longest and most sensible chat I had with him, although I have no proof that all he said was true. I again put it straight to him that there was a right of way for 'All purposes at all times' reserved to the cricket ground in 1968 and that there was a fair chance we would be buying the ground. Of course, we would then lay claim to the right of way and as soon as I heard anything regarding this I would let him know. His reply surprised me and again I have no proof that he was telling the truth or whether he would have admitted it, but he said 'Frankly I am just as fed up with it as anybody but it is them next door, who want the lock keeping on. If it was left to me, I would take it off tomorrow'. So with this statement ringing in my ears, I again told him as soon as I received any information I would contact him.

After all the celebrations of the 75th Anniversary I think most of the officials were looking forward to a quieter life the following season but far from this it was probably one of the most antagonising years in the Club's history with angry confrontations around every corner. However, it was pleasing to see most members stood together and saw it through, and now most look back and feel it was also the year that probably ensured the Club had a proper future to try to improve.

The AGM in January was well attended and most of the officials were prepared to carry on, the only changes being Greg Lisle appointed treasurer, with Fred now in his 46th year with the Club, carrying on as his assistant. Jamie Hart and Ian Brooke were appointed 1st XI and 2nd XI captains respectively. Both had come through the junior ranks.

This was just the start of many meetings, discussions and events which the Club and its members had to carry out in order to fight for our survival, and at the same time carry out our cricket activities at both junior and senior levels.

Just to start the ball rolling, Tony Hutter came forward with an ambitious plan to take two junior teams to tour Australia at Christmas 1996, and being aware of Tony's enthusiasm and ability to organise, this would go ahead. Also, Mike Hart and myself met the council members designated to dispose of the ground, and over a glass of whisky had reached an agreement to purchase at £17,500. John Walsh enquired how this valuation had been arrived at, but M. Hart, who is a valuer, stated it was difficult to value a cricket ground but we offered £15,000 and they asked £20,000, so we had both agreed on £17,500. It was proposed by Roger Moore and agreed by the meeting for the purchase to go ahead. Shortly afterwards I wrote the following letter to Trevor West with a copy to Mr and Mrs Mosley. At the time most people thought this was wrong, however, it certainly stirred things up, and we got a true idea of what and who we were up against.

Further to my recent conversation with you regarding the Cricket Club's offer to purchase the cricket ground, I understand that this offer has now been accepted.

I would therefore respectfully suggest, that as we are now approaching the stage when work must start on the cricket ground for the beginning of the season, plus the fact that the Club is being threatened with expulsion from the Cheshire cricket league, that the lock on the gate is removed, so as to avoid the obvious confrontation and unpleasantness, which there is apparently destined to be.

I would point out that when the lock was put on, both Bernadette and Ivy assured me that this was for a couple of months only, and as this lock was put on the gate in October, I would expect this promise to be honoured.

It would be the hope of the members of the Cricket Club that when this transaction is completed, some dialogue between all parties could be considered, to see if both short term and long term an improvement in relations could make some progress.

After putting copies of this letter through the letterboxes of both the West and Mosleys on my way home, by the time I arrived home, Kit asked me to ring Mrs Mosley, which I did. She thanked me for sending them a copy and asked me how much we were paying for the ground, but I refused to tell her. I told her to phone M. Hart, but as far as I am aware she did not do so.

A few days later I received a letter from Mrs West virtually stating that they were not willing to compromise in any way and would not remove the lock, so I could only come to the conclusion that my conversation with Trevor when we had bags of top dressing ruined was pure fabrication. Shortly after this I was informed that Mr and Mrs Mosley had put in an offer of £2,000 above any figure we were prepared to pay.

142

However, we will never know what the outcome would have been had they purchased the ground. In their letter to the parish council they had stated they would allow the Cricket Club to continue. However, with only a few years on the lease to go, plus the fact the problems had started, not over driving cars across but that it was totally unacceptable for the Club to be controlled by people at the entrance to the ground.

As far as we were concerned it was just a kneejerk reaction, and I could see that no thought had been given to who would look after the ground if it went into private hands, plus the fact that no grants or loans would have been available and certainly the rank and file, plus junior's parents had their own thoughts, and maybe they were completely wrong but a general feeling started rumbling round that our neighbours were trying to get the Cricket Club out of the village and the people who had ashes of their dear ones on the ground were most upset.

It was proposed at the meeting that we appoint a solicitor as soon as possible to get on with the transaction as not only did we not trust our neighbours, there were members on the council who saw this as a possibility of the Cricket Club making more progress which they had always opposed all the 45-plus years that I had been involved.

The big problem now was finding the money. Firstly, the deposit and then the balance. One of the first things we did was to circulate houses and businesses in the area with the Test leaflets which shook a few feathers but also produced a few results. We also put in an application for lottery funds, plus a loan of £8,500 from Macclesfield Borough Council. As I was getting my Bus Pass later in the year I had seriously considered throwing in the towel, but with the possibility of buying the ground I felt once we could get this completed, the Club had at last a bright future, so as I had recently sold the property we had lived in for 27 years and had been refused planning permission to build at the rear, we had moved into a rented cottage, so even though not wealthy by any standards, I offered to loan them the deposit so they could fasten the transaction as soon as possible.

Even though all this activity was taking place, as the person who did the ground work, I was getting more impatient regarding the gate being locked. As anyone who takes care of grounds knows well, a lot of the members think you go to the ground about half-an-hour before the game to get everything ready, so I had written a letter to our neighbours and was prepared to deliver this as soon as necessary.

1995 was of course the 50th Anniversary of VE Day, so being on the village hall committee as well as that of the Cricket Club, I had suggested the village hall, school and Cricket Club should join in

TEST at Pott Shrigley

Just as we at Pott Shrigley Cricket Club were ending our 75th Anniversary season, little did we know that our sternest 'Test' yet, lay just ahead.

You may have seen in the press recently, that our access to the ground has been challenged, a gate erected across the entrance to the ground and since October 1994 a lock and chain now bars our way in threatening the very existence of our club.

Pott Shrigley Parish Council are the present owners of the ground but now say that their funds will not run to finance any legal action required, therefore, the Cricket Club has offered to buy the ground to enable us to expedite matters and to safeguard the present facilities and ground conditions now enjoyed by all in the area.

Strenuous efforts by many local cricket lovers have seen the ground steadily improve since Archie Brown laid and cut the first wicket in the early days of 1919 to its present high standards with pitch covers, one of the best squares for miles around and outdoor junior practice wickets reflecting the clubs emphasis on youth.

We must not let events at Pott Shrigley mirror other local events, where individuals, here one minute, gone the next, have not taken into account the good of the community.

Pott Shrigley Cricket Club has over the years combined with Church and Village in many activities to raise funds for the benefit of all and hope this will be allowed to continue.

In order to help us win this 'Test' we at Pott Shrigley Cricket Club appeal to you to support us in any way you can through Donations, Ball Sponsorship or just your vocal backing in order to ensure the future of our club.

Please make all cheques payable to:-
"POTT SHRIGLEY CRICKET CLUB"
and return to Mr. G. Lisle, Treasurer,
POTT SHRIGLEY CRICKET CLUB,
15 Charter Road, Bollington, Macclesfield,
Cheshire, SK10 5NU.

Thank you.

The leaflet we produced asking the public for help.

events which included a street party, 'Kwik cricket and fun day' plus a 1940s night in the village hall.

The chairman reported that after our last letter to both the Wests and Mosleys, they were prepared to look into the idea of finding a new way in. Ian Brooke proposed and B. Brierley seconded this but G. Lisle and S. Higginbotham were against. The chairman also agreed to limit cars to essential traffic and visiting teams at weekends.

In March we received a lengthy four-page letter from Mike Mosley, suggesting compromise regarding the right of way, but as this included a demand to give up claims to the right of way and only concerned the few yards on his property (then we would have to negotiate with the Wests for the rest of the way) we totally rejected this.

In the meantime I had delivered my letter to the Wests. Trevor must have quickly read it because he came out in his usual aggressive manner, flinging his arms about, so I quietly asked him to calm down, and if he had something to say, to go and put the kettle on and invite me in for a cuppa. To my surprise he did. As I got inside, Bernadette gave me a bit of a verbal broadside and reached for the pile of photographs she had taken. I told her I was not interested. I felt like informing her that she probably had as many mug shots as the FBI but she did not seem blessed with a sense of humour. Anyhow, Trevor asked her to go and make a cup of tea, and I probably stayed for over an hour and had a reasonable conversation, but at the end of this, it was apparent that Bernadette held the view that no one should go on to the ground with a vehicle without her permission. However, I did say to them that if the various bodies would agree we would see if we could help with getting a new way in, and in discussing this they started talking about giving a piece of land to park the cars on out of sight in the hollow at the end of our field. I said this was a non-starter, as we were not going to work and spend for a way in that did not even go onto the ground. Again I have no proof that what she said was correct, but the gist was that neither the Mosleys or some members of the parish council would agree to a way onto the ground. She then started quoting about Mike Hart being an estate agent and people of this ilk could be on the lookout for building land. I informed her that I was certain that was not the case, but I did throw in the fact that the Mosleys, who had only been in the village a couple of years had put in an offer to buy the ground. So I suppose Mike, who had been 20 years in the village, was just as entitled.

Bernadette then started quizzing me about whether it was true that the Cricket Club and the parish council had not got on well together. I admitted we had not seen eye to eye with the council in general as some members would always stand in the way of any progress, and instead of thinking of the Cricket Club and the way the ground was maintained, as an asset, there always seemed to be an inbred opposition to any progress.

I also informed them as chairman of the HPJCL that whether people liked it or not, it was our duty to provide cricket to as many juniors as possible and just to prove how respected the junior section was, Pott Shrigley had been selected to send a 'Kwik cricket' team to take part in the lunchtime entertainment at the England vs. South Africa Test Match. Just as I was leaving Bernadette informed me she used to love watching cricket on the television but since coming to live in Pott Shrigley she no longer bothered. I said I was sorry to hear that, and departed. On my way out I called at the Mosleys and told them of my discussions with the Wests and that I would contact the Peak Park and ask them to send a planning officer down to give a decision regarding making a new way in. A few days later two officers informed me of the date and time they would be attending. I passed this information on to both the Wests and Mosleys but neither bothered to attend, so it was left to M. Hart, Colin Bourne and myself to discuss the matter. We showed them where we proposed to get into the ground but they were not impressed. We then moved to the legal entrance to the ground and they simply stood at the bottom gate and said as far as they were concerned, the track was there from the road, and even more so it came from the centre of the village and carried on to the cricket ground, and this was where you would expect it to be and certainly no permission from them would be granted to alter this.

At the March meeting the secretary read out a letter from G. Hackney, who was unable to attend and had sent a letter stating it was time we started taking the lock off. There were still a few doubters, and I had to remind people forcibly that the season was now only three weeks away and I had no equipment on the ground, not even a mower, which had gone for service, and we had not been able to bring it back.

One problem we had was the size of the lock and chain. Even though a local car body repairer had loaned us a big pair of cutters, we were looking at a quick SAS-style operation, so once again the man who always had the answers and equipment for all occasions, said 'On Wednesday morning, 8.30 a.m. prompt, a couple of volunteers and a note from the Club instructing me to remove it'. So dead on the dot, with three members of the Club on hand, up drives John, the van door flung open, generator out and grinder cutting off the chain. I had put our letter informing John to proceed through the West's letterbox but they were not at home. Mrs Mosley came out but she had the dog with her and it was frightened of the generator noise

146

so she could not get near enough to say anything until the chain lay in pieces on the ground. A few days later Mike Hart received a bill for the chain, and a copy of a letter they had sent to the police, stating Mr Brooke had damaged the chain and they had a witness to prove it. About the same time a few of us were having a discussion at my home when we had a visit from the Old Bill. We had informed both the local PC and Inspector Allen at Macclesfield police of our intentions and had also shown them the letter from the solicitors informing us we could remove the lock. However, I had not seen this constable before but he had obviously come down from meeting the Wests and Mosleys who had informed him it was 'A footpath only'. He had been shown a copy of our lease with the parish council. We told him that things had been altered, and the council and ourselves had agreed on changes, which as far as we were concerned was a matter between the council and ourselves. He then stated that one of the parties was going to erect iron posts across the track, so we informed him that these also would be removed and suggested if they were so certain they were entitled to impede our access, they should take the matter to court instead of threatening people with injunctions and generally interfering with our members private lives. In our opinion they were trying to get the police to do the work for them, a situation we were not happy about.

They had also told the policeman that I had been offered a key and had refused it. I stated I felt I was entitled to make this decision. As secretary of the Cricket Club I certainly could not accept a key for my personal use when I considered their actions irresponsible, as I had informed them in a letter, and to block the access for everyone, including emergency vehicles by erecting iron posts defied belief.

As expected a new chain was then put on the gate which left me with another problem: that of getting the two machines back to the bowling green to get the green ready for the start of the season. So it was left to John and myself to make another 'Raid'. Unfortunately there were roadworks going on in Bollington which delayed me and by the time I arrived, John was on his way back with Trevor shouting something at him, so I asked what was his problem, and he said he had contacted the police who had told him to wait for them, but obviously John was not listening, and the machines were dropped off at the bowling green and John had returned to base. A short while after the local beat bobby, PC Hancock, turned up to take particulars.

At our meeting on 10 March it was apparent that the lock was going to stay in place and with John waiting for the police response to the incident regarding removing the lock, it was proposed that we engage solicitors and get them to take out an injunction to make them remove

147

the lock. However, as the council still owned the ground and would not agree to this course of action, we would have to keep removing the lock. We did get a bit more publicity when Paul Allott, who was fronting a local cricket programme for Sky Sports turned up with a crew and filmed us removing the lock and interviewed M. Hart. He then went to interview our neighbours but both parties were not at home. Paul apparently contacted the Wests later, but got one of the usual answers about the property being sold to them by a member of the Cricket Club.

At the meeting on 1 May a letter was read out from MBC confirming they agreed with our repayment plans for a loan of £8,500 to help pay for the purchase of the ground. As yet we had not put in for a lottery grant and life was very hectic indeed with Tony Hutter

Paul Allott lending Sky Television's support during the lockout.

also trying to raise money for the Australian junior tour. The chairman had also had another meeting with the Mosleys with similar results that any agreement was to be made with the proviso that we give up our claim to the right of way.

VE day was celebrated in the village in good style with a 'Kwik cricket' competition and fun day on the ground and once again the Club quarter-master, John Jackson, went to town and from his vast array of equipment at Heatherdale, produced two huge Second World War American army trucks with drivers, to circle the ground. The kids loved it, but I do not think the neighbours were impressed. The street party was moved into the school as there was an easterly wind blowing across the ground. A 1940s dance and social proved to be a success in the evening with Greg Lisle doing a superb job as DJ and turning out some decent music.

The next May Bank Holiday saw a successful Junior Day which added about £500 to Cub funds, which only proved what a good junior section Tony had organised and one which we should do everything in our power to assist.

Meetings were coming thick and fast as we were now in a position to put the deposit down for the ground and with the interest-free loan of £8,500 from MBC now secured, if we could get some lottery money, the future would be brighter. But until everything was signed and sealed, knowing how things worked in Pott Shrigley, you could not be sure, and when it was stated that Mrs Mosley had booked the village hall for a public meeting on 31 May, we decided we must get the transaction signed as soon as possible. So at another specially convened meeting on 27 May, M. Hart stated the contracts for the purchase of the ground were now ready for signing. Four trustees had to be appointed so M. Hart, myself, G. Hackney and J. Jackson were elected, and we were now ready to proceed. Unfortunately John, always a bit difficult to contact, had gone away to Wales for a few days but he would be back on the Wednesday. We did manage to contact him and told him he must be at the solicitor's office on Wednesday morning.

The reason for Mrs Mosley booking the village hall had now come to light. Two of the councillors who had now broken rank with the rest and joined the Wests and Mosleys in calling a meeting to protest that the sale of the cricket ground was not in the best interests of the parish. While these people may have been genuinely concerned, it was to say the least annoying that the negotiations had been going on since October 1994, with a price agreed in January 1995, not that this surprised some of our older officials, who had now made up their minds that if the matter was not brought to a satisfactory conclusion,

Ann Hackney turns the clock back during the anniversary of VE Day.

then as far as we were concerned, the Club may as well be wound up. We had been asked by the parish council to help them fight the situation over the right of way. It had cost the Club £1,000 to do this, plus all the worries and general abuse people had had to put up with. In a letter from one of these councillors which was sent to the Club, one paragraph states that this did not justify the abuse, verbal and sometimes physical, that followed. No mention was made of the fact that I was threatened on several occasions.

Another aspect which we found to be distasteful was that the meeting was only for persons on the current electoral roll, who were entitled to attend and speak, which excluded people like Fred Wrigley, Graham Hackney and myself who had helped the Club to progress from an organisation that could not have possibly survived in today's world to the Club that had recently appeared on the front cover of a book about the best village clubs in the country.

With all this in mind and the thought of the Club's future being left at the mercy of a meeting at which probably 95 per cent of the participants hadn't a clue about cricket or the work that went into keeping the ground up to an excellent standard, we decided all steps must be taken to sign the contract before this meeting took place. The following morning the deposit was taken out of my bank account and the contract signed. The solicitors had also received an anonymous donor's offer to meet the next payment, should problems arise.

The signature which made us the proud owners of our own ground.

On the night of the meeting to which we had not been invited, and which we knew was a waste of everyone's time, Colin Bourne was given an agenda by Mr Mosley, and informed the gathering that the agenda was not of much value as it had been overtaken by events, as the Cricket Club had paid the deposit and signed the contract. From accounts of the people who had been invited to attend there was a

151

stunned silence until Mrs West called the chairman 'a traitor' and threw a wobbly. I gather quite a few people did have a say, including our chairman M. Hart, who lived in the village and both his sons and son-in-law had played for years. His two daughters scored and wife Margaret organised the teas, so this was probably better than the outsiders having a say.

Mike received a letter from Councillor Kathleen Penny dated 1 June 1995 asking the Club to consent to the withdrawal of the contract and in return the residents of Pott Hall Farm would write in their deeds (at their expense) that the parish council's right of way would never be challenged as long as they remained owners of the ground. This should satisfy the council as the right of way had always been their main concern. My own view was and always will be that had the Cricket Club been treated fairly and a more sensible approach taken, then the problem need not have developed to these proportions.

The member of the Club who had suffered most with the illegal act of locking the gate was John Jackson who had been arrested by the police. I had gone to the police station with John and was not pleased by their attitude as they had only been shown a copy of our lease with the council, so we had to go to more expense and get the solicitor acting on our behalf to help. I was at John's early one morning when PC Hancock arrived and informed John all charges had been dropped and apologised.

Another problem encountered was with our lady president, Lily Tute, who was now 78 years old and had had a hip replacement in early April. Lily just lived for her cricket at Pott Shrigley and she had missed a few games, with the gate being locked and not being able to get to the ground as she was unable to walk very far. When I arrived home one Saturday lunchtime, Kit said that Lily had phoned to say she had contacted Mrs West who said if I went and knocked on their door and asked they would allow her across. I phoned Lily back and reminded her that the dispute was about these people dictating who could, or could not use the access and if she was keen on going to the cricket I would take her, and wheel her across in her wheelchair. However, when we arrived at the gate, which was locked, Mike Mosley saw us and said he would send a key out. But before he got to the gate Mrs West appeared with her key – whether it was a genuine offer to assist or the fact that PC Hancock appeared on the scene, I am not sure. In the confusion (we were playing Woodford) one of the visitor's wives had gone across in her car. As soon as PC Hancock went back the gate was locked again. A little later Mrs Mosley came and spoke to Mrs Tute and informed her that when she wanted to go home, she must send someone down to their house for the key.

152

A wet Saturday. The President and Secretary make their way from the ground during the lockout.

Naturally we had no intention of doing this. We had refused to on the way up, so we would wheel Mrs Tute down on the way back. However, we were left with the problem of the lady from Woodford with her car locked in on the ground, so it was a matter of taking the lock and chain off the gate, but as we started this operation, Mrs Mosley arrived to unlock the gate, so we decided that keeping quiet was the best option. But the lady from Woodford came out with a right mouthful of all the years she had been coming to Pott, and finding a situation like this, was deplorable, and we had to agree with her.

With the ground now in our ownership we were well aware that all would not be plain sailing. A few scare stories were circulating round the village that we would be hiring the ground out almost every day, so the schoolchildren would not be able to use it. We did meet representatives from the school to set their minds at rest. As anyone with any knowledge of sports grounds is aware, you could not have people playing every day with about 80–100 games played in a year. It was

153

difficult to find enough tracks as it was. Other people were mouthing that the ground should have been sold to the school, who at present used the ground virtually very time they wanted, which cost them noting. Had they purchased the ground and we had departed, where were they going to find a few thousand pounds to maintain the facilities? One had later to see the simple remark made by Lord Denning, a lover of village cricket, when asked to give support to a village club with problem neighbours: 'They tend the ground well and keep the outfield short'.

In an effort to try and find an amicable solution to problems regarding the right of way, Mike Hart organised a meeting with Mr and Mrs Mosley and the Wests on Friday 9 June. I was unable to attend owing to other matters, so I asked John Jackson to do so. Our opponents were still busy finding ways to make it as difficult as possible for us to raise the funds to buy the ground and had another trump card up their sleeves in the form of councillor Farrand, who had asked that the loan application be brought back to the committee for discussion on 21 June. It was felt someone should attend the meeting (although not allowed to speak) to have some idea of what went on. It was a bit like being in the House of Commons with Mrs Penny and Mrs Stewart sat on one side of the hall and Fred and myself on the other. All it achieved was to put getting our hands on the money back a week or two.

Opening the batting was Councillor Roy Harrison, JP, who had always been a keen sportsman, playing cricket at minor counties level. He had also been a football league referee. By the time he had finished a rousing speech regarding Pott Shrigley of the past and present, highlighting our continuing dedication to junior cricket, councillor Farrand's remarks seemed to lack any conviction. In fact they seemed to be a bit of an embarrassment and did not receive a word of support. However, as we left he did come over to us with Mrs Penney and Mrs Stewart and advised us to sell the ground back. It would have been easy to blow up but we just informed them we had a committee to make decisions like that.

Arising from the meeting which John and Mike had with the neighbours a 'without prejudice' draft agreement was presented to the committee but as this virtually excluded junior players and parents, the committee would not agree to it and Ian Brooke proposed that we require access for *all* matches. However a second draft was then negotiated with provision for those who supervised juniors. They would be allowed to drive across with a view to parents collecting and delivering children being restricted, and although there was some opposition, this draft was agreed.

154

Mike now had keys for the lock and had given one to Geoff Lockton, a junior manager and as a Colts Cup match was being played Geoff had got there early and together with a league official and umpire, Dave Lawson, had unlocked the gate and driven across. By all accounts he had been accosted by Mrs West and ordered off the ground. The key was wrested from them. How she managed this, I never found out, as their combined weight would be about 30 stones and neither of them were mild characters. However, although Bernadette was probably about 8 stone, she had put the fear of God into them.

Shortly after this on 27 June, Tony Hutter had organised a game against an Indian under 19s, team. Naturally Pott juniors were not good enough to take on a team of this standard so several players from around Cheshire had agreed to turn out. It turned out to be a glorious sunny day, the ground looked a picture with a few cars at the bottom, and in the school dinner hour one of the teachers brought some of the children across. I had taken Mrs Tute up after lunch – she still had her crutches but never missed a chance of going to cricket and loved every minute of it. Most of the spectators were full of praise for the effort and organisation that Tony had put into getting a game like this to Pott Shrigley.

However, they were later shocked and surprised. I was taking Mrs Tute home about 4.30 p.m. and got out of my car to open the gate. As I got back in the car, Mrs West drove in and instead of going into her own driveway, drove straight at my car and finished a few inches away. She then came out with such a tirade that it brought the game to a halt. It was as well Lily could not get out of the car, or else I fear the crutch would have been used for other purposes.

I wrote a letter reporting her behaviour to the police and at the next meeting it was passed that it be sent. Now, a lot of concern was being voiced about the wisdom of trying to reach an agreement with these people and there was even more concern that solicitors fees were still increasing. So the general feeling was that as the junior season was now almost over, and we were using the track at the weekends, we should let the matter rest until the closed season when hopefully something could be sorted out. Just to prove how silly and unpredictable things could be, the following week the Indian party came back and a Club side played the coaches and people who had helped with their tour. We had not unlocked the gate to save any embarrassment and when we noticed the bus stopped at the gate blocking the entrance to the West's property, we felt sorry for the driver. But suddenly the bus went onto the courtyard at the front of the barn and the driver came across to the ground. Fearing the worst, we asked if he had got into trouble, but he said, they had told him to park there.

With Tony's plans for the Australian tour now taking shape and the Club also trying to raise money for the purchase of the ground, life was hectic. In quick succession we held a midsummer ball at Adlington Hall which was a big success. The popular local MP Nicholas Winterton was in attendance, and he gave our ambitious project his support.

Shortly after this a successful quiz night was organised by John Walsh and Steve Higginbotham at the Ash Tree. With the landlord supplying pie and peas. This proved a good fundraiser. Greg and Andy had now got a lottery syndicate working which was also helping Club finances.

In early August another problem came to the fore which I had complained about for several years but it had fallen on deaf ears and nothing was done about it. I had been at the ground for most of the day when the Water Board turned up to replace the meter, which until a few years back was on the pavement, but had now finished up in the Mosley's garden. When I left work was still going on.

I was organising one of the junior teams that evening and they were playing away. As anyone knows this can be a bit of a task, getting everyone together and then making sure they arrive home safely, so it was about 10 p.m. when I got to my house. Kit welcomed me with a request from our chairman asking me to go to Pott and turn the water off as the Water Board had phoned to say there was a burst pipe and we were wasting two gallons of water per minute. To say I was not pleased was an understatement as you would have thought an organisation who were spending millions telling people to save water would have had the commonsense to leave it turned off.

However, I went up to turn it off and as it was now dark, it was a difficult job. They had put a different type of meter in, and I had not a clue what I was doing. When the meter had been on the pavement you could leave your headlights on. I went round to Roger Bailey who lived in the church cottages, to borrow a torch. Mrs Mosley came out and suggested I should ask before going on to their property but I was by now not in the best of moods, and informed her if it was left to me, I would have a bulldozer put through the meter and right of way put back in its original position.

The following day after I had calmed down, Mike Mosley was in the garden when I went to the ground, so I had a chat with him and we both agreed the most sensible way to proceed would be to have the water supply re-routed round the gardens and the meter moved onto the pavement. I also informed him most the Club's members were not happy with the situation as it was regarding the right of way. The big problem now, after nearly two years of negotiating and appearing to get nowhere, was that even though most of the members had stuck together, even joking about events, now they were getting the feeling that if things did not improve, there could well be an exodus, as most people involved with a Club like Pott have responsible jobs and the last thing they want is a lot of aggravation in their leisure hours.

At the August meeting I had written a letter to send to the neighbours stating that from the 1996 season we would be using the access for all games' maintenance and special events, and should they wish to take the matter to the courts, we would contest it. However, other people felt further attempts should be made during the closed season to continue dialogue, and this was approved, with M. Hart, J. Jackson, F. Wrigley and myself forming a deputation to meet as soon as possible. It was sometimes difficult at this time to be able to concentrate on what we should be doing, which was playing and enjoying cricket.

However, during what was once again an average season, there were two outstanding performances, both against Holmes Chapel. On 24 June at Holmes Chapel, Mark Dean and Warren Barlow batted through the 45 overs and scored 240 runs for 0 wickets. Unfortunately the game petered out to a tame draw and while it was, a great performance, my own view was from a winning the game point of view, probably an earlier declaration would have produced a different result. In the return game at Pott Shrigley, Rick Mattock took all 10 wickets, and as far as we know this was only the second time this feat had been performed by a Pott member. Mark Dean had an excellent season with the bat scoring 713 runs with an average of 50.92. Matthew Tarr was top wicket-taker with 45 wickets and Rick Mattock and John Nuttall were on 32 wickets each.

At the September meeting John Walsh, who had arranged and captained a team against Bramhall in the last game of the season, stated Mrs West had spoken to him regarding spectators driving across when we had come to an agreement that spectators would not be allowed to drive across, and he said to her that no agreement had been passed by the committee.

One thing all the problems did achieve was to cancel the annual bonfire for the first time since the early sixties. Quite a number of locals were very disappointed about this but in some ways it did a good turn, as people said they would be prepared to help in future if the event was reinstated.

We did however have a successful sponsored cycle ride along the old Macclesfield to Marple railway, now The Middlewood Way. The president, Mrs L. Tute, organised another race night and hotpot supper to put more money into Club funds. The junior section finished their year with a well attended barbecue.

Warren Barlow (left) 126 not out, Mark Dean (right) 106 not out, helping Pott
Shrigley to score 246 for 0 at Holmes Chapel in June 1995.

Another sad loss to everybody and even more to me, was having my
faithful dog Beauty put to sleep. She had been a familiar sight to
everyone. She came to all the games and while I was still playing,
never came onto the field of play until the players were leaving at
teatime or at the end of the game, and then she would rush on fussing
everybody. I got her from Windyway Kennels, a local dog rescue
centre, and shortly after some new people moved into one of the
church cottages, and started to bring their dog onto the cricket
ground. Beauty and him hit it off right away, always playing together,
and they looked very much alike, and after chatting with the people
regarding the dogs we realised they were brother and sister.

1996 started the same as the previous year had finished with discussions with our neighbours and a deputation from the committee

meeting at Pott Hall Farm in early January. I had come under a certain amount of criticism for not showing much enthusiasm for attending these meetings, but I was not prepared to agree to anything that was detrimental to the Club's future, as with all the talk of reorganising cricket in Cheshire we had to look forward, plus the fact we had purchased the ground together with a right of way 'For all purposes at all times'. In my opinion, whilst not totally ruling out compromise on some aspects, I would personally not be happy giving in to all the restrictions they were trying to impose. We had suffered from too many petty rules with the parish council as landlords, and to agree to another batch, some of which were unworkable, would be lunacy. One such restriction which I was against, and made my objections quite clear about, was to restrict access to six cup matches. In the present league I felt a lot of people knew we never played six cup matches at home, but to me that was not the problem, it was the fact that we were allowing them to dictate in this manner, and I was not going to be a party to this, as I considered the league we played in, and the number of cup matches had nothing to do with them. I was less pleased when one of the persons present stated, when I made my views known, that we were acting like schoolchildren. At the next committee meeting I asked the chairman to read out a letter regarding refusing to attend any further meetings on this subject.

At the AGM Jamie Hart was elected 1st XI captain, and Ian Brooke 2nd XI captain. Also, now we owned the ground, we had not got the 50 per cent from the village clause, so we could get rid of the dead wood, which over the years had been a farce.

In the High Peak league I was now chairman with Steve Amison as secretary. Tony, as treasurer of the league had now decided the tour to Australia should be run as a HPJCL tour as he had got players from other clubs in the league. There were a fair number of players and organisers who were helping members at Pott Shrigley. I cannot think any club in the country could get about 30 juniors to find the money and be available for a project like this.

At the meeting on 26 February, the chairman stated agreement had now been reached to divert the water pipe and have the meter re-sited on the pavement. The work was to commence on Saturday 9 March. John Jackson complete with JCB, Roger Bailey, G. Hackney, G. Lisle and myself were to assist. However, this again turned out to be a real shambles. When I arrived, John was halfway down the track, but was having a cup of tea Mrs West had brought him. As we did not have the pipe I said I would go to Plumbcentre and collect it. Wanting to make sure I brought the correct dimension of pipe, I called on Ian Hughes the ex-water inspector, but when I arrived back at Pott, John was sat in the cab of the JCB. He had now been informed by Mrs West, not to proceed beyond the gate, so we all had to pack up and go home.

At the March meeting Mike Hart stated the agreement to divert the water pipe had been reversed by Mr and Mrs West who wanted some kind of agreement regarding the right of way. But as we had bought the ground together with the right of way no document should be signed that interfered with this in any way. There was another meeting arranged with the Wests and Mosleys on Friday 29 March. M. Hart, Fred Wrigley, John Jackson plus John Walsh were present. John was one of the few members who appeared to have kept on fairly good terms, particularly with Mrs West. I had stated in my letter that I would accept any agreement they made and the committee ratified, and that we arrange for the officials of the Club to meet on Monday 1 April to decide on any agreement that had been reached. John contacted me after the Friday meeting to inform me they appeared to have reached some agreement but he would be calling on them on Monday just to confirm it all before our meeting. However, when he arrived everything had changed and more demands were being made, so as far as most people were concerned the talking had come to an end.

I made it quite clear to everyone that the acceptance of keys must be sorted out in a proper manner as I was not going to be responsible for ensuring the gate was locked or unlocked when required.

The problem with the water pipe almost led to one of the worst tragedies the Club has seen. Some people had said that this burst may be on our ground but I could not agree with this, as we had had a couple of bursts before and the water had come to the surface, but to try and locate whose ground it was on, we needed to dig down, cut the pipe and put a bung in it. And if the meter was still going round, it was most certainly under their garden.

Knowing how difficult it can be to dig exactly at the right place we enlisted the help of Ian Hughes, (ex-water board inspector) to see if he could come up with some high-powered technique to help. Instead he asked us to bring a metal coathanger from the pavilion, broke it in two pieces, and walked slowly along with the pieces of the hanger in front of him until they started moving, and thus established where the water pipe was. A couple of days later Graham and myself went to dig down just inside the gateway in the West's field after enquiring from the Water Board as to the legality of doing this. We were informed that it was our right to dig a yard either side of the pipe. I left Graham digging as I had to go and mow the bowling green, and in the evening he phoned to say he had found the pipe, so the same night I

160

phoned Bryon Holmes, our old stalwart when it came to helping the Club in the plumbing and glazing department, and he said he would go and chop it off and put the bung in the following morning.

I was working on the bowling green the following morning when I noticed Bryon coming in his van looking a bit pale and dishevelled. He got out still shaking. It was the electricity cable he had cut with a hacksaw, and luckily he was wearing rubber-soled shoes, but the shock had blown him out of the hole. It was not until after he had left me that the full implications dawned on me as to the tragedy that could have happened, all for the sake of getting onto a ground to play the game of cricket. I was not over pleased when several members received letters from Mrs West virtually saying it was our fault for getting an inexperienced man to repair the pipe, as Bryon was already on the pension. He had started work as an apprentice plumber at the age of 14, and had run his own business for over 40 years. He had probably been in more ladies bathrooms in Bollington than anyone.

Bryon had always been a friend, ever since we attended school together. He was always the school prankster and never seemed to grow out of this, making light of most things. I remember telling one of the ladies on the village hall committee about the incident, who said she went out with his elder brother at one time and sometimes they took him to places with them, and what a little horror he was. They had once taken him on a day trip to Blackpool, a typical 'little brother' on the boating lake bugging them all the time, and giving them the works on the dodgems.

As we got into our teens, almost everyone went to Rhoda Dawson's School of Dancing, to learn ballroom dancing. Rhoda, a typical dance teacher, always dressed to kill and had all the female assets for the job. She used to dance with the boys and Eric, her partner, with the girls to show them the steps. Rhoda ensured you held her in the classical ballroom pose before you started and Bryon's little prank was to start with his hand on her bottom and without any expression, she would lift his hand higher and carry on with the lesson.

Years later I remember him getting us in trouble with doctor, John Coope, who was a great organiser and a lot of people felt he was in the wrong vocation. He should have been an orchestra conductor. He had organised several festivals in Bollington which had seen the forming of a festival choir which he conducted. At the same time I had been instrumental in forming a traders association of which Bryon was a member. I do not suppose it achieved much as most of the meetings took place in the local pubs, but it was in the days of the corner shop, before all the cutthroat competition, and it became a friendly organisation that most business people enjoyed.

161

The main event everyone looked forward to was an annual dance when some of us went to the Conservative Club the night before to decorate the room. We always had a net full of balloons fastened to the ceiling. One of the problems that came up was that Dr John had a choir practice on the same night and never finished on time. Bryon always had a moan about this and on one evening we were blowing up balloons in the kitchen which had a serving hatch to the main room where John was at the front of the choir and had them humming a tune softly so Bryon got the largest balloon he could, blew it up as big as possible, and let it go through the hatch just missing Dr John but making him jump out of his skin. John was not impressed and told us we were acting like children.

Bryon seemed to have a love-hate relationship with these doctors. He always did their plumbing, he had a bedside phone and would always go out on emergencies. Once when the phone rang in the early hours of the morning it was the doctor who asked if he could go and attend to the overflow to the tank as it was running and keeping them awake, but he informed them to drop two aspirins in the tank, wrap it up warm, and he would call round in the morning.

Back to our problems with the water. We had now established that the burst was on the neighbours' land, but it was frightening to think what a tragedy could have happened.

With the Electricity Board having repaired the cable we had now to join the pipe together so we could at least get water when necessary, so back to Bryon who, with myself, went up on Good Friday morning to join the pipe. I think the next 20 minutes or so were the silliest of the entire saga. We took the van to the side of the hole, and as usual at Pott, if you dig a hole almost anywhere, it fills with water, so I was down the hole bailing out with an old paint can when I noticed the Wests approaching. Trevor was not looking in the best of moods so I told Bryon not to get involved and to say nothing. I just carried on bailing out with them demanding to know what I was doing, which was obvious, but I just ignored them, so Trevor threatened that if we joined the pipe he would cut it. Bryon simply stood there with a grin on his face and asked me what we should do. I told him to join it up. At this point Mrs West went hot foot towards the house. I think Bryon felt she may be going for some weapon, but it was obvious to me she was going for the camera, so when she came back he was straightening his hair in the wing mirror, then started looking in the van for a joint, and after a few minutes with camera at the ready for action he turned round and said, 'you will never believe this but I haven't got a joint of that size with me.' So we came home, Bryon not getting his picture on the wanted list after all.

When I got back home I phoned 'the quartermaster', John Jackson, and as usual he did not disappoint. He produced a joint, came and coupled it up and I filled in the hole. So the next time they had a look, the job was done and the threat of digging it up and cutting the pipe never materialised. So we did not need Bryon again. I was pleased to see the hole filled in as I had a few nightmares of finding Bryon dead down the hole.

Getting away from the cricket, one of the local farmers, Harold Wainwright, whose entire family seemed to revolve around sheep, turned up on my doorstep with a border collie dog called 'Biff', who they had sold to someone from Manchester, and of course collie's and cities don't mix, and Harold felt I looked lost on the cricket ground without a dog. Biff looked a bit tatty. He was on a piece of old chain and wet through, but an easy dog to get on with. But as we were thinking of going away for a few days, I told him to bring him back the following week which he did, all clean and shiny. Biff made himself at home straight away, so we now have another resident Cricket Club dog, not quite Beauty for not going onto the field of play, but if he sees or hears anything on The Nab, he's off so fast that hardly anyone sees him.

In April, with the season about to start, we had a letter from Mr and Mrs Mosley regarding the water, stating they would be away for the first three weeks of the season and no work must be carried out on their land, so we decided we would just carry on turning the water on even though it was wasting gallons.

We were still concerned about the financial aspects of paying off the balance to the council and the ever-increasing legal fees. No help seemed available from the various sources we had applied to, so once again we met the ever-helpful officials from MBC, Tony Foggarty and Tony Riddington, to see if a further loan could be obtained. However, with things looking a bit glum in the financial department I opened the post one morning, and with a note stating 'To help the Club with the problems with the neighbours' was a banker's draft for £5,000. If the donor reads any of this account, the Club will always be grateful.

We also had an offer from a local farmer and councillor that we could lay a new water pipe across his land from a supply he had near a cattle trough in the roadside opposite as he did not now use it. With agreement with the Water Board, we could have the meter and supply transferred to the Club. With water being wasted at approximately 2 gallons per minute, Mike asked the Water Board to come and advise us, but on the morning we were to meet the Water Board inspector, he contacted us to say Mrs West had informed them they would not be allowed on their land.

I was personally aware that relations between our neighbours were not perhaps as close as they had been and that they were probably not using the same solicitors, and soon we received a letter from another firm (this being the third to be used) again threatening us with an injunction should we transgress. So, three years and three solicitors later, we were back to where we started. The opinion was that we just ignore their threats. We then received a letter by recorded delivery on 23 May from the solicitors representing Mr and Mrs Mosley.

With a threat to cut off the water and electricity, and threats of injunctions from the Wests, we decided enough was enough and we would be prepared to take the matter to the courts. We had the offer from Geoff Barber for the use of a water supply but decided to call their bluff and let them do the dirty deed, which, as their solicitor had threatened, they would do in 28 days. So with all this in mind, we agreed to pay £1,000 for advice and then study this with a view to the matter going to court.

In order to let people be aware of what was going on, and to canvass as much support as possible we called an open meeting on Friday 21 June on the cricket ground, this being the deadline for taking steps to remove services.

We had a printed notice sent round listing the happenings over the last three years. Unfortunately we listed all these events together with the names of both parties and received a letter from solicitors representing Mr and Mrs Mosley stating that it contained allegations directed jointly to Mr and Mrs Mosley and their neighbours Mr and Mrs West, who they did not represent and demanded an apology be circulated to any parties who had copies of the original notice. Even though this was discussed and some advice sought, we decided to take no action.

With the threat of having no water I took the liberty of informing the school that the Cricket Club would not be responsible for the state of toilet facilities or any problem that may arise that required water for the school sport's day and other school events.

In early July we received counsel's advice and after most members had perused this we felt happy that if the matter went to court, it looked as though our position was strong, but we now had to get as much evidence to back us up as possible.

Once again the season was going by with officials hardly having the time to think about cricket and once again, regarding the access, the section worst to suffer were the juniors, but again all sections were doing well.

I was assisting the under 17s and got involved in a controversial decision when standing as umpire in the Colts Cup semi-final. The opposing umpire, an experienced player, gave one of our best batsmen

Lawyers brought into cricket dispute

SEE YOU IN COURT

THE FUTURE of village cricket in Pott Shrigley is on a sticky wicket as a two year feud threatens to end up in court.

by Ben Smalley

The club has been playing on the ground in the village since 1919 - but two years ago they were denied vehicle access by two neighbours who own the land leading to the pitch.

Club treasurer Gregory Lisle said: "The residents own the land at the entrance to the pitch. That is not in dispute, nor is pedestrian access. What is is vehicular access. They say there is no right of way and have erected a locked gate.

"Every time we need to access the pitch we have to cut off the padlock, which is soon replaced by another. It's childish, I know, but what else can we do."

The club has three main concerns. If there was an accident an emergency vehicle may struggle to get access, it has parking problems - especially if there is a wedding in the village, and it needs access for ground maintenance equipment.

Mr Lisle added: "Our groundsman Derek is approaching retirement and can't go lumbering heavy machinery over the gate.

"We have spoken to the planning department at the council about arranging alternative access to the ground but they said no on the grounds that we already have access and to sort it out between ourselves.

"The residents won't back down and neither will we. The only way it will be settled, unfortunately, is in a court of law. We can't really afford the fees to go to court - but we'll find them if we have to."

Mr West, one of the neighbours involved, said: "In the deeds to my property it is stated that pedestrian access only is allowed to the cricket club. They want to bring all of their players across my land in cars and this I object to.

"I have offered them a key to the gate for access for maintainance vehicles three times and each time they have turned it down. We have had to put up with two and a half years of harrassment from these people, barely any of whom live in the village. If they want to go to court, let's go to court."

The report on our dispute from the *Messenger* in 1996.

out, stumped off a no ball. I protested but was not 100 per cent certain. He was confident that he was right and at the end of the game we lost by one run, and when I later checked the rules I was apparently right and as both teams had lost nine wickets the game should have been a tie. In fact, the opposition had only ten men. I did discuss the matter with league officials who felt the only suggestion they could make was for us to ask the opposition to replay the match, which I did, but was disappointed to hear no more from them.

The Club team of the season was the under 15s who won the Cheshire Cup but unfortunately failed by one run to take the honours in the HPJCL.

Once again Tony Hutter had fixed up a game with a young Indian team. We had also organised the village match and hoedown in the evening to which we had invited the Indians. Unfortunately, the Pott

Pott's kids spring surprise success

HAVING won a close semi-final three days earlier against the previously unbeaten Barnton, Pott Shrigley arrived at Weaverham Cricket Club to play the hosts in the Final on Sunday July 14.

Skipper, Con Allday, lost the toss and was invited to bat. David Bates and Con Allday opened and from the outset attacked the bowling.

Con fell when the score was 16 and Matthew Street joined David in a partnership of 48 runs in a little over six overs before Matthew was caught for an entertaining 18. David was going from strength to strength and was now joined by James Hutter.

A further 41 runs were added before David was bowled for a sparkling 51. With the score at 105 Jonathan Keep joined James and this pair, both still playing under 13 cricket, remained undefeated taking the score to 13? three wickets with James

The successful Pott Shrigley team celebrate their shock win

28 not out and Jonathan 10 not out.

Good calling and running from all the batsmen had put Weaverham under pressure and given Pott Shrigley a score to defend over 20 overs.

If Shrigley supporters were happy with the batting, they were ecstatic over the bowling as Matthew Walker supported by James Hutter ripped out the

Weaverham top order.

Matthew produced a superb delivery to hit the off-stump of Weaverham danger man Steve Elsdon and Weaverham were tottering at four wickets down for just eight runs.

To their credit Weaverham staged a fightback and Shrigley were relieved to take the fifth wicket after a 26 run partnership. Opening bowlers Matt

Walker and James Hutter returned three for 19 and two for 15 respectively.

Jonathan Keep and Danny Hall kept a tight rein on runs conceding only 12 runs from four overs with Danny picking up a wicket.

Tom Eastwood and Con Allday came on to bowl the final overs following a run-out and after a shaky start Tom took the eighth wicket with the total on 66. Con, still disappointed with his earlier batting, wrapped the game up with two wickets in two balls, dismissing Weaverham for 68.

The bowling had been supported with excellent fielding and throwing and the team were a credit to Pott Shrigley Cricket Club and to themselves in winning this Trophy for the first time.

Team: Con Allday, David Bates, Matthew Street, James Hutter, Jonathan Keep, Matthew Walker, Tom Eastwood, Ben Richbell, Danny Hall, Robin Stamford and James Brockington.

The *Macclesfield Express* reports on our winning final in July 1996.

weather was at its worst and a few overs only were bowled the following week. A game had also been arranged with a young Australian team and the weather was just as bad. Everyone blamed the umpire, Dave Lawson, the well-known 'Rainman' of Pott Shrigley. It was a pity the weather spoiled these two games in an otherwise good summer.

With the Club now armed with counsel's advice and the ground now belonging to us; we now had a very nice sign made by one of the junior's parents, a local man, so we sent this to the parish council for their approval, but when it had the packing removed, it read 'Pot Shrigley CC' so it had to be returned for the extra 'T' to be inserted.

However, before we erected it, Mike Hart wrote to the police informing them of our intentions in the hope that it would not get vandalised in any way, but this didn't have much effect as in a few days it had been damaged and like the top dressing nobody ever owned up.

At the August meeting it was decided that we put a temporary water supply across the field so the supply in the Mosley's garden could be turned off and the wastage of water stopped. When we were issued with a bill of £900 you began to realise what a waste of water and money the Club had been an innocent party to.

People were doing as much as possible to help with the fundraising

Our right of way sign.

and Janine and Mark Frost organised a treasure hunt and barbecue at their home, and this caused another silly confrontation at the gate. Janine had taken the chairs from the pavilion to the event, only to be confronted by Mrs West. Whether she expected Janine to carry about 30 chairs one by one across to the pavilion approximately 300 yards away, I do not know, but they would then complain about people being rude to them.

With the end of the season approaching we were, as usual, in the pack below the leaders and the game against local rivals Woodford was played on a very wet day and though we had the covers on, the water had run under at one end. But, after a bit of mopping up the umpires allowed the game to go ahead. It was a superb game which the visitors won in the last over, but when signing the results sheet, the umpires wrote a bit of an essay about the wicket being dry at one end and wet at the other. After all the effort that had been put in someone scribbled over this and when the sheet reached Dave Lawson, who would fine you if you didn't cross your Ts, we were asked for an explanation. So in something akin to a scene from *Kavanagh QC* we argued that if the league required 'umpires remarks' there should be a portion for these and they should not be allowed to write remarks on the back in this manner. Most Clubs agreed with us so Dave didn't get the chance to levy a fine.

Once again the cricket had shown a lot of promise with players who had come through from the juniors. Doug Martin excelled with an average of over 50 once again, reminding us that his preference to lacrosse (in which he represented his country) over cricket was a loss to the game and Pott Shrigley. Mention also must be made of Jamie Hart who as well as being captain finished with 607 runs. Richard Mattock again showed his consistency with the ball taking 51 wickets.

The 2nd XI were also on the trail of honours until a typical Pott Shrigley performance saw them close to bottom at the end of the season.

In August our friend Geoff Barber sent copies of a proposal that part of the land at the bottom of The Nab next to the cricket ground be put in trust for the village organisations to use as they felt best. G Hackney proposed that we go along with this idea. At the same time I had put in an application to borrow a further £6,000 from MBC as an interest-free loan as all other applications for grants had met with no success.

With Mike Hart now getting evidence together, naturally as longest serving members of the Club, Fred and myself, had most knowledge of happenings over the years.

I had written a four-page letter of evidence which I had directed at the Wests and Mosleys, and on seeing Mike Mosley one lunchtime and bearing in mind his poor health I offered to put him in the picture regarding the Club's intentions, and if he wanted a chat, he should come across to the ground in the afternoon. Mike duly arrived. I had taken the minute book with me, into which I had penned the counsel's report, so I opened the page and gave him sight of this, not allowing him to read it but informing him of the general advice given. He stated that their counsel may come across with something different, so I said, 'Well that will be out of our hands'.

I also informed him that the threat of removing the water and electricity was what people considered the most disgraceful act of the whole dispute and it had not made them many friends, particularly as this threat was taken no further. He hinted that he was not well at the time and was not aware this was going on.

I also allowed him to read my evidence and informed him that the council held a lot of evidence which was at our disposal. We sat about for an hour discussing things, always in a sensible manner, and before

168

he left he asked if he could take the letter of evidence to show to the Wests. This I agreed to, as long as no copies were taken. He then thanked me for giving him all this information and took the evidence to the Wests at The Barn. I stayed on the ground mowing the outfield, and from what I could make out there appeared to be a long discussion (or argument) taking place. About an hour later, Mrs Mosley came across with the letter of evidence and asked if we could still talk. My answer was short and simple '*No*'. Once again maybe everyone may not have been in agreement but it again had startling results with the Wests putting their property up for sale and the officials of the Club being served with a writ for defamation against Mr and Mrs Mosley for displaying the notice entitled 'Shrigley cricket – a thing of the past'.

After discussing the matter with our solicitors it seemed the best advice would be to apologise and offer a substantial sum. An offer of an apology and token sum was refused, so a more substantial sum was offered and accepted as an out of court settlement and the letter of apology posted at the various places. The whole thing was a sad incident of life in a small so-called peaceful hamlet called Pott Shrigley.

A final incident before the property was sold as far as the Cricket Club were concerned was a little bit disappointing because even though we had been regularly cutting the lock and chain off, no other damage had been done to either property, but in October I went to the ground and someone who was obviously as fed up as everyone else with the dispute had taken a chainsaw to the offending gate and cut pieces out of it. I don't think it was a member of our Club as the cricket had been finished for a few weeks and, as most officials are aware, once the cricket season is over, most of the players melt away.

However, with the annual bonfire taking place back on the ground, this proved to be a big success, one of the best turnouts for years with a folk concert and the village hall using their outside licence for selling beer, even though Brian Buffey had received a phone call warning him not to. Everyone enjoyed the event on the cricket ground with John Jackson again to the fore, fixing the lighting etc. and with proper toilet facilities, and a room for the first-aid persons plus the ability to fence off the top of the field for the firework display.

With The Barn now up for sale some felt the dispute with the council and Cricket Club may have turned prospective buyers off, but this did not seem to be the case. As we were preparing for the bonfire two interested parties came across for a chat. One, quite an elderly gentleman, said he was a big cricket fan and the idea of just going across his field to watch a match appealed to him. I later had a phone call from a Mr Kevin Holiday (a builder) who asked if he could call and have a chat. The thing that seemed to concern most people was the prospect of having a bar in the pavilion, but apart from the fact that in the deeds of the sale to the Cricket Club, this was not allowed, the idea of having a bar in such a remote spot could be a catalogue for disaster in today's climate.

At a committee meeting on 25 November, Nigel Reeves (auditor) proposed that the committee should indemnify the five officials for cash or damages if awarded against them by Mr and Mrs Mosley. However, our increased offer to settle out of court was accepted in early December and most involved were relieved that this matter was over. The dispute had gone on for four years and cost the club nearly £10,000.

We left for Down Under on 12 December. The travel arrangements had been made for both the HPJCL and the mid-Cheshire junior league, so the least expensive way to travel had been sought but it turned out to be a bit of a long, protracted journey, leaving Manchester airport on the evening shuttle to Heathrow with a night in a hotel near the airport. Then, an early flight to Rome to get the lunchtime flight to Sydney via Bangkok. However, we then experienced one of those frustrating delays when the jumbo jet was delayed for six hours. During the flight from Bangkok we were informed that as there was a night-time curfew for Sydney, we would be diverted to Melbourne where accommodation would be provided overnight, and the party would leave on the first flight to Sydney, which meant only about four hours sleep. Being the only two oldies in the party, we decided we would have a lie in and spend the day sightseeing around Melbourne even if we had to pay our own fare.

However, when we went to check out, David Walker, who was dealing with the tickets for our party, had left them at reception, so we took them to the Quantas desk and explained what had happened. They were very helpful, and told us we could travel on any flight to Sydney so we left on the last flight, got our tickets and boarding card and travelled onwards thinking there had been no problems. Not until we were returning did we encounter any.

The one worrying thing was when you are in a party like this you tend to follow the person in front and not bother with much detail. We knew the hotel was called Barker Street Inn or something like that, but most of the bus and taxi drivers were immigrants. We gave one of these this name but he seemed a bit vague. We were in the taxi for ages, then he turned and there was Barker Street. It was Barker Motor Inn and we were pleased when we gave our name at reception and they provided the key to our room.

Even though I was chairman of the league I had not volunteered to help with any duties, so we decided to see as much of the area as possible. Sydney must be one of the best cities in the world for public transport, with buses, trains and ferries running a superb service. One can see how Sydney was chosen for the 2000 Olympics.

With Christmas almost upon us, and never having spent a Christmas away from home, it all seemed very different. We spent a couple of days in Canberra and the surrounding area. When we arrived back in Sydney the station was festooned with Christmas decorations, looking really like Christmas. But it didn't feel like it at all, and when we went to join the throngs at Carols in the Park with thousands of people sat on the grass and the temperature in the seventies it didn't feel quite right.

The Christmas dinner which had been arranged for us had plenty of meats and salads etc. and as we were helping ourselves, I heard John Bridgford, a local farmer, who had come along with us, asking for Brussels sprouts.

We had bought some rolls and finished up in the park in the afternoon eating them with bananas. Worse was to follow when we could not find anywhere open for a meal in the evening, so we made our way to Circular Quay and finished up sitting outside McDonald's having chips and a Big Mac. While we sat there I happened to say 'I wonder how "Biff" is going on for Christmas' to which the reply came 'he is probably doing better than us'. And this was confirmed a few weeks later, when I met one of Bryon's grandsons. There was a lot of tail wagging and the boy said "Biff didn't we have a good time at our Christmas party?", Bryon's wife, Olga, said Bryon had taken him out on Christmas Eve and they were gone for so long, she thought he had got lost. Apparently he had met another old school pal and local character, John Platt and they had smuggled Biff into The Lord Clyde, even though no dogs were allowed. I saw John a while later and he asked if I still had the collie dog who really liked a drink of beer, so I think Biff finished up with an excellent Christmas.

We did spend New Year's Eve with the cricket party in the hotel and did get into serious conversation with a couple of Australians who had come over with the Australian boys in our summer and how they had enjoyed the game at Pott Shrigley, and felt that some caution should be exercised in England and not to go headlong down the Australian way of grade cricket and do anything to spoil our village Clubs as there was nothing like it in their country. In fact most parents who had accompanied the boys seemed a little disappointed that most of the games were played in parks on matting wickets with no real Club atmosphere and even though all the parks contained artificial wickets, there did not seem to be much going on on the

171

HIGH PEAK
JUNIOR CRICKET LEAGUE

Australia Tour

December 12th 1996 - January 5th 1997

SOUVENIR BROCHURE

The cover of the smart brochure for the junior tour of Australia in 1997.

Derek Underwood
England and Kent

I am only too delighted to be asked to write an intro to the Australian Tour Brochure.
I am pleased to hear that the fund-raising for the tour is going well. I am sure it will
be a trip of a lifetime for everybody involved.

I was lucky enough to visit "Oz" on 3 full England tours, and have subsequently hosted
several tours, taking people 'down under' to watch the test matches.

The first time I visited Australia was in 1970 when Ray Illingworth was Captain.
It was a very tough competitive series, but in John Snow, we had the trump card as he
was at the time the best fast bowler in the world. In addition we had the strong batting
line-up of Boycott, Edrich, Luckhurst, D'Oliveira, Knott etc. We went on to win the
series 2-0, winning both tests in Sydney, which for me was the finest cricket ground I
ever played on - How sad the Hill has now gone.

Touring Australia 4 years later the Aussie were still smarting from their defeat. This
time they were ready for us with all guns blazing! This tour heralded the wearing of
helmets and we lost the first 4 test matches easily. In the last Test when neither Lillee
or Thompson were fit, we came back to win comfortably at melbourne but it was all too
late.

Hospitality will be superb but on the cricket front competition will be fierce. If you find
yourself in a good position don't let up for a moment as the Australians are tough
competitors and are good at recovering.

In all Australia is a great country. One thing for sure is that you will want to return.

Have lots of fun and good luck.

Derek Underwood MBE

Derek Underwood's introduction to the Australian tour brochure.

cricket scene. In fact we spent a few hours at Mosman, sat in the park on the Saturday before coming home. It is a beautiful spot with two cricket pitches but there was nothing going on. Shortly after coming home, I read in *The Cricketer* that it was where Alan Border had started his cricket, but the club had since folded.

Our personal problems came on the way home. David Walker, who had been in charge of the tickets, had flown home leaving the return tickets with Sheila Kirk and when we arrived to board the coach to the airport, Sheila met us and said, 'You have got your own return tickets', which we did not have. Obviously, they must have kept them at Melbourne when we did not travel with the main party, but the Alitalia representative at the airport made us empty our cases out to search for them. We never did find them, so we let Sheila do all the explaining at various airports while we stood about looking a bit vague.

6

"The Nab Witches"

1997 saw little change in officials but the expansion of the Cheshire county league meant that four clubs would be taken into this league from the Cheshire league which meant that four clubs would be promoted that year, so when the Wests moved house early in the year and Rachael and Kevin Holiday moved in, proving to be easy to get on with for the first time for almost five years, it seemed we could get on and enjoy our cricket even though there was still a lot of money to be found.

We were now fairly certain to get an interest-free loan of £6,000 from MBC plus a grant of £500 to help with re-routing the water pipe so we again appreciated the help given to us by the borough council, and with Roy Harrison, JP, now mayor of Macclesfield, honouring us with his presence at the annual dinner together with his wife Ruth, and making a first-class speech, it was appreciated by all the members. Mrs Margaret Duffy, leader of the council, was also sympathetic to our cause.

With us now owning our ground we were determined to get full value. We were now prepared to use it for more events. As far as we were concerned the right of way was for all purposes relating to the running of a Cricket Club and with all the petty restrictions of the parish council now behind us, we decided to organise a 'six-a-side junior festival' on spring Bank Holiday Monday in construction with the HPJCL and also a senior 'sixes' on 13 July.

We were now getting the various junior sections organised and it was beginning to look as though the under 15s were going to be the section to struggle. A few who had been on the Australian tour were now joining other Clubs, so in order to keep this age group going I said I would be manager and try and get a team together.

Our lady president was as always adamant that things should be done and look efficient. She presented us with a new Club flag. Her dedication to the Club was always an inspiration to everyone. At the March meeting I informed the committee that the legal department of MBC had sent the agreement for the additional loan to be signed, but

175

they had not changed the names of the borrowers, so I had returned it for alteration.

With Geoff Barber's offer of the piece of land at the bottom of the cricket ground now looking like going ahead another parish meeting to get people's views on this had been called. Of course I got an invite, and with most people appearing to be in favour, this seemed to me to be a generous offer to improve the area, but as usual I felt there would be undercurrents as anything new in Pott Shrigley is usually taboo, as we had always found out.

On the playing members side the treasurer brought to light that three first team members had not paid a subscription for the previous year and with the Club so much in debt, this did not go down well. Ian as league rep. stated that according to league rules, they were not eligible to play, so the committee banned them until their debts were cleared. However, these debts were collected, so with two fairly strong teams plus a good under 17s team a good start to the season was made. It was felt this could be an important year to try and get into the first division, as with new Clubs joining the league the playing strengths of these were not known.

I managed to get an under 15s team off the ground in a Cheshire league cup match at Peover. We arrived in a storm and to get the match over played eight overs a side. They bowled and fielded quite well but the batting didn't quite last the eight overs. Still, we got the thing off the ground. The lads did improve during the season, particularly when one or two of the under 13s came into the side, especially Jonathan Ward's brother Oliver, whose masterly spin bowling proved too much for some of the teams and again proved to me the difficulty juniors have with this type of bowling.

In May the financial position began to look clearer with the treasurer receiving the £6,000 second loan from the MBC and £300 towards the new water pipe and the first 'Junior sixes' proved a big success, together with a car boot sale yielding over £1,000 for Club funds. Also, one of our local members offered quite a large donation to improve some part of the Club's equipment, so a new sightscreen was felt the most important item for replacement.

The biggest flop of the season was the Village Hall Match, which over the years we had always tried to keep in our social calendar, but when the barman Brian Buffey was the only member of their team to turn up, it was obvious this event was becoming a waste of time.

As chairman of the HPJCL I received a long letter from the father of one of our junior's, regarding a stupid incident in a game against Gawsworth which had got a bit out of control, so I was asked to write to two of our lads warning them about their future conduct.

176

With Kevin Holiday now putting a fence down the side of the track and the trench that John had excavated to divert the water pipe, the entrance to the ground was now better than ever, and it was proposed a letter of thanks be sent to Kevin.

Two other events that met with some financial success were a senior 'Sixes' and a barbecue at the bowling green. This unfortunately was the last, as the secretary of the Bowling Club had just realised I had been on the pension for a couple of years.

With all the teams doing quite well it looked as if the club may finish with a few honours, but as usual at Pott Shrigley, we failed to receive and made a bit of a mess of things and finished second best, with the under 17s finishing runners up in the HPJCL and finalists in the cup, and the under 13s doing the same. We also now had an under 11s section who gave a good account of themselves.

The biggest disappointment was on the first team. With four Clubs getting promotion we had been up with the leaders all year but slipped a bit towards the end of the season, so the last game against Knutsford meant which ever team won they would gain promotion. With John Nuttall and Mathew Tarr bowling well, Knutsford were reduced to 36 for 6 but managed to get 119, which was not a big score on our ground, and when Mark Dean and Jamie Hart had put on 39 without loss in the first ten overs it looked easy, until Mark was needlessly run out. What happened next was best forgotten. We lost by 20 runs. Mrs Tute, who had specially made the effort to attend after an illness, was not impressed and I got a bit of earache on the way home.

So, at the end of what had seemed to be a promising season, things turned out a bit of a disappointment. I suppose one of the worst aspects of league cricket is that someone always suffers these sorts of disappointments, and probably as we had one of the youngest teams in the league, it was harder to accept. So, the closed season seemed lacking, with poor attendance at the dinner, the players meeting and the indoor nets.

The bonfire was again a big success, with no problems of the gate being locked and no aggravation, plus another helper when Rachael from The Barn helped with the serving of refreshments. In general there was more help and interest from the village. Gerald Barton was always willing to help, and fixed scaffolding and a canopy at the front of the pavilion which improved the look of the thing as well as providing a cover for side stalls etc.

At the 1998 AGM virtually all the playing officials were changed, with Dominic Lisle 1st XI captain and Rick Mattock vice-captain. Nathan Bull was 2nd XI captain, Geoff Lockton vice-captain, plus Robert Street, Sunday captain. His son Mathew offered to manage the under 17s and though noted for being a bit on the wild side he did a superb job winning the respect of the lads and the club officials.

Early in the year I attended a meeting at Grappenhall CC regarding the forming of a Cheshire pyramid league system, even though I personally had a few reservations, particularly regarding the travelling. But it appeared this project was going to get off the ground and I was surprised that no other club in the Mellor Braggens cricket league had a representative at the meeting.

At the league meeting I proposed the league make progress along these lines, but made the point that there should be a uniform registration policy or none at all. This to ensure that all Clubs were competing on a level playing field. I suppose one word could sum up 1998: 'WET'.

Before the season began we at last got to grips with breaking up the sightscreen. It had done excellent service even though when the ground was wet it took about eight men to move it. Having done such a stout job of making it, we cheekily asked Don to come and dismantle it. Never one to let the grass grow under his feet, he arrived with cutters, and managed to get it into two halves away from the base on which we intended to put the new screen. We left the two halves at the edge of the ground thinking it would be easy to get a scrapdealer to collect them, but together with the wet weather and the weight of the things it frightened even the most herculean Steptoe away and it was June before we eventually got the thing carted away. Gerald Barton offered to weld us scaffolding together and we purchased a 'Tillnet Screen' and tied it on. One man can move it, and it proved to be a job well done.

Greg had now got an architect to draw up plans for a new pavilion and in April he submitted them to the Peak Park planning authority, a procedure always viewed with trepidation as Greg's account implies:

So what of the future? Will Bluebell Wood echo to the sound of leather on willow into the next millennium? Well, for a small club we are nothing if not ambitious. In February 1998 Mike Hart, Derrick Brooke, Greg Lisle, Kevin Halliday and Plumber Chappie met in the pavilion to discuss ways in which we could improve the facilities. Various options were discussed and eventually the urge to call for Fred Dibnah became too strong and it was decided to demolish the existing shed and build a state of the art emporium of excellence.

I don't know how I drew the short straw, but it has somehow fallen to me to coordinate the planning application and Lottery appeal. At first I set about the task with great zeal attending

178

meetings and gathering information on how best to go about securing funds and gaining planning permission. I have found however, that whenever dealing with officialdom, time seems to take on a new dimension and all sense of logic seems to fail. Chris Tyrell drew up the plans fairly quickly and all was well apart from a brief digression when members felt it was unnecessary to have more toilets than Buxton Opera House! Having not counted the toilets whilst at the opera I was at a distinct disadvantage. The plan that was adopted from several schemes was the one with the fewest toilets. The motion was passed, and the seeds of an idea began to take on tangible form.

The next question was to whom do we submit the plans? An easy enough question you would think, but you'd be wrong. Was it Macclesfield Borough Council or the Peak District National Park? Both the respective authorities claimed to have jurisdiction over planning in Pott Shrigley. However it was eventually decided that the land on the side of the road nearest the Peak Park came under Macclesfield Borough Council and the Peak Park would obviously deal with the land on the far side of the road away from the Park. Obviously!

At this point I should have realised that it would be wise to redraft the plans in the form of a Disney theme park complete with monorail. How foolish of me to want to take down the old pavilion and replace it with another pavilion. Our planning officer's knowledge of cricket could easily have been transcribed onto the back of a postage stamp with plenty of room to spare. One suggestion was that we could reduce the tea room size by half if we had the away team eat tea first and when they had finished everything off the home team would be welcome to fight over the scraps. Now why didn't I think of that? Why not go the whole hog and have alternating changing rooms and showers.

There then followed a complete pantomime of a performance with various versions of the plan being drawn up. It was all to no avail and eventually we were advised to withdraw the plan. The local community had raised only one objection. The following week an article appeared in the press referring to the plans as 'too grandiose'. And so it was back to the drawing board and the building size was reduced by ... wait for it, 3ft. The new building had to be made to look as if it was an old building with an extension added on the back. A novel idea, but not one that any of the committee felt bound to agree with. Still, we went along with it, as by now if they had asked for it to be constructed in the style of the Taj Mahal out of balsa wood, we would have agreed.

179

The new plan was resubmitted, looking remarkably similar to the very first plan that was drawn up. Even down to the clock on the roof, which had remained throughout despite the reservations of the planning officer. Even more amazing was that this time there were no objections and the plan was passed with no conditions attached. The whole process had taken over a year and given me a valuable insight into the workings of a planning department. Remind me to build my new house on the opposite side of the road.

At the same time that we were trying to obtain planning permission we were also trying to secure funds from the Lottery. To receive Lottery funding there is an inevitable application form to fill in. You cannot apply for Lottery funds until you have planning permission and have quotations for the building work. You cannot get quotations until you have a more detailed specification of the likely work involved and the materials that are going to be used. Needless to say, progress on this front was slow. So slow in fact that we are on our third Lottery application form, the previous two having time-expired. At the time of going to press various local builders were being invited to tender for the building. One thing is for sure, we will keep persevering and the pavilion will get built – I'm just not sure when.

As the season went by and became wetter and wetter both teams were doing well in the league, and the under 17s were winning every game they played. They also had the best run in the Village Cup ever, getting to the final of the Cheshire and Clwyd group, where we lost to Mere in front of a good crowd at Pott Shrigley on one of the few fine days of the year.

Another first in 1998 happened when we played Bollington for the first time in a league encounter, and even though we tried to get some public interest in this game and Slater Harrison sponsored the 1st XI match, there isn't the same interest in Bollington as there was in time gone by. Pott had the upper hand in every game, the 1st XI winning both games, and the 2nd XI winning one and getting a winning draw in the second game where the last two batsmen managed to hold out. I did watch the 1st XI at Bollington, where a couple of regular spectators joined me, one having a moan that he thought he would never see this day happen. I must admit I felt a bit smug and my mind went back to when I first went to Pott and had to put up with the jibes about how many runs were scored when the ball went down a rabbit hole.

With the season going well on all fronts it was sad when our presi-

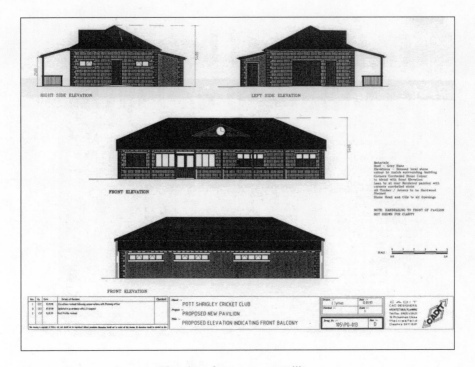

The plans for our new pavilion.

dent passed away on 19 August. Of all the presidents who had graced this office, her devotion to the Club was second to none. The number of times she phoned Kit up to discuss the Cricket Club must have gone into hundreds, sometimes just to inform her that she had managed to purchase some cheap teabags on a special offer. She hardly ever missed a game, and on the previous Sunday I had taken her to watch a friendly at Hale Barns. We had come back to The Coffee Tavern at Pott Shrigley for some tea and we could tell that she was not feeling well, but she insisted on going back after tea to watch even though it was only a friendly. So, we had a drink with the lads in the bar and unfortunately it was the last. When the 1st XI won promotion a few weeks later it would have been nice to see her sat on her favourite chair clapping them in, but it was not to be, and even though she was sometimes a bit controversial and usually called a spade, a spade, there was a lot of respect for her, not only from our own players but from the opposition and league officials.

The form at the end of the season still left a lot to be desired. The batting all through the league seemed poor, the wet wickets not

181

Flag flies at half mast in tribute to ex-mayor

FRIENDS and family have been paying tribute to a long-standing councillor and former mayor of Bollington.

Lily Tute, who celebrated her 80th birthday in May, died suddenly last Friday.

The town hall flag — which was lowered last week after the death of Neville Birch — will stay at half mast as a mark of respect.

Lily was town mayor in 1985 and served as a Conservative councillor for thirteen years until 1995.

Last year's mayor Claire Crosby said: "She was one of the first people I met when I came to Bollington — in fact she helped me find somewhere to live.

"Lily attended all the council functions, even when her health was failing — she was a super lady and will be very much missed."

She stood for council after the death of her husband Lewis and was a strong campaigner to save the viaduct when it was threatened with demolition.

She was also president of Pott Shrigley Cricket Club and a member of the NSPCC committee.

Lily's daughter Cath Drabble said: "She worked very hard for Bollington — she was born in Hurdsfield but lived here for 59 years so she was considered a local.

"She was a very active member of the Methodist church and sang in the choir."

Claude Harlington, Bollington town clerk said: "Lily was a very kind person — if you asked her to help you she would do anything.

"She was a very good town mayor and a good chairman — when Neville died she called me straight away to suggest we put the flag at half mast."

Lily leaves two sons and a daughter, 10 grandchildren — who will all be together for the first time at her funeral — and 5 great-grandchildren.

The funeral will be at Bollington Methodist Church at 2.15pm on

Lily Tute

Friday (August 28) — donations will go to the NSPCC and the Rheumatism and Arthritis Council.

Sadness as Pott president passes away

Unfortunately for Pott Shrigley their president Lily Tute passed away last Friday at the age of 80. She had been president since 1991.

Her enthusiasm for the club was immense, she watched every game and took great pleasure this year watching the under 17s.

Her commitment and work for the club was second to none, organising race nights and her own Presidents evenings.

A minutes silence was observed at Saturday's game, and what would be a great tribute to her and her predecessor would be if Pott Shrigley 1st XI could clinch promotion to the First Division.

Words alone cannot say what a lovely lady she was and her presence at God's little acre will be sorely missed. Her funeral is to be held at Bollington's methodist church, Wellington Road this Friday at 2.15pm.

The *Macclesfield Express* reports on the death of our President in 1998.

182

We're going up

Division 1 – 1st XI				
Team	P	W	D	L	Pts
Bredbury St ...	22	12	5	2	357
Prestbury	22	10	7	3	315
Oakmere	22	8	7	4	277
Offerton	22	7	7	5	262
Styal	22	7	6	5	261
Winsford	22	6	3	8	241
Lindow	22	7	4	9	229
Weaverham ...	22	7	7	7	215
Chelford	22	4	7	9	212
Christleton	22	5	8	6	206
Knutsford	22	6	3	10	192
Davenham	22	1	6	12	119

Division 2 – 1st XI				
Team	P	W	D	L	Pts
Mere	22	14	4	2	335
Pott Shrigley ..	22	10	5	4	276
Lymm O'ton ..	22	9	7	4	270
Bowdon Vale..	22	8	5	5	265
Barnton	22	8	4	8	249
Holmes Chapel	22	6	8	4	232
Sandbach	22	8	1	11	217
Bollington	22	6	3	10	206
Ashley	22	4	6	10	180
Malpas	22	4	5	9	180
Woodford	22	5	8	8	176
High Lane	22	3	4	10	145

ON Saturday High Lane were the visitors to Pott Shrigley for the last game of the season.

Nerves were running high as all Shrigley had to do was to win and they would be promoted to the first division.

High Lane elected to bat first and disaster soon struck when Hart took a good slip catch off the Bowling of Mattock in the first over.

Brett then had Cooke caught by Lisle and High Lane were struggling. Both Mattock and Brett were bowling well and Brett had Davies caught by keeper Lisle for one.

Mattock then had Bailey brilliantly caught down the leg side by Lisle and Shrigley knew that victory was only round the corner, Matt Tarr playing in his last game for Shrigley before jetting off to Australia came on to bowl and bowled his customary wide.

Matt will be sorely missed next year but we wish him and Amanda all the best. High Lane were bowled out for 57 with Mattock bowling excellent finish-

High Lane 57 all out
Pott Shrigley 1st XI 58-1

ing on six wickets. Hart and Dean opened the batting for Shrigley and these two took the score to 20 when Hart was caught for ten.

Mattock joined Dean and these two scored the necessary runs with Mattock hitting a massive six to win the game.

So at long last Shrigley have finally made it and I would like to congratulate all the players for their hard effort during the season especially when their captain was quite hard on them (sometimes). The celebrations began in force with the champagne flowing freely. The lads then went to Bredbury Hall but the details of that night have been sent to the Sport.

Thanks to the tea ladies and especially to our scorer Denise for an excellent job all year and to Derrick Brooke, our groundsman, the lads are now looking forward to October 16 for the league dinner. Well done again to everyone concerned.

DOMINIC LISLE

Pott Shrigley win promotion in 1998.

helping, and with some horrendous batting performances it again came down to the wire with having to beat High Lane in the final game. They were bottom of the league having struggled for several years and the game finished as a bit of an anticlimax, with High Lane only mustering 54 runs. The game was over by just after 4.00 p.m. so celebrations started early.

With promotion the under 17s won the Meller Braggins Cup, the High Peak Junior League and the Kirk Cup. Jamie Hart had organised a successful tour to Hampshire where that Jack of all trades John Jackson, who had only played about four games was star batsman. The under 15s, 13s and 11s had all performed well with one of our under 11s starring for Cheshire on several occasions. What a difference a bit of success makes! The room was full to overflowing at the players' meeting and 20-plus players went by coach to the league presentation evening.

Chairman M. Hart, who was on the bonfire organising committee, reported in September that the bonfire would be held on Hallowe'en night, and gave an insight into this by stating he had a novel idea of flying witches coming down off The Nab hill, so together with the ever-willing John Jackson, a test run was organised a couple of weeks before the event, with a rope attached to a tree part way up The Nab and the other end attached to the roller on the ground. The witches were made from old clothes, but the first trials were not very successful, so we tried putting more weight on, but all this did was pull the rope down and they ground to a halt in the centre. So we then decided it would have to be something lighter, like plastic, and we would try again the next week.

On the following week the new breed of witches arrived: basically bin liners with bits added here and there, and of course broomsticks. After a few technical adjustments, and being a still morning weather-wise, things worked quite well. Unfortunately, as most people are aware, the weather was horrendous at the end of October and with the ground flooded on the Friday and the forecast even worse for the Saturday, we reluctantly decided to put the event back one week. A big disappointment to all concerned, especially as from the enquiries we had had, a big crowd was in the offing.

The Saturday following produced a much drier day, but with a force-nine southerly wind blowing. A large crowd turned up. The witches were meant to appear from various quarters, the idea being to tie a big sparkler on them and follow them with a spotlight, but with the wind against them they could not get them to move, so we had to put a string on them and pull them, wind-assisted, up The Nab. Some of the younger children looked a bit apprehensive and when a witch burst out in flames half way up and dropped out of the sky, just missing John working the spotlight from his van, probably a few of the younger ones had nightmares.

During the closed season yet another crisis arose in the village. A plan to fell some of the trees in Holme Wood had been approved, so once again I was invited to a parish meeting and realised how sensible we were to get the ground signed over before a lot of trash could be talked by parishioners who had not much knowledge of what they were talking about. When the bluebells were brought into the discussion I made my exit. I learned later that I had missed the best bit, when John Jackson more or less informed the meeting they were being a bit vindictive to the owner, as earlier in the meeting the chairman had called him a charming man.

So with 1999 rapidly approaching and the annual dinner coming up at which the four trophies the Club had won in 1998 would be on view, and past captain Alan Sherratt as the after-dinner speaker, comedian and auctioneer, it ended a successful year.

The 1999 season started well with both teams winning their opening games against Chelford, who had suffered an exodus of players during the closed season, so it was obvious that harder battles were to come, and unfortunately this was proved correct with the only two victories coming against Chelford. Two victories in the Village Cup were obtained before a poor batting performance against Pont Blyddyn put an end to further progress.

The second team looked capable of finishing in a good position, and with three games to go were in a good place for honours but fell away badly and finished sixth, losing to Bollington in a keenly contested semi-final of the League Cup. There were some good individual performances in both teams with Nigel Reeves, Jamie Hart and Nathan Bull all completing centuries.

Once again it was left to the juniors to fly the flag with the under 15s joint champions and a very good under 13s section finishing runners up in every competition. Unfortunately, due to losing a number of juniors a couple of years back for the first time in almost 30 years, we did not enter the under 17s, but again entered the under 21s Cheshire Cup. However, after beating Congleton in the early round by one run, we lost to a very strong Neston side in the semi-final.

Once again, as usual, the duels with Prestbury proved interesting affairs. The 1st XI game at Prestbury was particularly tense. Prestbury were the eventual champions, batting first. In their usual belligerent style they hit over 240 runs in 40 overs and with 50 overs to get the runs, Pott once again found themselves in a good position. With captain D. Lisle and last man M. Street at the wicket and 18 runs needed, they decided to play for a draw even though the game had already taken over six hours with the ball getting lost every few minutes. I left, thinking Mathew's temperament was more suitable for swinging the bat and going for the win. However, he did finish unbeaten.

Mathew and Robert, his dad, live at the Old Vicarage, and are the nearest members to the ground, so he has come through the junior section and played a large part in the organisation of the older juniors, which is probably the most difficult section to organise. A bit of a character, his pedigree coming from a long line of solicitors, he appeared to have broken the mould as one of his tutors described him as 'A lovely lad but a bit of a loose cannon'.

Another junior to hit the headlines was young Richard Hough. Apart form winning the under 12s batting award, he performed well in the HPJCL representative games, with a ton not out in one game. I had played with his granddad in the 1940s.

With better weather most of the organised competitions were successful. A Caribbean evening at Mark and Janine Frosts home and

185

the annual bonfire were huge successes with well over 1,000 spectators paying for admission to the bonfire, and a few who didn't please Rachael from The Barn at the entrance, by sitting on her fence and not paying an entrance fee. Annoying, but you always get a few people like that.

7

The New Millennium

Once again it was that Pott-bred man, for all seasons, John Jackson, who converted his barn into the Shrigley Dome and had a bonfire and fireworks on the hill going up to Bowstones, a hill which, legend has it, got its name when the area was all part of Macclesfield Forest. At that time the inhabitants went to the 'Stones' to bend and make their bows. From here on a clear day the Mersey is visible. A large family gathering attended from OAPs like ourselves to babes in arms, with a disco provided by the defunked 'No Parking' trio, of Greg, Andy and Stuart, but I think there were complaints at the length of the queue waiting at the 'Body Zone' for a plate of Anne's hotpot.

With the festivities going well, at about 11.45 p.m. it was time to make our way to the bonfire only to find the cloud and mist rolling off the moors and the visibility about ten yards. However, a large number managed to find their way to the bonfire area. As the clock struck 12.00 p.m. the usual festivities followed with a circle of shadowy figures singing 'Auld Lang Syne' and looking like a scene form *Wuthering Heights*. However, just to prove the age of romance is not dead the young man next to me produced a ring and proposed to the young lady by his side, and from what I could see, he was accepted.

I did get details of another party taking place on the top of The Nab, where the Holidays and the Gibsons, who live on either side, met and opened a bottle of champagne, but I think Kevin's account of this would take first prize in a 'Where were you at midnight on New year?' competition, when he stated that the weather was much better up there, and they took their clothes off and danced round the trig point. Rachael and Caroline deny this.

Plans are now in hand for a millennium celebration weekend and it appears that The Village Green Project may be ready for the next millennium in 3000 AD. Colin Bourne's account tells all:

The village without a green

In bygone days and for many years, the whole of Pott Shrigley was owned by the Shrigley Estate. On Tuesday 11 of May 1920, the local firm of Messrs Turner & Son of Macclesfield were instructed to offer for sale by auction at 2.30 in the afternoon at the Macclesfield Arms Hotel, 47 lots belonging to Shrigley Estate. These consisted of farms, quarries, cottages and a coffee room tenanted by Mr I. Cotton at a rent of £10 p.a. The whole lots offered in total 1,468 acres, 2 roods and 39 perches, producing a rental of £1860 8s 3d per annum.

Some lots changed hands but others failed to tempt a buyer. At the time, Pott Hall Farm, in the centre of the village, consisted of 153 acres let to Mr J. Wainwright at a rent of £180 p.a. It is not mentioned in the sale particulars that the farm at one time doubled up as farm and village pub, known as The Lowther Arms. This property failed to find a new owner and continued to be run as part of the estate. Later on it was farmed by the Boon family until 1968 when it was again offered for sale in five lots, but excluding approximately two acres of the Show Meadow adjoining the village school.

Since that sale in 1968, the various lots have changed hands more than once. Nab Wood, the old Pott Shrigley and Bollington Golf Course, the Race Field, not forgetting the Hollow Meadow adjoining St Christopher's church, now in 1999 all belong to Geoff Barber of Norman's Hall Farm.

Geoff's family and farming connections stretch back many years into Pott Shrigley history. Many of his family chose St Christopher's as their final resting place. Both Geoff and Claire, his now deceased wife, desired to give a little thank-you to the village in perpetuity by way of a parcel of land adjoining the church. This they considered would secure for the future any of the church's land requirements. To the Barbers surprise the offer was not taken up, possibly because there was a lack of positive clarity regarding access to the site at that time, in 1991.

As time went by, Geoff's desire to give the land to the village had not diminished and a new idea was born. He would offer the land as a village green to be administered by three trustees to be elected or re-elected every five years. One trustee from the village hall, one from the Cricket Club and one from the church, so as to strike a balance for all walks of life.

Geoff called an informal meeting at his farm of interested parties. Present were Geoff Barber, Phil Whatmough, Michael Hart, Keith Meecham and myself. Several more meetings took place looking at ways of funding and access use of the proposed green. Also, importantly, planning permission would be required for change of use. Penney Hart very kindly volunteered her skills to draw up the plans necessary to apply for planning and also possible grant monies. Various forms of grant were looked at.

On 24 June 1996, a meeting took place with The Countryside Commission, to look at possible funding for a millennium village green. The conditions that would be imposed, if we chose this option, would be dictated by the fund providers and would throw the doors open to the general public rather than just parishioners. Instead, the committee secured a promise of a grant of £2,000 from Rural Action, which would be sufficient to get the project started.

Having progressed this far, it was time to put the idea to the parishioners. A public meeting was called in the village hall at 8 p.m. on 7 May 1997. Fifteen per cent of the entire parish attended, and everyone had their say. There was unanimous support for the project. It is worth putting on record one young parishioner's comment, 'Let's take up Mr Barber's offer before he changes his mind.'

Then the committee presumed they had authority to proceed with a planning application, which they paid for out of their own pockets. In due course, the splendid plans produced by Penney showed landscape details and the new access, which could never be disputed, were submitted together with the application to the Peak Park planners in December 1997. It took until 13 August the following year, 1998, to get the planning committee out for a site visit.

By this time, some attitudes had changed in the village and the doubters had reportedly expressed their fears that a village green would somehow devalue the freehold of their properties. Six letters of objection, including one from a Canadian resident, were sent to the planners. The parish council had no objections; likewise, Macclesfield Borough Council. Cheshire County Highways had previously been consulted about the design of the proposed access; they also had no objections.

The site meeting was a very hurried affair. The chairman gave his brief address standing on the access to the rear of the church. The planning officer John Scott said his piece which most certainly confused most of those present, with his remarks about the new access needing three metres of infill to bring it up to the required level. He then elaborated by saying that to achieve proper sight lines, 70 metres of established hedgerows would have to be removed in either direction; whereas Cheshire County Highways said the hedges must be maintained at a maximum height of 1 metre. It is little wonder that the full planning committee, faced with that kind of report from their officers, refused planning consent.

All being hardy, resilient types, the village green committee decided to appeal to the Ministry of the Environment. In due course, their inspection took place on Monday 15 March 1999. In his report, the inspector recognised Peak Park as the overriding authority on planning matters within the conservation area. He upheld their decision to refuse permission, mainly on the grounds of access.

The village green committee, once again after licking their wounds, displayed their determination to carry on regardless and submitted a new revised application to the Peak Park planners in April 1999. Who can tell, it may just be third time lucky.

The next bad news and setback is with all the unforeseen delays, the £2,000 grant money from Rural Action is no longer available. It is a very generous offer indeed that has been made to the parish and I suggest that we should all stand high enough to accept the gift on behalf of future generations; and in the meantime for our own enjoyment.

So we end the story with Fred in his 51st year and myself at 50, both with sons who are committee members and players. Other families, like the Hackneys, Barlows, Harts, Tutes and Lisles are all involved and have sons playing cricket. I suppose, some, as always, may think the old times were the best, but I am sure cricket must move with the times to survive. I hope there will always be room and people to carry on the tradition of village cricket, and that my account of Pott Shrigley Cricket Club may help to keep this traditional part of old England alive.

Finally, even though at times there have been disagreements, at the end of the day, most members and supporters have a bond with Pott Shrigley that has attracted them to the village, whether to play cricket, worship at church or attend the primary school, and so keep the village institutions alive.